Chronicle

Chronicle

essays from ten years of television archaeology edited by Ray Sutcliffe

Richard Atkinson   David Collison   Basil Greenhill   John Hale
R. G. Harrison   Kenneth Hudson   Paul Jordan   Henry Lincoln
Magnus Magnusson   Tony Morrison   John Julius Norwich   Colin Renfrew
introduction by Glyn Daniel

British Broadcasting Corporation

First published in 1978 by the
British Broadcasting Corporation
35 Marylebone High Street
London W1M 4AA

ISBN 0 563 17483 8

Printed in England by Jolly & Barber Ltd, Rugby

Contents

Acknowledgements

Page 10 A. F. Cobb
13 (top left) National Maritime Museum;
(top right) A. F. Cobb (bottom)
16–21 photo Marion Morrison
22 photo Tony Morrison
23 (top) Bristol City Museum
(bottom) photo Marion Morrison
24 photo Marion Morrison
29–32 National Maritime Museum
34 (top) Gordon Cramp;
(bottom) Professor Sverra Marstrender
35–6 Professor Sverra Marstrender
37 National Maritime Museum
38 Bremerhaven Maritime Museum
40 R. G. Harrison
44 (top) taken on Kodak radiography film by courtesy of
the Ministry of Cultural Affairs of the United Arab
Republic and the Laboratory of the Musées de France
44 (bottom) R. G. Harrison
47–9 R. G. Harrison
54 Peter Hall
57 Mrs E. Marinatou
58 Hirmer Fotoarchiv
59 (top) Hirmer Fotoarchiv; (bottom) Peter Hall
60 National Museum, Athens
61 Hirmer Fotoarchiv
62 (top) Hirmer Fotoarchiv; (bottom left) Greek National
Tourist Office, Athens; (bottom right) Hirmer Fotoarchiv
63 (top) National Museum, Athens; (bottom) Greek
National Tourist Office, Athens
64 (left) National Museum, Athens; (right) Hirmer Fotoarchiv
65 (left) Hirmer Fotoarchiv; (right) National Museum, Athens
70 Roger-Viollet
71 (top) Roger-Viollet; (bottom) Paul Jordan
73–6 Roger-Viollet
82 Giraudon
85 John Glover
87 Henry Lincoln
88 John Glover
91 Henry Lincoln

94 Joya Hairs
97 Gordon Cramp
98–9 Peabody Museum, Massachusetts
100 Giles Healey, Museum of Mankind
101 Joya Hairs
102 A. P. Maudslay, Museum of Mankind
103 (top) Gordon Cramp; (bottom) A. P. Maudslay,
Museum of Mankind
104 Museum of Mankind
105–6 Joya Hairs
107 Peabody Museum, Massachusetts
109 Joya Hairs
110 Museum of Mankind
111 Joya Hairs
112 (top left) Dept of the Environment;
(top right) Colin Renfrew; (bottom) Gordon Cramp
115 Gordon Cramp
117 (top) Museum of Mankind; (bottom) Colin Renfrew
118 Colin Renfrew
119–20 Museum of Mankind
121 Colin Renfrew
123 Roger-Viollet
124 Gordon Cramp
125–6 Colin Renfrew
131 (top left and bottom right) Faversham Society;
(top right) A. J. Percival; (bottom left) Northern Mill
Engine Society
133 (top) Ch. Leva; (bottom) Anders Jespersen
136–7 Landesdenkmalamt Westfalen-Lippe
140–1 Radio Times Hulton Picture Library
142–3 BBC
147–50 Radio Times Hulton Picture Library
151 BBC
152 Radio Times Hulton Picture Library
160–2 BBC
163 Malcolm Murray
165 Eric Eden
167 (top) BBC; (bottom) Eric Eden
168 BBC
169 Malcolm Murray

Introduction   Glyn Daniel

In the autumn of 1952 my telephone in Cambridge rang and a quiet, hesitant and slightly quavering voice announced that it belonged to a BBC producer called Paul Johnstone and asked if I could spare time to come to the Lime Grove Studios and take part in the trial run of a proposed new quiz game to be called *Animal, Vegetable, Mineral?* Reluctantly I agreed, and as we travelled back from Shepherd's Bush to Central London after the dry run, Sir Mortimer Wheeler and I agreed, sadly, that such a programme could never succeed. Three weeks later we both found ourselves in a live transmission of the programme and we appeared constantly on it for nine years until it came to an end in 1960. Paul knew better than we did what the TV audience should be taught to like, and how he could mould archaeologists and anthropologists to give them educated entertainment.

This was the beginning of an association which grew into a firm and warmly appreciated friendship. I soon got to know that the quiet and unassuming manner concealed a strength of character, an organisational and administrative ability, a sense of purpose, integrity, quiet determination, and great technical skill. Paul was convinced that television could and should teach as well as entertain, and yet, in venturing into the *haute vulgarisation* of archaeology and history, and later astronomy, he demanded and achieved the highest possible standards of scholarly accuracy and honesty, as perhaps one might have expected from a man who had emerged from reading History at Oxford with a First Class Degree.

Born in 1923, Paul went to Stowe School where the head boy during one of his years was another name now famous in broadcasting circles, namely Noël (now Lord) Annan. When the war came Paul joined the Royal Navy and rose from a volunteer Able Seaman to be a Lieutenant in command of his own gunboat, a motor launch in the Coastal Forces Then, three years at New College, a little school teaching, and, after a spell with BBC Radio, he joined BBC Television in 1951 and became one of its pioneer documentary producers, working with devotion and distinction until his untimely and much lamented death in 1976.

In a quarter century of television production he made an enormous contribution to establishing the name and nature and serious role of television, and made archaeology and history popular, interesting and absorbing. His obituary in *The Times* of 17 March 1976 said of *Animal, Vegetable, Mineral?*: 'It was an instant and spectacular success. Libraries found that neglected shelves of archaeological books were suddenly empty.' *AVM* gave birth to full-length archaeological documentaries under the title *Buried Treasure*. We hatched this series together and travelled all over Europe to make the programmes: to Italy to film the Etruscan towns and tombs, to France to photograph the treasure of Vix and the stone rows and megalithic tombs at Carnac, to the Orkneys to film Maes Howe and Skara Brae. My most vivid memory of those happy *Buried Treasure* days between 1954 and 1959 was when, in Copenhagen and in the presence of Princess Margrethe (now Queen of Denmark), Paul made Sir Mortimer Wheeler and myself taste a reconstruction of the last meal eaten by Tollund man two thousand years ago, before he was ritually hanged.

In 1966, the BBC, in its wisdom, created an Archaeological and Historical Unit, with Paul as its Director. He asked me to be his archaeological adviser, although by then I had become a Director of Anglia Television, and this I was happy to do for the next eleven years. I only took part in a few of the programmes which his unit put out under the title *Chronicle*. One was about Glozel, that strange forgery in central France which came into the news again in the last few years because Thermoluminescence dates suggested that some of the obvious forgeries (or obvious to an archaeologist) were made two thousand years ago. Glozel is not very far from Vichy and I well remember visiting hotels and restaurants in Vichy with Paul demanding Vichyssoise soup, before we realised that it was not a French dish but a potato and leek soup invented in the Waldorf-Astoria in New York. Another programme was about Lepinski Vir and we travelled together in adjoining and interconnected compartments on the Simplon-Orient from Calais to Belgrade, endlessly talking about archaeology and broadcasting. And the last programme we worked on together was about Colonial Williamsburg. I had been tremendously excited by this remarkable piece of archaeological research and reconstruction and was full of admiration for the work of Ivor Noel Hume, and had visited the site when I was teaching at Harvard. Paul came to America during my Harvard period and showed a series of *Buried Treasure* and *Chronicle* programmes there and elsewhere, to the astonishment and delight of his American audiences. We then planned the Williamsburg programme together, and three years later made it, although at that time it was sadly clear to me that his energies were flagging. But his interest and enthusiasm survived to the end.

Apart from his great role of *haute vulgarisateur* of archaeology on television – and his standards were never vulgar (in the English sense of that word), and always very high – he made three extremely important and original contributions to archaeology itself. First he embarked on novel and exciting archaeological experiments. He dressed me up in a tight-fitting and very hot garment of cow-hide designed by Brian Hope-Taylor and made me run about in Skara Brae. He reconstructed, as I have said, the last meal which Tollund man ate. He tried out replicas of Sumerian chariots. He got sixth-form schoolboys to punt replicas of the blue stones of Stonehenge up the Avon and drag them on sledges across Salisbury Plain. He

was fascinated when I told him that in Roman times geese from the territory of the Gaulish tribe the Morini (and I have a house in their territory between St Omer and Calais where Paul came to stay with us) were walked off to Rome where they and particularly their livers were a Roman delicacy. 'We must organise a goose-walk', he said at once, and this was the origin of his famous and fascinating programme in which geese walked along the Ridgeway; his calculations during these experiments showed us that the figures given for the journeys of geese from the north of France to Rome were accurate. It was while we were planning the goose-walk that we discovered that turkeys walked from Norfolk to Smithfield, and suddenly remembered together an object that had appeared on *AVM?* which we hardly believed possible, namely the little leather bootees which the turkeys wore for these walks; geese having larger harder feet had no need of these.

Paul's experiments in archaeology led to the sea which remained all his life one of his loves. He organised the building of a replica of a Bronze Age boat in Norway; this experiment was a great success and of the greatest value to serious archaeology. He organised the building of a curragh in Ireland and its sailing across to Wales. I knew that he was a don *manqué* – but lost to what a good cause, and I encouraged him to write; which he did – papers in *Antiquity*, a book called *Buried Treasure* based on the programmes, and eventually a book on prehistoric seacraft to be published next year. This book will be a mine of information and of informative comment for all archaeologists. He became, through his programmes and his intelligent preparation for them, an archaeologist in his own right, and it was a great pleasure to his friends and colleagues when he was elected a Fellow of the Society of Antiquaries. Mortimer Wheeler once said to me, 'Paul would have made a good professional archaeologist with his intense attention to detail and his visual appreciation of everything.'

Experiments; the sea. His third great serious contribution to archaeology was persuading the BBC to film a total excavation from beginning to end. He chose Silbury Hill and his cooperation with Richard Atkinson in the excavation of this curious monument is a tribute to the intelligent ideas of the BBC, the enthusiasm of Paul, and his friendship with Atkinson. That they never found the original burial (if there was one) is neither here nor there: they showed the world how excavation took place, its problems and difficulties, its hopes and despairs. It was a major effort of expository archaeology.

In his bachelor days and away from the studio and the archaeological filming in the field, he came on several holidays with my wife and myself. We wandered about France, Switzerland and North Italy, seeing churches and old towns, and occasionally the odd megalith, visiting art galleries and markets, and picknicking by the sides of rivers and in woods. He married Barbara Clegg in 1962 and had three children, Adam, Rufus and Jemima. It was a very happy marriage and he was devoted to his wife and children. These essays reflect some of the things he did while he ran *Chronicle*. We, and his wife and children, can see them as a reflection of a man whose loss we all mourn, but who, in his years at the BBC created a tradition and achieved something which many professional archaeologists thought, wrongly, was impossible. I quote the last words of David Attenborough's address at the memorial service for Paul in St James's, Piccadilly: 'His archaeological programmes from the early days of *Buried Treasure* right through to today's *Chronicle* have been quietly adventurous, thorough, filled with a delight in the world – and true. So was Paul: he gave us standards.'

The Return of the SS *Great Britain*   Tony Morrison

Port Stanley harbour, a sheltered sound in the East Falklands, is accustomed to strange comings and goings. Its lonely position in the gale-torn South Atlantic 500 miles off the southern tip of South America has assured it a place in maritime history. In the last century many of the great sailing ships rounding Cape Horn on the trading route to the Pacific ran for the islands in bad weather, and some, like the *Great Britain*, an iron ship of the Industrial Revolution, remained there as hulks: fine ageing relics of a glorious age.

The Falkland Islands were involved in both World Wars. In December 1914 the Battle of the Falklands was fought around the islands, and during the Second World War the cruiser HMS *Exeter* called in Port Stanley before and after the *Graf Spee* incident off Montevideo, the Uruguayan capital. Now, with those heady days over, the people of Stanley are more accustomed to sleek research vessels, tourist cruise ships or the occasional call from round-the-world yachtsmen.

Pembroke Light, established in 1855, is on the most easterly headland of the Falkland Islands and traditionally first with the news of arrivals. On 25 March 1970 the message came that a salvage flotilla was approaching in clear weather. Not more than 1000 people live in Stanley and slowly at first, then in groups of twos and threes, the islanders gathered until a large crowd was watching the narrow entrance to the inner harbour. Their curiosity was mixed with sadness: the 'salvage men' they had been expecting for over a year had arrived to take away 'their Britain' – the most famous of all the hulks in Falkland waters.

The *Varius II*, a converted stern trawler of 1724 tons, had been brought from West Africa under the command of Captain Hans Joachim Hertzog, with his crew of fifteen. On board was a team of salvage experts from the Anglo-German consortium of Risdon Beazley-Ulrich Harms headed by Britisher Leslie 'Spike' O'Neill. Spike, who had been in the Falklands before on HMS *Exeter*, was partnered by Horst Kaulen from Hamburg, who at thirty-two had already travelled the world as a senior salvage officer. Horst was the expert in charge of the submersible pontoon, *Mulus III*, which had crossed the Atlantic on a tow behind the *Varius*. The *Mulus*, 2667 tons, was 250 feet long and 79 feet wide: roughly a quarter the area of an international football pitch.

The 'narrows' or entrance to Stanley harbour are only about 300 yards wide and can be particularly tricky if the wind is anything but a head-wind. On Wednesday 25 March the relative calm was interrupted only by occasional squalls with light rain, and the waiting crowd watched with quiet scepticism while Captain Hertzog edged the giant pontoon into the harbour and anchored it almost directly in front of the tiny red-roofed Christchurch cathedral.

I had chosen a high viewpoint from which to film the arrival. My position was well above the rows of white-painted, red-roofed houses lining the steeply-rising Sappers Hill on the southern side of the harbour.

'Can't see how they'll do it, che,' one burly islander turned to me.

'I reckon the old ship'll float like a sieve,' muttered another, finishing off with: 'The *Britain*'s all rust and rot – not a chance of doing it, they'll be gone home in a week, che.'

'Che' is the islanders' customary form of address. Bets, mainly in pints and cases of beer, had been laid heavily between the islanders. The Island council had

The Great Britain *at Port Stanley before 1900*

11

even asked for guarantees in case the wreck broke up and blocked the main channel.

I left the hillside and walked downhill to one jetty to join my wife Marion and *Chronicle* producer Ray Sutcliffe who had been watching *Varius* from water level. With them was John Smith, a resident of the islands for many years and now the local representative of the British-based *Great Britain* Project Committee. John had been reporting on the state of the hulk since the first pre-salvage survey made in the previous year and he was there to welcome another committee representative, Lord Strathcona and Mountroyal, ex-Royal Navy. According to *Who's Who*, Lord Strathcona's hobbies are gardening and sailing. On the salvage he turned his hand to carpentry, reporting for the local radio and writing for *The Times*. The *Daily Telegraph* was represented by his brother-in-law, Viscount James Chewton from the west-country Waldegrave family.

As we stood on the wooden jetty with the black-hulled *Varius* only a few feet away moving gently against rubber fenders, we were in the most general terms a motley crew and for five weeks we were to be thrown together energetically with the one, almost obsessive, aim of salvaging the *Great Britain*. Our filming would often have to take second place to the weather and the needs of the salvage, and so frequently the cameras would have to be put down while a rope or small boat was held steady. Although the doubters nearly had a field day in the last moments of the operation, all the Falkland Islanders were quickly caught by the enthusiasm. Radio operators, weathermen, aircraft pilots, fishermen, the Council, and the Governor and his wife, Sir Cosmo and Lady Haskard, all jointly directed their efforts to the salvage.

The story began in 1769, over 6000 miles away in Haqueville on the fertile plain of Vexin in Normandy, when on 25 April Marc Isambard Brunel was born. His parents, local tenant farmers of long standing, expected their son to enter the church, but instead he turned to engineering. Marc escaped from the Revolution and travelled to America where after a series of business deals he became chief engineer for the City of New York, returning to Europe in 1799. After his marriage in London in November of the same year, the 30-year-old Marc Brunel established an engineering partnership in Britain. In 1806 his son Isambard was born in Portsea, and from that moment some of the most brilliant and bold steps in Victorian engineering were guaranteed. The young Isambard Brunel not only designed bridges and railways, he also conceived remarkable new ideas for ships. His steamship, *Great Britain*, started in 1839, was to become a milestone. It was the first large ship to be built of metal. One thousand and forty tons of iron were used, as steel and the Bessemer Process for removing carbon from pig iron had yet to be invented. The *Great Britain* was 322 feet long overall, 289 feet at the keel (almost 100 feet longer than a Jumbo Jet). The ship was designed for good economics, and made the first crossing of the Atlantic with a screw propeller. Only a series of near-disasters affected her career.

The second part of the story leading to Stanley in 1970 began for the *Britain* after an eventful life, first with the route to New York, followed by trooping to the Crimea (between 1855 and 1856), and nineteen years on the Australia run. In 1882 she was converted into a sailing ship and then made four voyages to the West Coast of America. On 6 February 1886 she set out from Penarth with a cargo of coal for Panama. The route lay across the Atlantic towards the humid coast of Brazil: south-east of Santos in heavy weather, a small fire began – it was extinguished and little damage resulted. Captain Stap headed the *Great Britain* for Cape Horn and, in worsening weather and mountainous seas, the cargo slipped causing a strong list to port. Working in terrifying conditions, the crew shovelled the coal uphill in the 'tween decks, restoring some stability, but the wind and seas were immense. The top gallants were blown away and with the ship disabled, Captain Stap reluctantly turned for the Falklands for shelter. The ship arrived off Cape Pembroke at 3pm on 24 May 1886.

On examination the *Britain* was considered sound – a great tribute to Brunel's design, but the repairs were estimated at £5500. So for reasons which are not clear the Falkland Islands Company acquired the ship and converted the hulk into a floating wool store that was

The fitting out, photographed by Fox-Talbot in 1843

In mid-career, with three masts and new engines (1860s)

Beginning her third career as a floating warehouse (turn of the century)

13

used for the next forty-seven years. For that time the *Great Britain* was anchored in Stanley harbour and became a local landmark. Then in 1937 the hull, deemed unsound and apparently at the end of its useful life, was towed out through the 'narrows' and beached in a shallow bay of Sparrow Cove some 3½ miles away. The next day, holes were knocked in the bottom ensuring that the huge iron ship would not move again or endanger other vessels.

By the time that Hans Hertzog was anchoring *Varius* and the *Mulus* in Stanley, the *Great Britain* had been in Sparrow Cove for almost thirty-three years, exposed to the wind, driving rain and the daily rise and fall of the tide. The iron plating and iron frames had suffered the effects of exposure to air and sea water alternately over 24,000 times, a process which had left the structure weakened. Precisely how weak was a matter of conjecture and the *Great Britain* Project Committee relied upon the expertise of Dr Ewan Corlett, a naval architect, who had first proposed the recovery of the *Britain* in a letter to *The Times* in 1967. Dr Corlett visited the Falklands in 1968 to make a survey of the state of the vessel and to suggest ways for effecting the salvage. After diving and testing the plating ultrasonically he reckoned the iron structure was sound and he was convinced the ship could be refloated. Leslie O'Neill, when he visited the Falklands on behalf of the salvage consortium, concurred with Ewan Corlett's estimate of 80% success and, on reporting his findings to the committee chaired by Richard Goold-Adams, a cheque for £150,000 was signed by Jack Hayward, OBE, to underwrite the cost of the work.

Behind the scenes other wheels had been turning, and a detachment of Royal Marines based in the Islands for training were given the official chance to try their hand at some of the salvage work. Their commanding officer, Captain Malcolm McLeod, put a diesel-powered workboat, the *Marauder*, at the disposal of the team and for *Chronicle* to use as a camera platform, so that we could then manoeuvre independently of the larger salvage vessels.

Thursday 26 March was cold. A keen wind was causing a gentle chop on the grey water of the harbour when Ray Sutcliffe, Marion and I set out for Sparrow Cove ahead of *Varius* and the *Mulus*. Stanley harbour is a long inlet running almost due east-west and surrounded by low hills of grey rock, covered by white grass and low bushes to the water's edge. Once through the 'narrows' the *Marauder* was turned northeast and Sparrow Cove lay almost directly ahead. The *Britain* was beached far into the cove on the east side. A small pebbly promontory acted as a natural breakwater to the seaward side of the hulk and it was also a landing-place for Chris Bundes, the local farmer and owner of a small green hut which became the *Chronicle* 'office' in times of emergency.

The sunken remains of two iron scows were half exposed near the beach and as we approached a pair of black cormorants shuffled nervously along the rusting iron of the *Britain*'s stern before hurriedly leaving in a rapid flight across the calm water. We were ahead of the *Varius* and had time to pass around the *Britain* before going ashore to set up the camera. The hulk was resting in the same position as it had been beached thirty-three years earlier: dull and grey, it showed half above the water and supported three massive wooden masts, the centre one bearing a huge spar. The hull was sheathed in pitchpine, 3½ inches thick, an addition made in 1882 for no reason which has ever been fully explained. One suggestion is that the wood was a protection against ice floes in the southern Atlantic or to prevent fouling: another which also seems plausible is that the wood afforded protection, albeit expensive, against damage by the lighters used for trading in ports such as Iquique and Antofagasta on the Pacific coast of Chile. In 1970 the wooden sheathing, bolted and caulked, was virtually intact; only the planks covering the bulwarks had been removed.

We glided along the port side towards the bow. The 41-foot-long bowsprit that had been on the ship when it was towed to the cove had rotted and fallen some time after the ship was scuttled. It was recovered by a local diver the year before the salvage. The bow loomed twenty feet above us, bearing the broken end of the bowsprit and its iron mounting. On the starboard side, almost parallel to the shore, the wooden sheathing was broken by a jagged vertical crack which extended from the gunwale to the water. (Divers later found that this crack almost reached the centre-line.) The iron plates of the hull had also broken, though precisely when no one was sure.

It was this large crack which was of prime concern to the salvagemen. The weakness was introduced when the Falkland Island Company cut through the main longitudinal iron girders to make a side opening into the hull for loading wool bales. In effect, the top corner of the hull was destroyed to make the opening and even the top flange of the hull girder was cut into. As testimony to the strength in Brunel's original design, the hull did not break until long after it was beached. One story from farmer Chris Bundes told of a stormy night in a small boat when, alongside the lee of the Britain, he heard 'a sharp ear-splitting report'. The noise was not explained immediately, but a visitor later described the crack. The hull might have survived had it not been for the scouring action of the tides that shifted sand from under the bow and more from under the stern. In the later years in Sparrow Cove, the vessel was supported only amidships, and in marine terms it was 'hogged'. The strain on the already-weakened side caused the crack and later opened it considerably. The scouring and hogging continued after Ewan Corlett's visit and a grave concern for the Committee was the possibility that the strong bottom girders, plates and a wooden keel (seventeen inches deep and twenty inches wide – added in 1852) would break: the Britain would then fall into two halves.

The whole problem was exacerbated by the weight of the masts, over twenty tons apiece and probably the largest masts ever built for a sailing ship. During the winter of 1968 John Smith, aided by local fisherman Mickey Clark, wedged the main mast and secured the spar to lessen the movement. He also regularly monitored the crack. The shift in just one year was ten inches down and ten inches wider. The Britain was actually digging its own grave.

As John Smith explained 'live' over the island radio, the salvage operation would be attempted in three phases. Firstly, to strengthen and patch the hull generally, and to lighten it by removing the masts. A second stage of pumping out and refloating – a bold course but one supported by the salvage survey: 'the hull is in good condition for floating', it stated. However, the engineers had no intention of risking the Britain afloat for too long, and the third stage, easing the old vessel over the submerged pontoon, would ensure the safety of Brunel's ship. Finally the pontoon was to be floated again thus raising the Britain above the sea.

Varius arrived in Sparrow Cove with the Mulus. The pontoon was positioned end on' to the port side of the Britain, almost amidships. The crack was directly opposite on the starboard side. The Varius took up station with her port side to the Mulus and bow on to the side of the Britain. The Britain was dwarfed probably for the first time since the World War I cruisers of the Royal Navy had been in Stanley harbour. The tranquillity of the cove was soon replaced by bustle: the hum of powerful dynamos, the hiss of cutting torches, and a clatter of metal. The salvage, the first of its kind ever attempted, was started immediately.

Day 'One', Thursday 26 April, was filled with intense though unspectacular activity and the decks were cleared for action. Once the Mulus and Varius were anchored firmly, a diver went into the stern of the Great Britain to examine the scuttling holes. Water from the tide slopped in and out without obstruction and patches had to be prepared. A team of Marines built wooden walkways across the old weathered decking which, being wooden and laid in the 1882 refit, had rotted. Not surprisingly, the old planks were in a lethally dangerous state after eighty-eight years: soft, sometimes moss-covered, or with patches of island 'white grass' growing in places. In parts they were so rotten that a false step would mean an instant plunge into the watery iron pit fifteen feet below. On the steel deck of the pontoon, Horst Kaulen's team prepared an A frame, or 'sheerlegs', of tubular steel that was to be raised at the end of the Mulus near the Britain. The sheerlegs were to be used as a simple crane, or as a support to each mast in turn as they were removed.

Sunrise was clear on the Friday and the weather remained fine all day, so warm that even in those sub-antarctic latitudes it was a day for shirt-sleeves, and good for filming the first dramatic moments. Sergeant Tony Stott of the Royal Marines climbed the mainmast to the X foretop, to the main spar, a hollow-metal tapered construction 105 feet long, which, with an iron bridle, weighed between four and five tons. The spar was hanging sixty-eight feet above the deck, and Tony Stott's climb, made with special 'climber's knots', was the first recorded climb of the mast since the days when the *Britain* was in Stanley. After nonchalantly declaring the view to be marvellous, he fitted the sling and pulley-block for a bosun's chair. Before the mast was removed, I was able to reach the top and photograph the ship from the mast, probably another record.

opened, allowing the huge spar, only three feet shorter than the wingspan of a Boeing 727 jet, to be lowered. If it had fallen in the gales of the previous winter, the centre of the ship would have been smashed. While everyone, spectators and engineers alike, heaved a great sigh of relief, no one noticed that the main mast was quietly burning. A fine plume of smoke was drifting across the cove. The flame of the gas torch had set alight the rotten timber which, fanned by a gentle breeze, was burning 'very nicely', to quote one observer. A crewman was hurriedly despatched to the top of the mast to attack the flames, first with pails of water hauled from over the side, and then successfully with a foam extinguisher. Night settled over a tired but satisfied crew: things were going well – everyone was settling in. The difficult work was about to begin.

View of the deck from the mainmast

Lowering the mainmast

Once Tony Stott was down the salvage crew fixed more tackle, including a heavy block with a cable to a capstan on the *Varius*. Next a salvageman with an oxy-acetylene torch cut through the chains, sending a shower of sparks across the deep blue sky. The cable took the weight, supporting the spar which was allowed to fall slowly: then the severed chain links

When Brunel designed the *Great Britain* as a steamship, he gave the ship six masts and named them after the days of the week: from bow to stern Monday through to Saturday. The largest of them was the lower part of No. 2 mast – ninety-six feet to the keel. Its top-mast added a further fifty-five feet – indeed an immense construction. The other five masts of the 1843 ship were hinged at deck level but probably could never be fully lowered. Alterations in 1846, three years after launching, added a 'top gallant' mast to No. 2; 1852 saw No. 3 mast removed, No. 4 square-rigged, and No. 5 totally removed. Only masts 1 and 6 remained as Brunel designed them. The alterations, according to Dr Corlett, added an increase of 75 per cent over the original sail plan. Then in April 1853 more changes were made and a conventional three-masted rig was introduced, with top gallants on all masts.

At that time the *Britain* was making her second run to Australia; she completed the journey to Melbourne in sixty-five days. The foremast was probably the original No. 2 from 1845, and the main mast from 1846. These then, less the top masts (removed when the ship was hulked by the Falkland Island Company), were the masts standing on 29 March 1970. None were hinged: all were stepped on to the keel and each was built from four trees looped with hinged iron bands. They were as large as any mast ever fitted in a sailing ship. The foremast 93 feet; the mainmast 95 feet (18 tons and 43 inches in diameter); and the mizzenmast $79\frac{1}{2}$ feet. They had carried 33,000 square feet of sail, almost twice the area of the exposed surface area of the *Mulus*. Working on the principle that what goes up must come down, the salvage team set to work.

My diary says: 'Mizzen mast – Sunday 29 March. Calm weather.' This was a most important factor as the Falkland Islands are notable for gales and sudden squalls and these could have brought disastrous consequences with over fifteen tons of mast swinging free. Plan One involved moving *Mulus* until the sheerlegs A frame was in line with the mizzen, and then using the frame as a crane for lifting. A hawser fixed to the mast by a wire strap would run from a winch on the *Varius*, and extra lift was expected from the tide raising *Mulus* against the side of the *Britain*. All proceeded according to plan. A chain saw clattered in the depths of the hull, wielded skilfully by Willy Bowles, a local carpenter. A length was cut from the bottom of the mast, and lifting continued.

Horst was directing, more like conducting a modern symphony: one hand to the winchman, another to the crew. The decks were empty. 'Up, up,' he shouted. The cable moved inch by inch. The hushed expectancy of the audience was suddenly rewarded with a sharp crack as the mast broke near deck level, swung on its pivot from the sheerlegs, and toppled slowly

and gracefully. The mizzen then crashed through the remains of the 1882 galley that Euan Strathcona had spent all day repairing as a store for the divers' gear. It was called 'The lord's Teehaus' by the German crew.

Horst, standing well clear, leaped almost three feet in the air, threw his hat on the deck, and jumped on it. My knowledge of German improved three times in as many seconds.

The danger signals were seen. It was decided not to attempt to lift the main and foremast. Instead, they were held by tackle to the sheerlegs and cut above deck level. A down-pull by a cable to the lower part of each mast allowed Horst to topple them with perfect control. By Wednesday 1 April, seven days into the operation, the three masts were down and the bedraggled remains of the rigging had been cleared. Late in the afternoon, Malcolm McLeod took us in *Mar-*

Mulus alongside the dismasted Great Britain

auder across Sparrow Cove to film the hulk, now sad and inelegant without the grace of proportions given by the masts and lone spar. The tallest part of the Falklands landmark had gone.

The next stage of sealing the crack and patching the holes had started, and work was proceeding almost unobtrusively on both fronts. Once again the salvagers had to be thankful for the massiveness of Brunel's original design. The ship was based on a strong iron-built platform, not a double bottom in the modern sense as it was not watertight, but a structure that provided enormous strength. Five solid half-inch girders ran longitudinally, and the frames to form the shape of the hull extend to the centre-line under the platform. Dr Corlett gives the details, including 'a flat plate keel 10 inches wide and $\frac{11}{16}$ths of an inch thick, an outer keel 20 inches wide and $\frac{7}{8}$th of an inch thick'. These features, plus the iron hull plating $\frac{11}{16}$ths of an inch thick, had lasted well. The various surveys and reports of the divers left little doubt that the *Britain*, once patched, would float again. A second starboard entrance cut originally for loading wool had not included the gunwale and was not a cause of concern.

Strapping the hull

Then the salvage engineers, with infinite patience and minds flexed for any eventuality, decided to strap the ship together with half-inch-thick steel plates. Three would be used: one at weather-deck level, and one each for the upper and lower 'tween decks bolted to the original iron stringers. All the wooden 'tween-deck planking had been removed before scuttling and inside the hull there was little more than the bare, rusting iron framework. The strapping plates had been brought to the Falklands on the *Mulus* and, though each weighed over a ton, the crew using Tirfor winches and sheerlegs moved them about like dominoes. The plates were drilled to match the strong iron stringers and duly bolted into position.

Plan One recommended that the aft end of the hull should be made watertight, then as it was pumped dry its buoyancy would raise the aft section while the section forward of the crack remained on the bottom. The crack would close, the strapping would be completed and the reduced crack would be patched. The engineers had to alter course half-way, when the after engine-room bulkhead (part of Brunel's original design) proved to be impossible to repair to a watertight state. The alternative was to strap the hull in the hogged condition and fill the crack with mattresses – 'an old Navy technique', explained Lesie O'Neill, 'But we'll need a lot of mattresses'. Thus with visions of people sleeping on bare boards, a call went out to

Divers preparing to patch the hull

18

Stanley on Thursday 2 April and twenty-four hours later twenty mattresses had been offered. The Marines went around the town collecting them and carried them to the increasingly busy salvage scene on *Marauder*, now firmly established among an attendant flotilla of small craft.

When the *Britain* was beached in 1937 seven holes were made in the bottom and around the raked stern below water level. The largest openings were about four feet by eighteen inches and by the time the mattresses were ready all the holes had been closed with plywood and special concrete. Pumps with a total capacity of 660 tons per hour had been swung from the *Varius* to the *Britain* and set on specially-built platforms in the now-empty cargo space.

In his seventh report for the island radio and speaking from the 'teehaus' John Smith, being the local expert, was asked for his impressions of the changes made within the first week. 'Staggering' was his reply. And he was particulary impressed by the apparent size the ship had assumed once the masts were out.

The final stage began when the *Mulus* was moved into a predetermined position in the centre of the cove. Pumping was started at low tide at midnight on Monday 6 April. This gave the machines a head start on the incoming sea as the *Britain*'s hull was then almost empty. By 7 am the next day, the *Britain* was clearly afloat, and the divers worked hard all the morning and into the afternoon, securing the many small holes that were concealed by the mud or had appeared in places where the iron plating was fragile. Also, as the experts had predicted, the crack began to close. By 3.30 pm the divers had finished and the ship was afloat with the pumps running lightly. But everyone was watching with growing concern as a south-westerly wind freshened and turned into a gale. White-topped waves rolled across Sparrow Cove tossing the many small craft that came from Stanley crowded with islanders for the great moment of refloating. The most powerful of the island boats then found themselves called upon to help as the *Britain* was blown from her beached position. Bow and stern lines had been fixed, but would they be enough? Chris Bundes had the most powerful boat, *Malvinas*, an

auxiliary fishing vessel, and he brought it up to push on the port bow of the *Britain* while *Lively*, a harbour tug and work-boat owned by the Falkland Island Company, was hitched up to the starboard bow to pull.

With no sign of the wind abating, Leslie O'Neill stopped the pumps on the *Britain* and over an anxious period of four hours the almost watertight hulk settled lightly on the bottom again. While *Lively* and *Malvinas* kept the strain from the shore lines, it was a nail-biting moment for *Chronicle*: what was probably the most exciting action in the *Great Britain*'s recent history was impossible to film. A storm-blackened night closed in quickly and only the powerful searchlight of *Varius* cut through the driving rain. *Chronicle* cameraman, stills photographer and director struggled through the gloom across the *Britain*'s planking onto the *Malvinas* and through the waves breaking on the shore. Nothing could be filmed and the *Britain* was fighting for a second life. Eventually at 1 am on 8 April, the film team retired to Chris Bundes' green hut on the promontory to clamber, with feelings of relief and despair, into sodden sleeping-bags. (As a crowning misery the bags had been dropped in the sea at some stage of the night's activity.)

Due mainly to continuing bad weather, the refloating was delayed for two days. Then on Friday 10 April at last there seemed a good chance of success. Pumping was started overnight. We made a filming sortie at 5.15 am in one of the Island's two Beaver floatplanes. A helicopter from HMS *Endurance*, the Royal Navy Ice Patrol Ship, hovered ahead. We looked down: at last the *Britain* was moving. With the high tide that day, the first attempt was made to manoeuvre her over the pontoon which was submerged about 400 yards south-west of the place where she had been beached.

At the first try there were many problems. The hull was heavy with mud and rubbish, including old cables and 'donkey' engines from the days in Stanley. The ship's draught as estimated for a docking was not attained, and the divers then discovered that the bottom of the *Britain* was sticking on the pontoon. The only line of action was to 'pull off' and move the pontoon into deeper water. But before a second attempt could be made, another gale struck.

Chris Bundes was the first with the warning. His barometer on *Malvinas* had fallen lower than he had ever seen it and the fall was sudden. This time, however, there was time to secure the *Britain* by lines, and the old ship was allowed to ride out the storm that lashed the tiny cove at Beaufort Scale 10 and higher. When Lord Strathcona described the *Britain* riding out its first storm for many years, he said over the island radio: 'Very well it did too – not a moment's anxiety all night.'

Once more Brunel's iron ship had not been beaten, and the salvage crew turned to the task of flushing out the hull with water and pumping out mud. On Saturday 11 April, a fine day with a keen though gentle wind, the *Britain*, lightened considerably, floated over the *Mulus*, pushed and pulled by a motley array of sea power. *Varius* nudged at the stern and *Lively*, *Malvinas* and *Marauder* pulled until only twenty feet of the old sailing ship were not over the pontoon. Later the same day, after more of the mud and rubbish had been cleared from inside the hull, the *Britain* slipped gently on to the pontoon, to stand firmly between tall 'dolphins' – 12-inch steel tubes, 33 feet high and arranged in two rows approximately the beam of the *Britain* apart.

But the surprises were not over. That night the watchman on the *Britain* heard a loud explosion. At about 2 am on the twelfth, as the tide receded and the iron ship settled on the solid bed of the *Mulus*, the crack closed even more until the massive steel strapping plates buckled under the strain of keeping it open. Two 1-inch bolts holding part of a plate snapped cleanly through and the *Britain* straightened; the 'hogging' disappeared and once more Brunel's massive iron structure had shown its strength. The same day the divers went down and closed the valves on the *Mulus*, air from compressors was pumped in and thirty-three years to the day, 12 April 1937, almost to the hour, that the *Britain* had been taken to Sparrow Cove, the bow was raised out of the water.

Another day was needed to raise the rear end of the *Mulus*, as the stability of what was virtually a floating cistern with a ship on top needed careful handling. The salvage was complete: the *Britain* was out of the

Inspecting the hull aboard the Mulus

water. The hull was surprisingly free of weed and growth, except for mussels: 'The *Great Britain*'s mussels are famous – the best in the islands' was one comment.

On 14 April, in the teeth of yet another gale, Captain Hertzog towed the *Mulus* triumphantly through the 'narrows' into Stanley harbour. Brunel's iron hull was standing six feet above the water and lay on the pontoon like a model ready for an exhibition. The operation had taken nineteen days. Another eight days would be needed to prepare for the tow to Avonmouth, the longest of its kind ever to be made.

With the *Mulus* and *Great Britain* alongside the East jetty in Stanley, the salvage crew had space to move and, working around the clock, the British and German engineers strapped and welded the *Britain* to the pontoon. The salvaged vessel was covered by insurance, but as Leslie O'Neill explained, he and Horst Kaulen felt the great responsibility of securing the *Britain* for the 'long and difficult tow through various climes'.

Then came the official transfer ceremony when the Governor of the Falkland Islands, Sir Cosmo Haskard, presented Lord Strathcona with the documents transferring ownership of the wreck. (As it was a Crown Wreck, the Governor in Council had to recommend to the Secretary of State that ownership should be transferred.) Referring to the long Falkland Islands associ-

The Great Britain's *bow being raised out of Sparrow Cove*

The tow home

ation with the wreck, Sir Cosmo reminded everyone 'that our oldest residents were children when the *Britain* came here'.

All too soon it was departure day: much flag waving, sad goodbyes, a flotilla as islanders followed in boats, people raced to the narrows, and the islands' Beaver aircraft dipped its wings overhead. A Royal Marine Hovercraft buzzed past for last-minute photographs. With Ray Sutcliffe I travelled as far as Montevideo on the *Varius*, and Marion went on the regular monthly service of the RMS *Darwin* two days later and reached the Uruguayan capital before us. Nigel Miller, *Darwin*'s captain, picked up the *Varius* and her tow on the radar at 9 pm on 28 April, and by 10 pm they had passed us. Marion said all they saw was 'just a glow on the horizon from the *Varius* searchlight'.

Only once did Captain Hertzog heave to on the nine-day trip, and for the film it was one of the most exciting moments. The salvage tug's workboat was slid down the stern ramp, and in brilliantly fine weather we made a wide turn around the *Mulus*. The massive bow of the *Britain* rose high over our heads: eighty-four years had passed since the proud ship had been on the high seas.

The 7400-mile tow across the Atlantic took sixty-nine days and Captain Hertzog averaged $4\frac{1}{2}$ knots.

But, with the film metaphorically under his arm, Ray Sutcliffe had taken the first available flight from Montevideo to London. There, with a detailed visual history of the *Great Britain* already in hundreds of separate pieces, the salvage sequences were spliced into a film story that had taken two years to make. A 50-minute programme was ready for the homecoming and was transmitted on 13 June 1970. But the story was not complete.

At Avonmouth extra strengthening and more patches were added. The *Mulus* was again submerged and Brunel's ship floated in 'home waters'. On Sunday 5 July a crowd of 100,000 gathered along the Portway built beside the Avon river through the limestone gorge at Sea Mills and Clifton. With a tug towing and small boats in attendance the *Great Britain* completed a stately final journey along the winding course of the river to where it passed beneath the Suspension Bridge, designed by Brunel but never finished in his lifetime. The crowds waved flags, traffic hooted and TV helicopters whistled by: the Risdon Beazley salvage crew stood proudly on the Great Britain returning the greetings. The welcome was spontaneous and it largely overshadowed the last, most symbolic events of the long journey, from the loneliness of Sparrow Cove with the spirit of the Falkland Islands.

(Lower) *Returning up the Avon Gorge to the dock from which she had sailed on her maiden voyage* (top)   23

The steamship *Great Britain* had been built in Bristol between 1839 and 1843 by the Great Western Steamship Company. A dock costing £53,000 had been constructed specially to accommodate Brunel's ship and the dock is still there, known as the Great Western Dock. It is close to the centre of Bristol, and on 19 July 1843 Prince Albert had been there at the launch. Thousands of people had lined the processional route from Brunel's Temple Meads railway station, while 30,000 people crowded on to Brandon Hill overlooking the dock. Cannons were fired and the list of guests was long and imposing.

On the evening of 19 July 1970, exactly 127 years later to the day, HRH Prince Philip stood on the stern of the *Great Britain*, watching with sharp interest as Brunel's ship was edged back into the dock where it had been built. The launch had been marred by the *Britain* sticking in the dock gates, but now the hull of the old iron ship slipped easily into the dock, but with only inches to spare. It was a momentous evening: Brunel's Great Iron Ship had been returned to its cradle.

The SS Great Britain *returns to her construction dock*

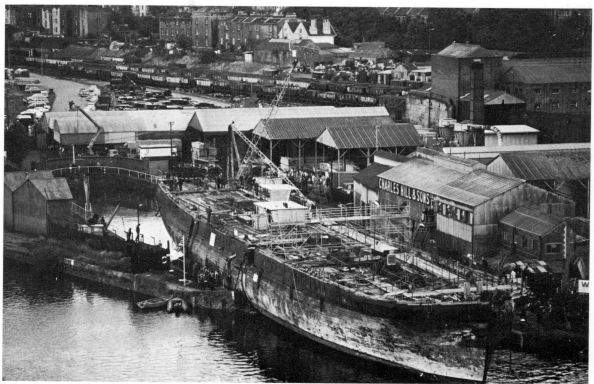

The Archaeology of The Boat   Basil Greenhill

Great as was Paul Johnstone's contribution to interpreting the work of archaeologists in general to the television viewer there was one special field in which he may be said personally to have played a large part in the creation of a new study. When Paul began his work as a producer, maritime history, and especially the history of ships, was very rarely touched upon on television. When he finished it was a popular subject, and it has remained so. One particular aspect of the history of ships, the archaeology and ethnography of boats and the early ships which developed from them, was almost unknown when Paul began in the late fifties. Now it is a discipline in its own right, a part of the complex of archaeological specialisms which cannot be ignored.

In many ways the subject of the development of boats and ships was the most difficult archaeological problem that the television of the 1960s had to handle. It is an esoteric subject, far from the daily experience of ordinary people. Other artefacts of man – pottery, buildings, tools, jewellery, fortifications, drainage schemes – had their own archaeological specialists, but the study of boats had not. Wooden structures, including boats, do not, of course, survive the centuries so well as metal, pottery and stone. But they do survive and are found, and the probability is that far more boat structures than is known have been found and ignored because they have not been recognised for what they are.

Initially Paul's interest in the archaeology of boats was a very personal enthusiasm. Besides all the other difficulties of introducing an entirely new subject of study, in handling boats and ships and seamen television had to overcome the classic alienation of the seafarer from the rest of society, and of the rest of society, the great bulk of mankind, from the seafarer. This is an alienation which extends by association to those who follow trades, like boatbuilding, which are closely allied to seafaring. The separate worlds of the seafarer and the landsman must have developed very early in the history of man's encounter with the sea. Essentially the seaman's world is cut off from the ordinary everyday life of most of us, so that the seaman thinks and behaves differently and reacts differently – very differently when his world was as specialised and exotic as that of the three-masted square-rigged sailing ship, built of wood and rigged with natural fibres, which was the standard world-travelling, sea-going vehicle until the second half of the last century. This world of men who fished from open boats; of men who carried cargoes and people to North America in the 1600s packed so tightly that those on board had only eighteen inches square each to call their own; of men who built up the patterns of European trade in medieval cogs and hulks, was so strange and different that it was not only another world, but also a closed world which most historians have preferred to ignore, fundamental though it was to human development.

To begin to translate the world of the prehistoric and medieval seaman and the boat builder, or some parts of it, into a channel of popular awareness and interest, to begin to convey a very special area of academic enthusiasm to the large and well-informed audience of the *Chronicle* series, required the certain conviction that it could be done. This Paul had in good measure. But it was his most difficult subject, not only because of the strange and alien nature of the content, but also because it was so new that little work had been done on it. There was so little to show, and what there was was not spectacular or beautiful, or even, at first sight, particularly interesting. Indeed, apart from the Gokstad and Oseberg ships at Oslo, there was almost nothing complete to show to audiences: nothing easily recognisable as a boat or ship, much less as an object of efficiency and beauty.

The remains of boats and ships are as a general rule not spectacular until much work has been done on them. They convey little or nothing, except to a very small number of specialists, until they have been interpreted by meticulous examination, measurement, recording and analysis, and illuminated by creative imagination. Paul Johnstone had to gain his audience's attention and interest while entirely new work was going on in a new field without spectacular results to demonstrate. He had to convey knowledge as it was generated; almost, to present thinking in the process of development. At the time he produced his early programmes almost nothing was available in print on the subject of the archaeology of boats. Now there is a good deal of material, popular, academic, and in the form of reports of finds, and quite widespread knowledge. As with his other work of exposition – but especially in this field, so much his own original contribution – many thousands of people have experienced the fascination and involvement of the subject which Paul Johnstone brought to life. In this they have been helped by his own writings. Besides his popular book, *The Archaeology of Ships*, he published original contributions in *Antiquity* and in the *International Journal of Nautical Archaeology*.

To illustrate the methods of the producer I shall summarise briefly the present stage of the study of the archaeology of boats and take a number of extracts from three programmes – programmes which Paul Johnstone himself rightly regarded as keystones in the exposition of the subject – to help the account. This approach will illustrate the way in which *Chronicle* used the existing, fragmentary material to convey the whole, and to show it in the wider world of the contemporary scene.

The archaeology of boats can never be archaeology in a narrow sense, because the study of the development of boats involves not only the remains of ancient boats but also of twentieth-century boats of very many different kinds all over the world. Thus it is archaeology according to Webster's definition: that is, 'the scientific study of the material remains of past human life and experience'. These remains can be buried in the mud of the Oslo Fjord or the mound at Sutton Hoo, or be found painted on a church wall in the Åland Islands; and their twentieth-century analogue can be seen carrying a cargo of firewood in the Gulf of St Lawrence or on the great rivers of Bangla Desh.

In the world of boats the ancient and modern coexist to a degree uncommon with man's artefacts. It is perfectly possible to find – in Bangla Desh for example – dugout canoes, highly sophisticated wooden boats, and several different intermediate kinds of boats, all lying together on the same stretch of river bank. These boats may be literally thousands of years apart in development. A very great deal is to be learned about the development of boats from the study of these contemporary examples – providing that it is not assumed that things were necessarily the same in the past as they are now, or the same elsewhere as they are in the place of study; and bearing in mind such things as the development of tools and their use – by using the contemporary as an indication of what is possible, and as a source of ideas for interpreting other information. Moreover, the naval architect with his calculations and graphs plays a large part in the new discipline – indeed his arrival on the scene has been one of the landmarks in development in very recent years.

The intensive study at Greenwich of recent finds is not only revealing information about them, it is generating new methods and techniques as it goes along. We are only now beginning to learn what questions to ask. Thanks to the work of Ole Crumlin Pedersen on Danish finds, of Arne Emil Christensen in Norway, and of others, we now know a relatively great deal, for example, about Viking Age shipbuilding within 250 miles or so of the Skaw, the northern tip of Denmark; and we know quite a lot about the development of boats in one or two other areas for very restricted periods. But when all is added up these are small fragments of the whole. We are right at the beginning of the study of a new branch of the history of man's activities. The confident statements of the writers of a generation ago on the evolution of the Viking ship or the Portuguese caravel have been undermined by recent discoveries and thinking. It will be a long time before they will be replaced with any degree of certainty. In this uncertainty, of course, the archaeology of boats is merely a very apparent example of a process going on in archaeology generally: the development of scientific method is leading to the questioning of many long accepted ideas.

But a number of new ideas are standing the test of constant reappraisal. It seems, for example, that boats all over the world began in one of four different ways. Some boats developed from rafts, some of them boat shaped, but still dependent for their buoyancy not on being watertight and thus enclosing air, but from the fact that the material from which they are made is much lighter than water, so much lighter that they can not only float themselves but also have reserve buoyancy to carry people and goods. Some developed from boats made by sewing a covering of animal skin or fabric on to a framework previously made of wood or bone. Some boats were made by stripping a continuous cylinder of bark from a suitable tree and forming a boat shape out of the bark itself. The shape was maintained by building a strengthening framework inside the vessel, usually of twigs bound together. But the largest class of boat, indeed the majority of plank-built boats which were used in the western world until the recent development of glass-reinforced plastics, came from quite a different source. This was the 'dugout', more properly the log-boat, made by hollowing out and shaping a log, and thus producing a basic boat-shape which could carry loads on the water in proportion to the wood cut out.

The four types of boat developed independently, probably several, indeed many, times over in different parts of the world in human history. In places they interacted, so that influences from more than one origin affected the shape and structure and development of later boats. The four origins appear to have had varying degrees of influence on the development of boats generally. The skin-boat and the bark-boat are really dead ends, susceptible of a surprising, but in the end limited, degree of development. The raft advances when it takes the great step of ceasing to be a raft and becoming a watertight vessel. Some authorities consider that in the raft is the origin of many of the vessels of the vast and complex boat culture of China – but not of Japan, where it seems certain that the indigenous boats have been derived from dugouts. On the other hand, the hollowed out log is susceptible to almost limitless development and the majority of the boats of the western world appear to be derived from it.

Hollowing out a log to make a log-boat was, like building a wooden house, a considerable undertaking. There had to be suitable trees near the water and there had to be time – which meant a sufficient surplus of food – and reasonably efficient tools. So a community which made log boats had to be prosperous and relatively developed. But it was possible to hollow out a log before it was technically possible to make planks and join them together to make a watertight boat-shape, and the idea of such a structure may not have been conceivable until the log-boat had shown the way. Slowly, as ideas and tools developed, planks were added to make dugouts wider and deeper. In this way the shell-constructed plank-built boat developed at different times, in different societies, in different parts of the world.

For it is certain that there are two great classes of wooden plank built boats in the world, those which are built of planks joined edge to edge and usually, but not always, joined to strengthening frames shaped to fit the completed or semi-completed shell and inserted into it; and boats and ships built of planks which are joined not edge to edge, but only to the supporting framework which is erected as the first stage of building. This type of building, a major technological breakthrough which enabled boats to develop into ships capable of world voyaging, appears to have taken place in the late 1300s and the 1400s.

But the great majority of boats in history all over the world appear to be in the former category. Indeed this 'shell construction', as it was dubbed by the Swedish maritime ethnographer Olof Hässloff, of planks joined together and formed to a boat shape in a way which has been likened to an act of sculpture, seems to have been the natural way to build a boat, and to have remained so to the present day over a greater part of the world where wood is still used as the construction material.

A log-boat that has been both expanded – that is, widened by having its sides forced apart after softening with fire – and extended, with planks on the sides, is capable of a variety of developments. It is still disputed, but Ole Crumlin Pedersen, the Danish naval architect and archaeologist, saw this as the origin of the Scandinavian clinker-building tradition, in which the planks of the boat overlap one another at the edges and are joined through the overlap, and which culminated in the Viking ships. By the second half of the tenth century the tradition had developed brilliantly to produce many different types of specialised vessels.

It now seems increasingly evident however, that the Viking ships were only a part, a very developed and specialised off-shoot perhaps, of a much wider north-European pattern of clinker-building traditions. After all, the Saxons fought the Vikings at sea and even allowing for the political bias of the Anglo-Saxon Chronicle defeated them; and extensive contemporary trading contact existed between Britain and mainland Europe to the south of Scandinavia. The Saxon invaders of the great migrations in the period roughly from AD 300 to 600 used large numbers of boats, and some indication of their degree of possible sophistication is given by the great Sutton Hoo ship, whose ghostly shadow was found in the rich burial-mound near Woodbridge in 1939. But until 1970 there was in Britain no major find at all of a boat of the Viking period, and certainly none of clearly non-Scandinavian origin, to cast light on the nature of building traditions outside Scandinavia at the height of the Scandinavian expansion.

In the cold autumn of 1970 the Kent Water Board were engaged in widening the Hammond Drain on the marshes between Whitstable and Faversham. In the words of Magnus Magnusson's commentary to the *Chronicle* programme – itself a memorial to Paul John-

stone – which recorded the events which followed:

'The driver of one of the excavators was Roy Botting. One day he came across some old timbers. They could have been anything. But Roy Botting was an avid *Chronicle*-watcher and he realised at once that it was part of an old boat.

'Members of the Canterbury Archaeology Society did some preliminary excavation and quickly recognised the importance of the find. They contacted the National authorities, and Basil Greenhill, the Director of the National Maritime Museum at Greenwich, came to lend professional expertise.

'The critical problem that had to be solved at once was how the boat could be salvaged. Winter was at hand with its high tides, and the Kent river authority was in a hurry to complete its drainage scheme before more flooding took place. No one could tell from a preliminary examination just how old the boat was. Nothing like it had ever been seen before. But one thing Basil Greenhill had no doubt about – this find was so important for the history of boats in Britain that it simply had to be saved.'

It was in fact Paul Johnstone himself who first told me of the discovery of the Graveney Boat, and he told me that he decided there and then to make the excavation a model case – to follow the find through with the cameras from first discovery to eventual display and publication. This decision proved of great material importance, because the *Chronicle* team under Ray Sutcliffe who recorded the rescue operation – 'in as cold, difficult, and generally beastly conditions as I have ever seen on an excavation', as Paul put it to me, also provided lights to enable excavation to go forward into the night, and some transport and communications facilities, even physical help as labourers at times when everyone was needed – and everyone was needed. Clerical staff from the National Maritime Museum's Registry, typing pool, Museum Assistants, distinguished Heads of Departments, on this operation everybody mucked in – literally. The result was a film which recorded the complex and difficult excavation step by step, with a commentary which brilliantly expounded in simple terms an extremely delicate operation:

Night-filming of the Graveney excavation

'Before anything could be done about lifting and conserving the timbers, the complete hull had to be surveyed and measured *in situ*. While the Kent River Authority went about its business nearby, teams of experts from the British Museum and the National Maritime Museum, working together for the first time, put up a tent to protect the timbers and archaeologists alike. Only the stern of the boat survived, and now the dismantling began.

'The frames, or ribs, were freed from the trenails that had held them for a thousand years, and carefully lifted away. Each frame, as it came off, was wrapped with moist plastic foam and sealed in a polythene envelope to prevent evaporation from the waterlogged timbers.

'As the rib-frames were being numbered and removed, the second phase of the operation got under way. There began the task of creating a plaster mould of the inside of the hull. With the ribs removed, the plaster would be applied to the strakes, the clinker-

The progress of the Graveney excavation:

(left) *after removal of the ribs;*

(below) *the keel during and after removal;*

(opposite) *the boat as first uncovered after cleaning.*

built outer planking of the boat. To prevent the plaster spreading, small bands of clay were moulded across the hull to separate the plaster into sections. The plaster was then applied to each section by hand.

'After three days of work all the ribs were gone, and the mould was complete, and itself ready for surveying. All measurements were taken from a common datum line, in order that the mould too could be correctly reassembled. Each of the nineteen separate and interlocking pieces of this giant plaster-cast jigsaw was recorded and numbered and then successively removed. It took another four days to remove all the sections. But now the exact shape of the boat as it lay on the mud had been recorded and the plaster mould could be used as a precise guide for reshaping the strakes after conservation. But first the strakes themselves had to be extracted from the glutinous mud.

Scale model of the bow half of the Graveney boat

'A plywood strip was inserted under each sodden timber to prevent distortion or breaking. Timber and plywood were then slid on to a solid plank, and only then carefully lifted free. The strakes, wrapped in wet foam and sealed in polythene and supported on plywood strips to preserve their exact curvature, were then fixed into crates. So every precaution was taken to ensure that the timbers of the boat could eventually be rebuilt in their correct and original position. Finally they set off on the long journey to Greenwich, to the tanks already prepared for their reception.

'Later investigation in a special laboratory in the National Maritime Museum would show that what had been salvaged in the frenzied fortnight was a unique example of a coastal-estuary boat dating from about AD 950.'

What the commentary did not bring out was that equally frenzied activities had been going on at Greenwich, where a special temporary research centre was set up in an old garage, equipped with huge steel conservation tanks which were welded up while the excavation was going forward. At the same time the nucleus of a research team was recruited, and the Graveney Boat Unit formed.

What had emerged from the mud of the Graveney Marshes was in fact just what we had been waiting for, a highly developed clinker-built boat or ship, contemporary with the Viking raids on Britain, but clearly stemming from quite different developments of the basic clinker-building traditions. After years of intensive examination and research the full report on this most important find has been published this year. Even more important, perhaps, was the fact that the necessity for the work provided the occasion to build and staff the Archaeological Research Centre at Greenwich, and for the first time in this country to put the archaeology of boats and ships on a full-time professional basis.

Although the main strands of the northern-European round-hulled, clinker-building traditions of the period before 1200, including that represented by the Graveney Boat, probably developed largely from the dugout, still the influence of the skin-boat in some local areas may have been significant. This was the matter about which Paul Johnstone had ideas of his own. Whatever its later influence may have been, he was quite sure that the skin-boat had played a large part in seafaring in northern Europe in the Bronze Age.

One of the difficulties was the simple fact that, although there had been much academic discussion about what was really depicted by numerous boat-like scribings of the Bronze Age on rocks in Norway and Sweden, nobody had ever set out to determine whether a skin-boat resembling these scribings could actually be built with the tools and materials available 2500 years ago. Paul Johnstone therefore set about encouraging and recording an interesting nautical-archaeological experiment carried out under the inspiration and supervision of Professor Sverre Marstrander of Oslo University. It was to be a double experiment carried out in front of the camera, an experiment both for the expert boatbuilder and for the film maker. Again in the words of Magnus Magnusson:

'It was a unique commission – to build a Bronze Age ship of the sun gods. The man chosen to realise·the idea was a third-generation Norwegian boatbuilder, called Odd Johnsson. The largest alder tree provided a keelson some twenty-one feet long. The bark is stripped off, but apart from that, the wood is quite untreated. The disadvantage of this, of course, is that the boat wouldn't last very long; but on the other hand, the Bronze Age shipwright would be able to start on a new boat without the delay of waiting for the wood to be seasoned.

'The next stage was to make the ribs that had showed through so clearly on the rock-carvings. Nine U-shaped frames were to be attached to the keelson, each one made from three separate round pieces of wood pegged together. One of the main problems was how to design the bottom of the boat. All the rock-carvings show boats only in profile and give no indication of what the bottom was like. Odd Johnsson decided on a flat bottom, for ease of beaching and load-carrying. There is little doubt that this is how the original boats must have been. But he had also decided to put the keelson inside the skin covering, with a keel outside for greater protection, which was rather more problematical.

'Putting the skin cover outside the keelson would mean driving pegs through the skin, when the keelson was fastened to the keel, and a Bronze Age boatbuilder would probably have been reluctant to do that because of the risk of making the boat less watertight. No metal of any kind was used in the construction of the boat, of course, and nothing that would not have been available to any Bronze Age shipwright. Apart from the wooden pegs, the only fastenings were lashings of rawhide. To cover all the joins and reinforce the pegs, yards and yards of these lashings were required. Leather lashings were the one factor that bridged the gap between the Bronze Age skin-boats and the wooden planked boats of the Iron Age, for the Nordic shipwrights used lashings right up to the days of the Viking longships.

'Every now and again, Professor Sverre Marstrander would leave his students at Oslo University and travel down to Frederikstad to see how this unique boat-building enterprise was progressing, and to give advice on the spot on the hundred-and-one unexpected snags that kept cropping up. It was a remarkable partnership between the intuitive skills of the boatbuilder and the intellectual insight of the archaeologist.

'Apart from his hands, Odd Johnsson used only four metal tools; an axe, a knife, a hammer, and an electric drill – this last simply to save time: had he lived in the Bronze Age, he would probably have had to use stone tools only, but with stone tools he could have done everything he set himself to do now – even drill holes, trim and shape wood.

'Once the construction of the hull was completed, there was still the major problem to be tackled – the problem of how to cover it. The skin hull was the basic factor of Professor Marstrander's thesis. But unlike

33

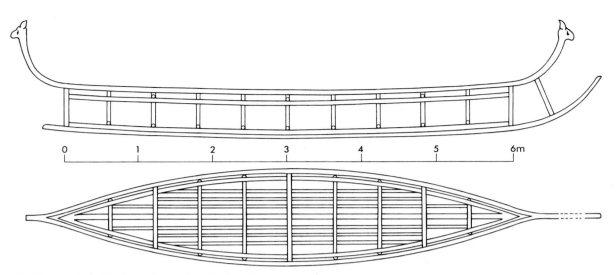

The Bronze Age skin-boat: (above) *scale drawing;*
(below) *Sverre Marstrander and Paul Johnstone* (left) *examine the nearly-completed boat.*

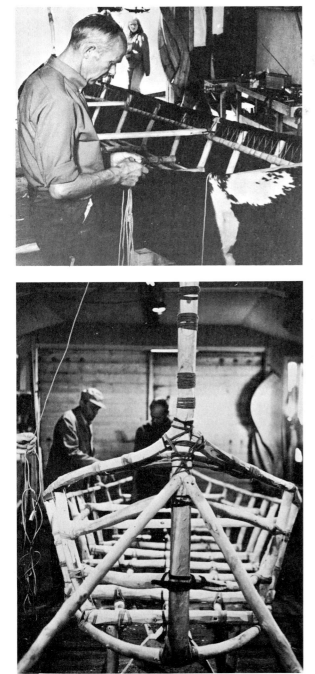

places like Greenland and Ireland, there was no surviving tradition of skin-boat making in Norway, so it too had to be improvised.

'For the material itself, it was decided to use cowskins that can be bought commercially at a tannery in Oslo: eight cowskins in all were required. The seams can easily be waterproofed by having grease worked into them; it is the skins themselves that are the weak point. That is why skin-boats are never left in the water longer than absolutely necessary.

'The eight cowskins had to be fitted together like a jigsaw puzzle. They were then cut into the right pattern and sewn together. Odd Johnsson did this job himself. He used an ordinary sailmaker's awl and thimble to join the skins by double seams through an overlap. It's not unlikely that in the Bronze Age the skins were joined by blind seams – the needle never actually going right through the thickness of the skins – just as the Eskimos do to this day.

'The final stage in the construction was fastening the skins to the hull. The complete covering, ready-sewn, was secured by continuous lacing through the edge which came over the top of the gunwale and down a little way inside, and then round the stringers along the inside of the hull.'

The boat took 200 man-hours to build. It was subjected to some tests with paddles in still, calm water which did not really establish that the boat was capable of carrying weights in normal choppy or rough sea, or that it would not tear itself to pieces if subjected to the strains of a voyage of any length. Paul Johnstone summed up the results of the whole experiment with his usual precision, but perhaps over-optimistically, and with claims that went too wide:

'The whole thing had turned out to be a highly satisfactory exercise. The tests do not of course prove that the Bronze Age rock-carvings of Scandinavia represent skin-boats. What they do show is that it would have been perfectly feasible and simple, with the resources of the time, to produce a skin-boat

(Above) *lacing the skins to the hull;* (below) *the completed framework of the hull.*

(Above) *The launching of the skin-boat;* (left) *sea-trials in calm water.*

which closely resembled the carvings and which in seaworthiness, load-carrying and beaching was decidedly adequate.

'And finally, they rule out any argument that only a planked boat could have carried out the sea journeys required in the Bronze Age. Professor Marstrander's boat had proved itself beyond question.'

The work which has been done on the archaeology of boats in recent years has led to some tentative general conclusions about the ways ships developed in the medieval period. It seems likely that the northern round-hulled clinker-building traditions began to be challenged in the thirteenth century by two other types of boat, both stemming from old, but very different traditions. The first of these was the cog. A flat-bottomed, wall-sided boat with straight stem and stern-post, her sides clinker-built, her bottom of planks laid edge to edge and not joined together, she came from a German-Frisian tradition which had been developing for many centuries. Big cogs, able to carry big loads, became an important factor in the development of the powerful Hansa towns and the pattern of trade they established throughout Northern Europe from the year 1200 onward. In turn the cog was replaced as the predominant type of big boat or ship in northern Europe by the hulk, which also stemmed from an old pattern of building traditions, perhaps centred in what is now the Netherlands. In time she too, and the cog, and the northern round-hulled, clinker-built boat, all gave way to something entirely new.

No recognised remains of a hulk have yet been found, but in 1962 the almost complete hull of a large cog, dating from about 1380, was found in the mud of the river Weser, in circumstances which made excavation particularly difficult. The cog was salvaged and is now almost reconstructed in the new maritime museum at Bremerhaven. Her rescue and subsequent conservation were made the subject of a *Chronicle* programme in 1974. The commentary to this programme summed up:

'This was at the time when some of the cities of northern Europe were organising trade on a scale that's never been known before; and they had got a

Full-size reconstruction of the midships section of the Bremen cog

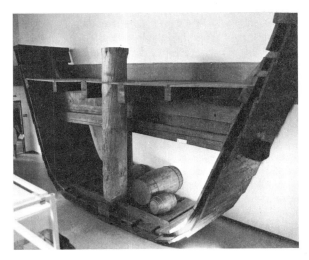

stranglehold on that trade by forming what you might call the first Common Market multi-national company – the Hanseatic League. And the instrument of their supremecy, the vehicle of their prosperity was the cog. The cog, you might say, was the juggernaught lorry of its day. And by the same token, the rivers and the waterways of the Low Countries in the Middle Ages were most precisely the motorways of today.

'The dominance of the cog, judging by the civic seals, lasted until about 1400, when a new type of ship begins to take over: the rounded hulk.

'The cog at its best could carry only 200 tons, the new giants could carry up to 400 tons of cargo. The whole cog formula – flat, keelless bottom, clinker-built sides, and a single sail – simply couldn't be scaled up any further.

'The answer lay in strengthening the frame of the

ship and in dividing up the canvas spread amongst several masts. Sixty years after the Bremen cog was built, three-masted ships, appreciably larger than even the hulk, were being built in Holland. The Bremen cog marked the end of the long era of single-masted ships.'

In fact the answer lay not so much in strengthening the frames of the ship as in revolutionising the whole approach to shipbuilding. Henceforth the cog and the hulk and the round-hulled clinker-built ship and their derivants ceased to be the principal vehicles of sea transport. The boat became a ship, built by erecting a skeleton of frames, covering it with a skin of planks not joined together at the edges, but made waterproof and strengthened by caulking and lining it with a positively twentieth-century speed; and the resultant ship could take three masts and was capable of world voyaging. In 40 years after its perfection, that is between 1480 and 1520, all the seas of the world were discovered and the dominance of western man assured for centuries. The wooden three-masted square-rigged sailing ship was perhaps the most important vehicle of transport in man's history. Its story did not

(Above) *The Bremen cog in course of reconstruction in the hall specially built for her at Bremerhaven;* (below) *hull construction: the three lowest planks are laid flush, while all the remaining strakes are edge-joined in the clinker tradition.*

38

end until 1945, when the last wooden three-masted barque *Eläköön*, owned in the Åland Islands, part of Finland, was converted from a sail vessel to be a motor ship.

Today at the National Maritime Museum at Greenwich there are specially-constructed laboratories and other facilities, and a small staff of conservators, scientists and archaeologists working under the direction of the Chief Archaeologist, Sean McGrail, is employed entirely on the study of the development of boats and ships before the great technical revolutions of the 1400s. Elsewhere in the Museum, the collection and correlation of evidence on the revolutionary developments of the 15th century – the period when it might be said that boats turned into ships – is going steadily forward. That it should be widely recognised now that these problems are very important as part of the pattern of the study of the development of European man is quite largely due to the meticulous care and attention that Paul Johnstone gave to them, and to the great efforts he made to interpret them, not only to the ordinary informed viewer, but also to many professional archaeologists.

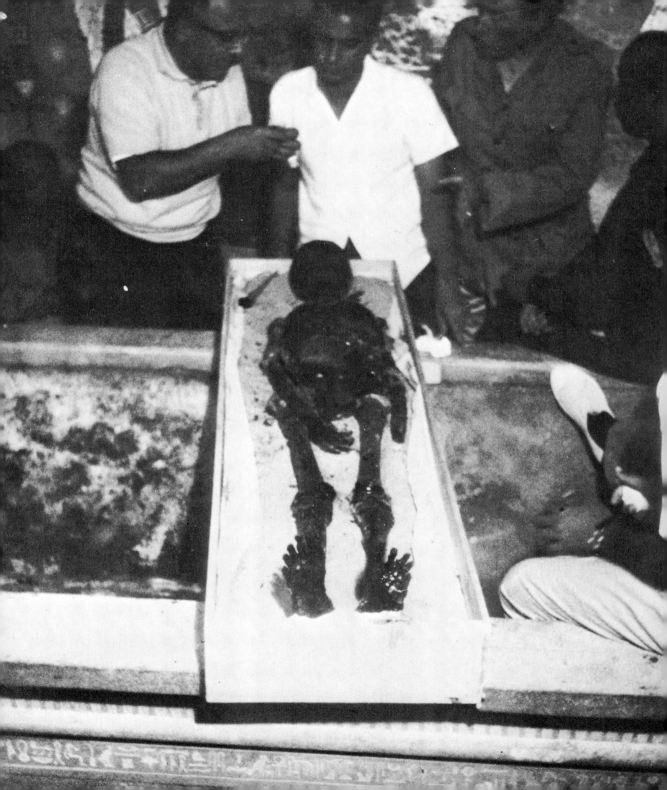

The Tutankhamun Post-Mortem

Every anatomist at some time in his career finds that he is approached by a forensic pathologist to advise on the identity or ageing of human remains and this happened to me with increasing frequency in the years between 1950 and 1960. Almost all the cases were unique, some bizarre, but the most extraordinary post-mortem in which I was involved occurred in 1960 when Dr E. Gerald Evans, Pathologist at the Caernarvon and Anglesey General Hospital in Bangor, invited me to assist in the identification of a woman who had become mummified. This was because the remains were found in a cupboard close to a chimney flue and the heat had progressively desiccated the tissues to produce a state of mummification. At that time there had been little experience of cases in which mummification of tissue had come to post-mortem in Britain, for obvious reasons. In predynastic times in Egypt, however, when a body was simply buried, the heat was often sufficient to cause mummification by simple dehydration.

Because of this experience with mummified human remains, it was later suggested that I might become involved in the reinvestigation of the remains in the Egyptian Museum at Cairo which had previously been thought to belong to the Pharaoh Akhenaten, although the Museum authorities were convinced that they probably did not belong to that pharaoh. Accordingly, with the assistance of a grant from the Wenner-Gren Foundation for Anthropological Research, it was possible to travel to Cairo in December 1963 to reassess the remains. While Egyptian mummies have been X-rayed before, this was certainly the first time that the remains of a pharaoh had been subjected to X-radiography. The remains were found to consist of little more than a skeleton, but as a result of extensive anatomical and anthropometric investigation, assisted by radiographic examination of the skeleton, it was possible to demonstrate that the person to whom the skeleton belongs could not possibly be of an age nor of a facial appearance, following reconstruction, which would have any resemblance to Akhenaten (Harrison, 1966). On the other hand, the resemblance between these remains and Tutankhamun was very close and had already been suggested by the late Professor Derry, who found a very close correspondence between the measurements of the skull of these remains and the head of Tutankhamun. As a result of the examination in December 1963, from considerations of physique, age at death and facial appearance, it was impossible to concede any resemblance between these remains and Akhenaten, and the only possible conclusion was that they belonged to Smenkhkare. It was known that Smenkhkare was a brother of Tutankhamun, and since the remains of Smenkhkare showed some interesting and rather peculiar anatomical features, it was thought advisable to re-examine the remains of Tutankhamun in order to assess the degree of conformity between the remains of these two pharaohs.

The re-examination of Tutankhamun, however, presented a much more difficult task than any reassessment of the remains of Smenkhkare. Tutankhamun is the only pharaoh whose remains still lie within his tomb, in the Valley of the Kings at Thebes, some 500 miles south of Cairo. Whereas there are excellent radiological facilities in Cairo, the only possible radiographic unit at which the remains of Tutankhamun could be examined is in the hospital at Luxor, on the other bank of the Nile away from Thebes. When the remains of Tutankhamun were first dis-

The mummified remains of Tutankhamun, in their bed of sand on a simple wooden tray, lie across the sarcophagus. Dr Zaki Iskander (left) *explains to Paul Johnstone the effects of mummification on human tissue.*

covered they were enclosed in three coffins, one inside the other. The two innermost, being the most precious, have been removed for museum display, and the remains now lie in the tomb, enclosed in the outermost of the coffins, which is in turn contained in the sarcophagus, covered by a sheet of plate glass in order that visitors to the tomb may observe the outermost mummiform coffin. Any re-examination of Tutankhamun would therefore involve reopening of the sarcophagus, a very complicated affair, and one which would certainly require very careful consideration by the authorities at the Department of Antiquities in Cairo and Thebes. Nevertheless, Professor Ali Abdalla, my colleague and associate in the Department of Anatomy at the University of Cairo, expressed his willingness to inquire of the Department of Antiquities if they would be willing to allow this procedure to take place. In addition, somehow or another, it would be necessary to have the use of portable radiographic equipment to X-ray the remains within the tomb, since it was unlikely that permission would be obtained to remove the remains from the tomb to Luxor Hospital.

Whilst Professor Abdalla was making the most extensive enquiries in Cairo, it became obvious that there would have to be some method for taking a photographic record of the anatomical and anthropological investigation. In addition, of course, there was the not inconsiderable question of financing the expedition. At this point, I contacted Reg Jordan, Head of North Region Programmes with the BBC, to determine whether it might be feasible for the BBC to assist me in this project. As a result Gordon Watkins, Head of General Feature Programmes of BBC Television wrote to me and suggested that his colleague Paul Johnstone would like to meet me and discuss the venture. In May 1967 I was very thrilled to hear from Paul Johnstone that financial aid, on the substantial scale which I had suggested as necessary, might be feasible. We agreed that we should aim to undertake the expedition in December of that year, although conflict in the Middle East eventually delayed the expedition until the following year. At this point in time, Mr Filce Leek, a dentist in Hemel Hempstead who was interested in the

pathology visible in the teeth of ancient Egyptian skulls, requested that he might join the expedition in order to examine the teeth of Tutankhamun.

In March 1968 the necessary permission for the re-examination of the remains of Tutankhamun had been obtained owing to the immense efforts of Professor Abdalla. Despite various spurious reports that the tomb area in Thebes was overrun with wild dogs, and that there was a danger of contracting rabies if one were to be bitten by one of them, Paul agreed in August 1968 that we should plan to undertake the expedition in December of that year. Meanwhile Professor Abdalla had obtained the loan of a very primitive portable X-ray apparatus, and, by the end of October, written permission for our projected expedition had been received from the Director-General of the Antiquities Service in Cairo.

Up to this point I had not realised just how fortunate I was in being able to be associated with Paul Johnstone in this visit. He took upon himself the complete organisation of the trip, and brought together a team of BBC staff who travelled with us in order to photograph the re-examination procedure as it happened, and arrange it for a *Chronicle* programme. The efforts of Professor Abdalla were also essential to this operation; not only did he obtain all the necessary permission from many authorities, but he was able to act as official interpreter and aid in finding accommodation and establishing good relations: Tutankhamun has a very special place in the hearts of Egyptians, just as he does in the minds of many British people old enough to remember the excitement of the discovery of his tomb in the 1922–26 period.

Organising the expedition for December 1968 proved to be very convenient for Paul, since the excavation of Silbury Hill was scheduled for April in that year and, as it happened, proved to be a protracted affair. Meanwhile permission to film the treasures of the tomb of Tutankhamun which are displayed in the Cairo Museum, was also obtained, in order to illustrate the life of the pharaoh in the subsequent *Chronicle* film.

The BBC team, Mr and Mrs Leek, and my own technician Mr Lyn Reeve and I left for Cairo on 30

November. We planned to stay there for three days to formalise the authority for permission to reopen the sarcophagus and to allow filming of the exhibits in the Cairo Museum. As it happened we were to become separated for these three days, since accommodation for Lyn Reeve and me had been arranged in the Nile Hilton Hotel, separate from the remainder of the party. This, however, allowed a close contact with the Museum and facilitated negotiations with Dr Gamal Mokhtar, Under-Secretary of State in charge of the Antiquities Service.

Our air-trip to Luxor on 3 December was uneventful, and we were all accommodated in the original Winter Palace Hotel. Next morning we were to establish contact with Mr Taher, Chief Inspector of Antiquities in Luxor, and the Chief Engineer of the Antiquities Service in the Valley of the Kings, Mr Salah Osman, whose organisation and assistance in the delicate procedure of opening the sarcophagus and coffin were invaluable. Later, we were very glad of the experience, expertise and advice of Dr Zaki Iskander, Chief Scientist to the Antiquities Service, in exposing the mummy, once the sarcophagus was opened.

It immediately became obvious to the BBC team that the crowding of equipment into the confines of Tutankhamun's small tomb, with cables snaking everywhere to floodlights, would present difficulties for them and for the Chief Engineer's staff in opening the sarcophagus and examining its contents. Nevertheless, the only damage which resulted was that a corner of the sheet of plate glass covering the sarcophagus was broken, and this has since been replaced free of charge by Pilkington Bros of St Helens.

Fortunately the tomb has a wooden gallery overlooking the sarcophagus and the camera team were able to confine themselves to it, so leaving space around the sarcophagus free for the operations of the Antiquities Service staff. The tense, excited atmosphere at the moment of exposing the outermost mummiform coffin has been beautifully recaptured in the *Chronicle* film. What is not shown, however, is the heat generated in the tomb by the workmen and investigators confined in the restricted space, all concentrating on their various tasks; the brilliance of the scene illuminated by the spotlights (and the heat from them if one came too close); and eventually, as the mummy was exposed, the sweet, almost sickly smell of the unguents in the hard resin covering the remains, which eventually permeated the tomb.

The outermost coffin fitted into the sarcophagus very closely, leaving only just enough room to pass a hand between them, and the greatest care had to be exercised in removing its lid in order not to damage the gold inlay on it. When this had been done, the remains of the pharaoh were found lying on sand in a simple wooden tray which Howard Carter had prepared to return Tutankhamun to his coffin in 1926. Lengths of rope which lay under the tray at each end had been used for lowering it into the sarcophagus. They could similarly be used by us in removing the tray.

The Findings

When the modern bandages loosely wrapped around the remains were removed it was immediately obvious that the mummy was not in a very good condition and certainly not in one piece. The most striking feature was the marked carbonisation of the tissues of the mummy, and the presence of black resin which still adhered to the rock-hard black tissues. In his description of the remains Howard Carter is at pains to point out that the mummy was in a very poor condition. In his report (1927) and in the extracts from his diary quoted by Leek (1972) he pointed out that efflorescence encrusted upon the inlay and surface goldwork, together with the tendency to swelling here and there in parts of the second coffin, suggests the existence of humidity, possibly from the mummy being wrapped and placed in the coffin before being perfectly dry. The mummy was firmly fastened to the base of the innermost (third) coffin by resin poured over the mummy in such quantities that it even overflowed to stick it to the second coffin. The outer bandages of the mummy had completely deteriorated ('one might say carbonised') from the action of the libation that had been poured over it. As a result, all attempts to remove the mummy and mask from the coffin were at first unsuccessful, and eventually it was only possible to separate the second and third coffins by turning them upside down upon trestles, covering the outside (second) coffin with heavy wet blankets, lining the third coffin completely with plates of zinc which would not melt at less than 520°C, and then placing primus stoves burning at full blast underneath the inverted coffins for three hours. An hour later the two coffins slowly began to fall apart. Carter claims that a temperature of 500°C was achieved, and one wonders therefore just how much of the carbonisation of the mummy is due to the poor condition in which it was found and how much to the extreme heat to which he subjected it. Nevertheless, it is very obvious that at subsequent post mortem examinations by Derry, the wrappings were in a state of disintegration, in many places reduced to dust, 'largely owing to the carbonisation brought about by a sort of spontaneous combustion due to enclosed humidity combined with heat'. The tissues were extremely brittle, and the abdominal wall, as well as the soft tissue of the limbs, showed numerous cracks, so that the tissue came away at a touch. Since the upper limbs were found flexed at the elbows and the right forearm was resting on the upper part of the abdomen, while the left forearm lay above it over the lower part of the ribs, it was found necessary to remove the limbs in order to free the trunk by working beneath it in order to withdraw the mummy from the mask.

Certainly at the time of our examination many parts of the mummy were distracted from one another. The head and neck were separated from the remainder of the body and the limbs, in addition to being detached from the body, were broken in many places. These appearances have been described by Harrison and Abdalla (1972) and may be summarised thus:

The right arm had been broken at the elbow, the upper arm being separated from the forearm and hand, which lay across the torso so that the hand lay on the lower left part of the abdomen. The left arm was also broken at the elbow, and in addition at the wrist, the lower ends of the radius and ulna [the bones of the fore-arm] being broken off. The thumb was missing from the right hand; this and the left hand were later found lying under the body in the sand of the tray,

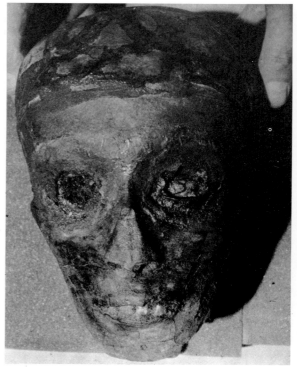

(Above) *Radiograph of the outer coffin;* (below) *the face of Tutankhamun.*

44

whilst the left forearm itself was found in cotton wool on which the sand tray had lain in the base of the coffin. The left leg was broken at the knee. The right leg was intact, but some indication of the fragility of the remains became apparent when, with the slightest movement, this leg also dislocated at the knee joint. The heads of the right humerus [upper arm] and both femora [thigh] had been broken off the remainder of the bone.

In the torso, the sternum [breast-bone] and the adjoining parts of the ribs had been removed, so exposing the thoracic cavity from which all viscera had apparently been removed and replaced by rolls of cloth soaked in resin. The right side of the abdominal wall is intact, but there is a curved oblique incision about 86 mm long in the lower left part of the abdomen, extending approximately from the umbilicus to the front of the hip-bone, which exposes similar balls of rolled up cloth soaked in resin.

The head and neck had been distracted from the torso at the joint between the seventh cervical and first thoracic vertebrae [the base of the neck]. The facial appearance is that of a young man, and the lips are parted in a smile, so displaying the upper incisor teeth. The tip of the nose is flattened. This is usual in mummified remains that have been wrapped, and is caused by pressure of the bandages. The eyelids are open, and expose desiccated eyes, sunken in their sockets. There is a circular hole in the lobe of each ear approximately 7 mm in diameter. The tissues of the face are contracted on the skull so that the cheekbones appear very prominent. All present at this exposure of the king's remains agreed with Howard Carter's description of a 'refined and cultured face' and a 'serene and placid countenance'. Much of the skin over the vertex of the skull had degenerated, but traces of the beautifully-woven skull-cap, even the coloured pigment from it, are still visible. One very significant and easily noticeable feature is the marked prominence of the occipital region [back] of the skull, very obvious on examining the lateral aspect of the head. The shape of the skull, in fact, approximates very closely to that of the skull of the remains of Smenkhkare from Valley Tomb No. 55. In addition,

there is an unduly marked prominence of the left occipital bone, forming an asymmetric protuberance some 28 mm in diameter. Some repairs to the head were visible in the form of wax between the atlas and the foramen magnum [between the spine and the base of the skull], and smooth, recently applied, but solidified, resin under the chin.

Because of the thick resinous deposit on most of the bones, and postmortem fractures in many of them, anthropometry of the remains (the measurement of the dimensions of bones of the skeleton) was not as easy as one might have wished. First impressions on the close conformity of the shape of the skull in Tutankhamun with that in Smenkhkare are confirmed. The diameters of the skull are almost identical: in fact, on placing an X-ray of one skull on that of the other, there is virtually complete conformity. The cephalic index also demonstrated that the type of skull (i.e. brachycephalic) is the same in each case. Only in the measurements of the facial skeleton is there some discrepancy, indicating that Tutankhamun had a slightly narrower face than Smenkhkare. Even the measurements of other bones of the skeleton show fairly close conformity. If there is any difference to be noted, it is in the more robust development of leg bones in Tutankhamun, and a slightly longer forearm. One very notable feature is the presence of epitrochlear foramina in both humeri [holes in the bones of the arms, just above the elbow joint]. These are also present in Smenkhkare, and indicate some degree of genetic affinity, for this variation of bone-structure – comparatively common in ancient Egypt, but found less frequently among modern Egyptians – is known to be genetically-inherited.

The disadvantage of the X-ray apparatus was that, since we did not know the characteristics of the machine, test exposures were necessary, preferably on site. Facilities for developing, fixing and washing the exposed films were, of course not available in the tomb, nor were they easily obtainable anywhere in the Valley of the Kings. On the first day of the examination of the mummy, it was therefore decided to take test exposures of the remains, and develop them in Luxor on our return in the evening. Fortunately, the commodious bathroom furniture in the older part of the Winter Palace Hotel at Luxor allowed the development of X-ray films in one receptacle, fixation in another, and washing in a third. The dense blackness of the Egyptian night served as an excellent darkroom, and while Mr Reeve coped with the films, other members of the expedition ensured that no intervening doors should be suddenly opened to allow a flood of light on the proceedings. Having determined the parameters of the equipment, it was possible to radiograph the remains the next day, for eventual development in Liverpool. Owing to the long experience and skill of Mr Reeve, all the films taken developed excellently on return.

The X-rays taken of the head and neck of Tutankhamun were very revealing indeed, and confirmed naked-eye impressions about its shape, which conforms very closely to that seen in the radiograph of Smenkhkare. The most prominent feature, however, is the presence of two dense shadows, the first along the vertex of the skull, and the second occupying the back (posterior) region of the skull. Each of these shadows possesses a fluid level, suggesting that fluid opaque to X-rays was introduced into the cranial cavity with the top of the skull downwards, and then with the body lying horizontally, so that the posterior region of the skull was lowest. In addition a small fragment of bone is seen in both lateral and frontal views of the skull, lying against the side of the skull. This, at first sight, looked like a piece of bone from the thin bony roof of the nasal cavity, and perusal of the frontal X-ray of the skull confirms that this bone has disappeared from both sides of the floor of the skull. This would be very understandable, and could fit in very well with known theories of the practice of mummification. It is a generally accepted view that an instrument was passed through the nostril, up into the nasal cavity to perforate or remove this bone, allowing extraction of the brain and the introduction of any preservation fluid into the cranial cavity. On closer analysis, however, after further X-rays became available for study, several main objections to this theory were apparent, and an alternative explanation suggested itself. This additional

analysis will be discussed in a future publication.

The radiographs of the skull also provide much useful information about the teeth. The left wisdom tooth in the lower jaw is just in the process of eruption, and the right one has erupted, but the upper wisdom teeth have not yet erupted at all. They would place the age of the skull within the early part of the age-range 18–22 years. Although the X-rays do not provide much information regarding the degree of wear of the teeth, they all appear perfectly normal and there is no evidence of caries, abscesses, or resorption of the roots of the teeth. There is some overlap (imbrication) between the two left maxillary incisor teeth.

The sinuses of the skull, clearly shown in the X-rays, are large, and typical of the male. The frontal sinuses are extensive, but not unduly so. The large size of these sinuses signifies life in a hot, dry atmosphere, and this is also seen in the mastoid processes, which are large and markedly cellular. In the frontal X-ray of the skull, the post-mortem packing of the nasal cavities with cloth is clearly visible, and this obscures details of intranasal features. The markings of veins inside the skull bones are also visible.

The radiographs of the thorax confirmed the fact that the sternum and most of the ribs on the front of the chest had been removed, and showed also that all the internal organs had been removed and replaced by cloth, which showed up on X-ray as a granular amorphous opacity. All the vertebrae are intact, including the epiphysial plates [the lines of increased density to X-rays on the upper and lower surfaces of the individual vertebrae]. This appearance would suggest that Tutankhamun did not die from tuberculosis, as had been proposed by some authorities, since destruction of the epiphysial plates often occurs in cases of very severe T.B. which ultimately prove to be fatal. Scattered about the thorax, and visible chiefly in the upper part of the X-ray, are to be seen small, circular faience beads. These were probably detached from the very fragile necklaces on the King's body when removed post mortem. Similar beads are also visible on the X-rays of the humeri.

The granular, amorphous X-ray appearance is also visible in the radiographs of the abdomen, and is again

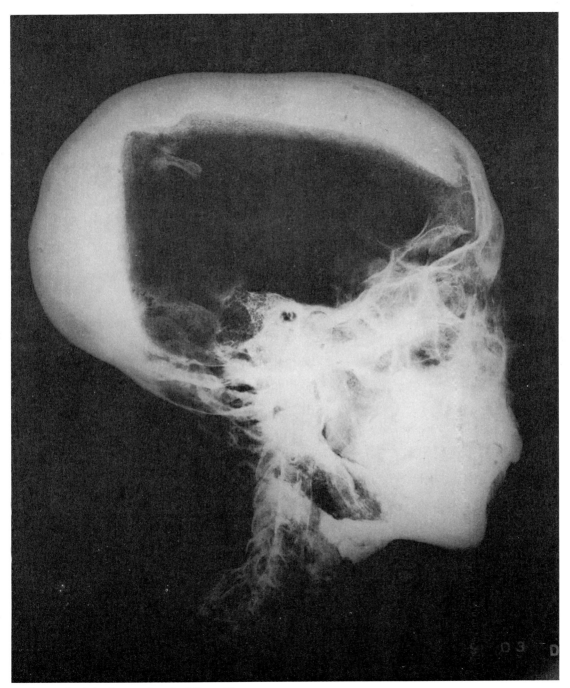

Radiograph of the face and neck of Tutankhamun

due to rolls of cloth soaked in consecration unguents which have been used to pack the abdominal cavity. In addition, the pelvis is filled with a more densely opaque oval mass, caused by a hard ball of solidified resin; the method of packing the pelvis in this way was not unusual in mummification procedures and has already been noted by Dawson and Gray in a radiographic examination of mummies in the British Museum. The lumbar vertebrae show no abnormality apart from post-mortem damage: the third lumbar vertebra is completely cut across horizontally as is, indeed, the majority of the abdomen at this level. This transection is very precise and has clearly been effected post mortem. There has been extensive post-mortem damage to the lower part of the pelvis, destroying the pubic bones. It is, however, possible to see the right greater sciatic notch and note that it is only about 50°, thus confirming the male sex. Most of the left side of the pelvis has also been destroyed post mortem.

The radiographs of the limb bones, apart from confirming the presence and site of post-mortem fractures, are not very informative. However, the medial epicondyle, a process at its lower end, shows signs of recent union with the remainder of the bone in both humeri. The line of union of the epiphysis for the head of the humerus with the shaft of the bone is also still clearly visible. These features would place the age at death at about 18 years. Damage to both ends of both clavicles prevents observation of their epiphyses and their exact length, and therefore precludes the use of these bones as an aid in estimating age and stature; their general shape and appearance, however, suggest that they belong to a young man.

There is also extensive damage to both ends of the radius and ulna of the left forearm. In the right forearm, however, it can be seen quite clearly that while the epiphyses for the upper ends of both radius and ulna have firmly united with the remainder of the bones, those for the lower ends are still separate and not united with the shafts of the bones. This also would place the age of death at about 18 years.

Similar damage to the bones of the legs also precludes their use in age and sex assessment, but the

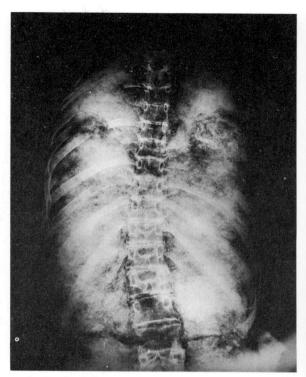

Radiograph of thorax

epiphyses at the upper end of the femur still show a line of union at their junction with the remainder of the bone. There is a trace of such an epiphysial line at the lower end of this bone also, and at the upper end of the tibia and fibula, showing that these epiphyses have more firmly united. The epiphyses for the lower ends of the tibia and fibula have completely united with the shaft of the bones, leaving no trace of an epiphysial line. All of these features would point to an age at death of 18 years.

The transverse arch of each foot is accentuated on X-ray, suggesting that they have been cramped slightly in width. There is no evidence of hallux valgus [bunion], the metatarsal and proximal phalanx of the big toe being in a perfectly straight line. The terminal phalanx is very slightly deviated laterally, however.

In all X-rays of the limb bones the soft tissue is visible as a very coarse granular opacity, suggesting

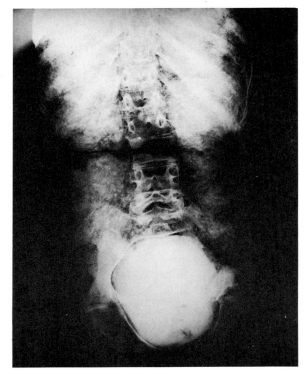

Radiograph of abdomen

precisely these three bones in five out of eight of its formulae. Nevertheless, all estimations agree closely in placing the mean height at approximately 5 ft 5½ in to 5 ft 7 in. The average of the readings indicates that the stature is 5 ft 6½ in. This estimation does not agree exactly with the measurement of the height of the mummy by Professor Derry as 5 ft 4 in. However, as Professor Derry pointed out, this measurement is probably less than the true height, owing to extreme shrinkage of tissues following death and subsequent mummification; he himself applied the formulae devised by Professor Karl Pearson to give a stature of 5 ft

Radiograph of left foot

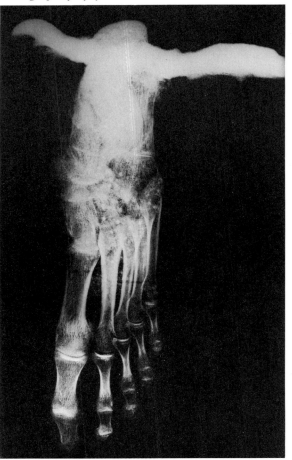

that the consecration unguents applied to the soft tissues are granular, or that changes have occurred in them over the ages to produce precipitation of material within the fluid.

At first sight it seemed that estimations of stature from the remains would be difficult, even disappointing, since the application of formulae for such estimations depends on a very accurate measurement of the lengths of long bones of the limbs; almost every long bone in the body had been damaged to a certain extent, particularly at the extremities of the bones, so that precise measurement was impossible. The only bones from which accurate measurements could be taken are the left humerus and the right radius and ulna. Those parameters of the reconstruction formulae involving use of just these lengths were calculated. It so happened that one of the estimations (that evolved by Trotter and Gleser in 1958) utilises the lengths of

6 in. When the stature of the mummy was measured during our examination in 1968, it was only 5 ft 3 in. Further shrinkage has therefore taken place in the period 1925–68, but this shorter stature may be accounted for in part by the post-mortem damage to the mummy. It is of interest that the heights of the two wooden statues of the young King, which stood on either side of the sealed door leading to the burial Chamber, are within a few millimetres of the height as estimated above by the application of formulae.

Since the chemical substances (polysaccharides) which characterise blood groups reside in all tissues of the body and not just in the red blood cells, it is possible to extract them from mummified tissues (even from the bones of a skeleton), attach them on to group O red cells of a living person and so estimate the blood group. Alternatively, more sophisticated analytical methods may be applied to the tissue extract. By such methods it was possible to investigate the blood groups of Tutankhamun and Smenkhkare and show that they both possess blood groups A_2 and MN (Harrison, Connolly and Abdalla, 1969). Taken in conjunction with other features, such as the almost identical measurements of the skull and the resemblance in facial appearance, a close kinship between the two pharaohs is strongly suggested; in fact a relationship sufficiently close as to suggest that they are brothers is the most acceptable. This application of a serological micromethod as well as anatomical and anthropometric analyses to investigate the affinity between members of a human population living over 3000 years ago, is perhaps unique and has led on to a much more extensive study of the inter-relationships between members of the family of Tutankhamun.

Thus, earlier theories that Akhenaten through his marriage to Nefertiti was the father of Tutankhamun have now been discarded in favour of the more acceptable descent from Amenophis III. The mother of Tutankhamun is less clearly identifiable, but two possible candidates have been suggested, namely Queen Tiye, chief wife and favourite of Amenophis III, and Sitamun, eldest daughter of Amenophis III. An opportunity recently presented itself to examine the body of Amenophis III and, since the remains of Queen Tiye and Sitamun were not available at that time, an investigation of Yuya and Thuya, the parents of Queen Tiye, was also made (Connolly, Harrison and Ahmed, 1976).

The results of these investigations demonstrate that all three mummified remains are group A and by differential exclusion A_2. Amenophis III, in addition, was shown to be group M (both of two fragments from Amenophis III yielded identical serological reactions), whereas both Yuya and Thuya were group N.

It may be argued that Queen Tiye, their daughter, would also have demonstrated the blood group A_2N. It would follow, therefore, that Sitamun, daughter of Amenophis III, and Queen Tiye would have had the blood group A_2MN.

By these analyses, Amenophis III and Queen Tiye could, therefore, have been the parents of Sitamun as well as both Smenkhkare and Tutankhamun – both previously demonstrated to have the blood group A_2MN. The possibility of Amenophis III and Sitamun being the parents of Smenkhkare and Tutankhamun cannot be excluded, but the probability of this event is slightly different: such a union would theoretically produce equal numbers of offspring of groups M and MN whereas Queen Tiye in any union with Amenophis III would always have created offspring with the blood group of Tutankhamun and Smenkhkare, that is, MN. There is some evidence in modern populations for an excess MN offspring (Moreton and Chung 1959) from the type of union which would have existed between Amenophis III and Sitamun and, therefore, the probability of such a union producing offspring of group MN like Smenkhkare and Tutankhamun, is slightly greater than that of the alternative group M appearing. However, since by inference Queen Tiye must have been group N, any union between her and Amenophis III would *always* yield offspring of this MN group, like Tutankhamun and Smenkhkare. Clearly then, with Amenophis III as father, union with either Queen Tiye or Sitamun would, in practical terms, equally accord with both Smenkhkare and Tutankhamun as possible offspring.

The 'Curse' of The Pharaohs

When making the exploration to re-examine the remains of Tutankhamun, not unnaturally members of the investigating team discussed the often-quoted 'Curse' of the Pharaohs, which was particularly related to the opening of the tomb of Tutankhamun. This arose from a story which was given great publicity at that time when Lord Carnarvon, who had financed Howard Carter in his search for tombs in the Valley of the Kings, became seriously ill and eventually died.

When one becomes interested in a particular research project, particularly if it is related to such a colourful Pharaoh as Tutankhamun, one immediately becomes identified with investigations into this Pharaoh. Not unnaturally, therefore, when Dr Geoffrey Dean became interested in the 'Curse' we entered into correspondence about it. The way in which Dr Dean became involved is connected with his interest in, and the treatment of, an illness which he observed when he was a Consultant Physician in Port Elizabeth in the Eastern Cape Province of South Africa. One of his patients became seriously ill after exploring a complex of caves in the Urungwe Native Reserve of Rhodesia, to see if it was possible to use the large quantities of bat guano in these caves as a fertiliser. These caves are occupied by many thousands of bats and contained, in places, over six-foot-deep deposits of guano. Dr Dean's patient became desperately ill shortly after examining these caves, and was eventually found to be suffering from a disease known as histoplasmosis. This disease is caused by a fungus that grows in the guano, is inhaled in the dried dust from it, and results in severe respiratory disorder. Dr Dean enquired about the death of Lord Carnarvon and discovered that it was from 'pneumonia of insidious onset', and he suspected that this might have been due to histoplasmosis. He further confirmed (in his article in *World Medicine*, 18 June 1975) that a number of other people had died from a similar pneumonia-like illness after working in the Valley of the Kings.

The passage leading to the tomb of Tutankhamun is now sealed – particularly at night – by a door, and no bats can enter it; but bats are known to frequent neighbouring underground passages. When Dr Dean informed me of his theory, I made enquiries from Dr Gamal Mokhtar, Under-Secretary of State and Chairman of the Egyptian Antiquities Organisation, who was able to make an investigation for me. Dr Mokhtar inquired from old people living in Kurna, who were present at that time. They said that a temporary iron door made of bars was used after the discovery of the tomb. Bats used to enter through this door and pass the night in the tomb and Mr Carter used to ask people in charge to get these bats out in the morning. The permanent door was only used six months later.

Lord Carnarvon worked for three months in the underground passage and ante-chamber of the tomb, and during a time when the passage was frequented at night by bats. Then, just after the opening of the inner chamber of the tomb on 17 February 1923, Lord Carnarvon developed lassitude, headache, breathlessness and enlarged glands, and became more and more ill. He returned to Cairo to the Continental Hotel, where bilateral pneumonia slowly developed. His health continued to deteriorate until he died on 6 April. We may never know for certain, but the evidence strongly suggests that Lord Carnarvon's death was due to inhalation of dust containing the fungus histoplasma from dried bat-droppings in the passage leading to King Tutankhamun's tomb.

One very cogent argument against the existence of a 'curse' is that it should surely have affected Howard Carter, the person who discovered and opened the tomb, or Professor Derry, the anatomist who first examined the pharaonic remains, more than anyone. Yet Carter lived until the age of almost sixty-seven, and Derry until he was eighty-seven. This is probably explained by the fact that Carter had a long exposure to tombs and excavations. At the age of seventeen (1891) he went to Egypt as assistant draughtsman on the staff of the Archaeological Survey of Egypt. Early in 1892 he joined Sir W. M. Flinders Petrie at El-Amarna and received four months training in the art of excavating. He then worked, as draughtsman, in tombs in Middle Egypt and later in the temple of Queen Hatshepsut. At the end of 1899 he became inspector-in-chief of monuments of Upper Egypt and

Nubia, with headquarters at Thebes. In 1902 he began excavations in the Valley of the Tombs of the Kings and later, among other discoveries, found and cleared the tomb of Amenophis I. By 4 November 1922, when he discovered the tomb of Tutankhamun, Carter had therefore probably been subjected to exposure to guano in a variety of situations. In addition, since he had spent a much longer time in excavating the tomb of Tutankhamun and had been gradually exposed to bat guano during his life, presumably he developed an immunity to the histoplasma organism, and therefore did not succumb.

Return

We returned to London on 11 December by a Qantas flight. One of the BBC team was convinced that the fact that we had to depart at 4 a.m., that the plane was late arriving, and that we had to wait about an hour in the plane before finally taking off, was all connected with the 'curse'. We could hardly have had a more pleasant flight home, however! *Al Ahram*, the leading Cairo newspaper, gave extensive coverage to the expedition that same day in an article written by Kamal El Mallakh, on the Editorial Staff of the newspaper and an archaeologist, who had visited Luxor to learn of our researches at first hand. His report indicated that Tutankhamun not only extends the history of Archaeology, but also influences medical archives more than 3300 years after his death.

As the closing part of the *Chronicle* film states, it is hardly surprising that Tutankhamun is poorly represented among the great relics of ancient Egypt, since he was a boy king who reigned for a short time in a troubled kingdom. Now, as a result of the investigation, we know at least that he was Smenkhkare's brother and that he was probably no debilitated invalid when he died. What started as an analysis of a relatively obscure Pharaoh has therefore now devolved into a thorough examination of the inter-relationships of the Royal Family of Egypt in the XVIIIth dynasty, and this was assisted in no small measure by the interest taken by the BBC, the *Chronicle* series and Paul Johnstone.

References

Carter, Howard (1927). The tomb of Tutankhamun. Vol. 2. (London).

Connolly, R. C., Harrison, R. G. and Ahmed, Soheir (1976). Serological evidence for the parentage of Tutankhamun and Smenkhkare. *Journal of Egyptian Archaeology, 62*, 184.

Dawson, W. R. and Gray, P. H. K. (1968). Catalogue of Egyptian antiquities in the British Museum. I. Mummies and human remains. (London).

Harrison, R. G. (1966). An anatomical examination of the pharaonic remains purported to be Akhenaten. *Journal of Egyptian Archaeology, 52*, 95.

Harrison, R. G. and Abdalla, A. B. (1972). The remains of Tutankhamun. *Antiquity, 46*, 8.

Harrison, R. G., Connolly, R. C. and Abdalla, A. (1969). Kinship of Smenkhkare and Tutankhamun affirmed by serological micromethod. *Nature, 224*, 325.

Leek, F. F. (1972). The human remains from the tomb of Tutankhamun. (Oxford).

Moreton, N. E. and Chung, C. S. (1959). Are the MN blood groups maintained by selection? *American Journal of Human Genetics, 11*, 237.

Trotter, M. and Gleser, G. C. (1958). A re-evaluation of estimation of stature based on measurements of stature taken during life and of long bones after death. *American Journal of Physical Anthropology, 16*, 79.

The Ashes of Atlantis

Magnus Magnusson

The legend of Atlantis, the fabled island that sank beneath the sea 'in a single day and night of misfortune' after a series of violent earthquakes and floods, is one of the archetypal legends of the western world. Its name is cognate with the Atlantic Ocean through Atlas, eldest son of the sea-god Poseidon and first ruler of the island. And people have searched for it tirelessly, in all manner of likely and unlikely places, because the story of a golden prehistoric age that disappeared in some ancient catastrophe appeals to a profound need in all of us: the need to know of a lost age of innocence, some lost paradise of the past.

The latest and, some would say, most plausible candidate for being the site of the original Atlantis is a tiny, enchanting Greek island in the Aegean called Santorini. It's a marvellously dramatic place. It is, quite literally, a volcano – one of the most violent volcanoes in the world, in fact. Once upon a time the island of Santorini, or Thera as the ancients called it, was twice the size it is today. Then, around 1500 BC, a titanic volcanic eruption tore the heart out of it. All that is left of it is the rim of the volcanic crater, or caldera, broken in three places in such a way that ships can sail in and out of it.

It was this eruption, one of the most massive volcanic eruptions on earth since the last Ice Age, that may have given rise to the legend of Atlantis. And this theory has been given added force by the spectacular archaeological excavations that have been going on there since 1967, revealing a rich and prosperous civilisation that had been buried beneath many metres of tephra (volcanic ash and pumice).

The historical value of legend, especially in relation to archaeology, is a rather touchy question in professional circles. But it has always fascinated me; and

when *Chronicle* began, away back in 1966, I was delighted to find that my interest was shared by one of the early *Chronicle* producers, Julia Cave. The first programme we made together was the story of Heinrich Schliemann, the 19th-century German millionaire who was convinced that there was a kernel of historical truth in the Homeric story of Troy. Orthodox classical scholars of the day pooh-poohed the idea; but Schliemann went out to Turkey and started excavating (in a hideously crude way) the ancient mound of Hissarlik – and found that it covered the ruins of a succession of great cities. He called it Troy; he even claimed that he had found Homeric Troy, and in the ruins of that city a great hoard of treasure which he called the Treasure of Priam. More meticulous and less romantic scholars have since shown that Schliemann's Treasure of Priam came from a much earlier city than Homer's Troy could have been, and purists point out that there is no proof whatsoever that the city was actually Troy – or, indeed, that Troy ever existed. But at least Schliemann had demonstrated the existence of a city civilisation in an area, and at a time, in which the Homeric 'legend' had been placed.

In the following year, 1967, we made a programme about Sir Arthur Evans and Minoan Crete, entitled *The Last Days of Minos*, tracing the story of Evans' magnificent obsession with Crete and his discovery of a hitherto unsuspected civilisation, which he called Minoan (after the 'legendary' King Minos), centred on the great palace of Knossos which he excavated and partly restored. He found ample evidence of a bull-cult at Knossos; and the labyrinthine structure of the palace, combined with some superb frescoes and ivories of acrobats somersaulting over the horns of a charging bull, drew him inevitably to the conclusion that Knossos was the origin of the 'legend' of Theseus and the Minotaur.

It so happened that also in 1967 the veteran Greek archaeologist Spyridon Marinatos started to excavate a site called Akrotiri on the island of Santorini, which lies some 65 miles due north of Crete. Marinatos had for long nursed a theory that the destruction of Minoan Crete, as evidenced by severe damage found at Knossos and other Minoan palace sites on Crete, had been caused by the eruption of Santorini *c.* 1500 BC. Julia Cave and I paid a quick visit to the excavation, just when Marinatos had started burrowing into the outskirts of what promised to be a new Pompeii: a large Minoan site superbly preserved under 150 feet of volcanic tephra. We promised ourselves that one day we would return to make a full report on this spectacular excavation. And return we did, in 1972. In the five intervening years, all the early promise of the site at Akrotiri had been more than fulfilled; and I still look back on that halcyon season of location filming, with Peter Hall as our cameraman, as one of the most memorable occasions that many years of filming for *Chronicle* has afforded me.

I said that Santorini is enchanting, and it is. It lies in the southern Cyclades, some 130 miles south of Athens, a twelve-hour journey by ferry. As the ship glides through a breach in the rim of the old crater into the caldera, the sight of Santorini is breath-takingly beautiful. High up on the precipitous tephra walls of the crater perch clusters of dazzling, white-washed houses. The only way up to the main township, Phira, is a tortuous zig-zag path negotiated by strings of obdurate and much-abused donkeys, who took singularly badly to all the filming equipment that we fastened precariously to their backs. It's a picturesque, idyllic-looking island, an island of grapes and wine, an island of 8000 people, living in narrow streets angled to break the sweep of the dusty wind. The hotel we stayed in, aptly named Hotel Atlantis, left absolutely nothing to be desired, a most welcoming haven after a long hot day on location.

But underneath this idyllic surface there still lurks the threat of terrible natural violence, for Santorini is in an area of alarming geological instability. Earthquakes

Nea Kammeni

are not uncommon. And out of the bay of the caldera, a small volcano is pushing its way up from the sea-bed 300 metres below the surface of the water. It's called Nea Kammeni – the 'New Burnt One' – and it has been growing in fits and starts for several centuries; it is the afterbirth of the stupendous eruption of *c.* 1500 BC. By now it is an island about one and a half square kilometres in extent, rising to a height of about 150 metres above sea-level. It is riddled with fumaroles from which clouds of gas and steam hiss sullenly. The great caldera of Santorini, some 13 kilometres in diameter, is filling up again with a new lava-mountain that one day will assuredly erupt in another cataclysm. It has already erupted on several occasions, in 1707, 1866, 1926, 1939, and 1950. The 1926 eruption and its attendant earthquakes destroyed 2000 houses, whose ruins can still be seen tumbling down the cliffs, and killed 48 people. It must be like having a time-bomb of unimaginable violence sitting on your doorstep, with no way of knowing when it might explode.

Such, then, is the setting for the latest theory about the origin of the legend of Atlantis. The legend itself has an impeccable pedigree. It was first written down by the Greek philosopher Plato in the 4th century BC in his *Timaeus*, and later expanded in his unfinished *Critias*. Plato claimed that it was based on a story told to his ancestor Solon around 600 BC, by a priest in

Egypt. This is what Plato wrote in the *Timaeus*, purportedly a verbatim account of what that Egyptian priest had said to Solon:

Many great and wonderful deeds are recorded of your state [Athens] in our histories. But one of them exceeds all the rest in greatness and valour. For these histories tell of a mighty power which unprovoked made an expedition against the whole of Europe and Asia, and to which your city put an end. This power came forth out of the Atlantic Ocean, for in those days the Atlantic was navigable; and there was an island situated in front of the straits which are by you called the Pillars of Heracles [Gibraltar Straits]; the island was larger than Libya and Asia put together, and was the way to other islands, and from these you might pass to the whole of the opposite continent which surrounded the true ocean; for this sea which is within the Straits of Heracles [the Mediterranean] is only a harbour, having a narrow entrance, but that other is a real sea, and the land surrounding it on every side may be most truly called a boundless continent.

Now in this island of Atlantis there was a great and wonderful empire which had rule over the whole island and several others, and over parts of the continent, and, furthermore, the men of Atlantis had subjected the parts of Libya within the columns of Heracles as far as Egypt, and of Europe as far as Tyrrhenia [Etruria]. This vast power, gathered into one, endeavoured to subdue at a blow our country and yours and the whole region within the straits; and then, Solon, your country shone forth, in the excellence of her virtue and strength, among all mankind. She was pre-eminent in courage and military skill, and was the leader of the Hellenes. And when the rest fell off from her, being compelled to stand alone, after having undergone the very extremity of dangers, she defeated and triumphed over the invaders, and preserved from slavery those who were not yet subjugated.

But afterwards there occurred violent earthquakes and floods; and in a single day and night of misfortune all your warlike men in a body sank into the earth, and the island of Atlantis in like manner disappeared in the depths of the sea. For which reason the sea in those parts is impassable and impenetrable, because there is a shoal of mud in the way; and this was caused by the subsidence of the island.

(Trans. Jowett: *The Dialogues of Plato*)

That is the core of the legend. From his other writings, Plato envisaged Atlantis as the centre of a brilliant and powerful empire. Its capital city was a marvel to behold for size and beauty. Its people were the fairest and noblest race of men that ever lived. They had worshipped bulls, which were sacred to their patron god Poseidon the earth-shaker ('In bulls doth the earth-shaker delight' – Homer). They were masters of the arts of writing, architecture and painting; their ornaments were of silver and gold and ivory, and their staple metals were copper and bronze. But they became greedy and vainglorious and were punished by Poseidon, and their land sank beneath the sea. This disaster had occurred some 9000 years earlier.

On the face of it there are seemingly insuperable difficulties in trying to identify Plato's Atlantis (a huge island continent much too big to fit into the Mediterranean) and the date of its destruction (c. 9500 BC, according to Plato) with the Minoan civilisation of the Mediterranean c. 1500 BC. But legend is by its very nature tantalising and imprecise; and it has been suggested by some scholars that Plato's dimensions for Atlantis, and its date of destruction, involved a consistent mathematical error to a factor of ten, which might be explained by Solon's ignorance of Egyptian mathematics: that is to say that if you reduce both the dimensions and the date to a tenth of Plato's figures, you get an island corresponding in size to Crete, and a date of c. 1500 BC! In this scenario, the legend of Atlantis enshrined Egyptian memories of events much nearer home: the eruption of Santorini, and the consequent disappearance of the brilliant Bronze Age civilisation of Minoan Crete and its capital Knossos with which, as we know from frescoes in Crete and Egypt, the Egyptians had close commercial contacts. Santorini was a Minoan colony; and somehow the eruption of the volcano, and the abrupt severance of ties with Minoan Crete, fused into the concept of Crete/Atlantis sinking into the sea.

Ever since Plato penned his account there has been controversy. Aristotle thought it fiction, and said, somewhat sniffily, 'The man who dreamed it up made it vanish'. But not even Aristotle's disdain made the problem go away. Professor J. V. Luce of Trinity College, Dublin, author of *The End of Atlantis*, reckons that there are over two thousand works dealing with the lost continent – which has been variously placed in America (of course), Morocco, Nigeria, Heligoland, Mount Olympus, the West Indies, and the submarine Mid-Atlantic Ridge, to name but a few. So let us pursue a little further the possible association of Atlantis with Minoan Crete and her colony, Santorini.

It is important to remember that in Plato's time the Bronze Age Minoan civilisation of Crete had been almost completely forgotten, except in legend. It is only thanks to modern archaeology that we know anything about it at all. We know that, more than a thousand years before Plato was born, the palace of Knossos was the centre of a great and prosperous island empire that ruled the Aegean Sea. Legend knew it as the home of the mighty King Minos of Crete. As Homer put it:

Out in the dark blue sea there lies a land called Crete, a rich and lovely land, washed by the waves on every side, densely peopled and boasting ninety cities. One of the ninety towns is a great city called Knossos, and there, for nine years, King Minos ruled and enjoyed the friendship of almighty Zeus.

But by Plato's day the glory of Minoan Crete had vanished without visible trace. It was not until the first decades of the twentieth century that Knossos and Minoan Crete were rediscovered by the genius of Sir Arthur Evans, who started excavating the great mound of Kefala, near Heraklion in Crete, in 1900. Evans was to devote his considerable private fortune of £225,000 to the Knossos palace he discovered, until his death in 1941.

At Kefala/Knossos, Evans found overwhelming evidence of a wealthy and brilliant Bronze Age civilisation, centred on a palace that was a marvel to behold for size and beauty. The royal apartments were magnificently luxurious: the Queen's Room was decorated with dolphins, all grace and light – and sophisticated plumbing! It had been a world of great wealth and craftsmanship and artistry: a world of vivaciously beautiful women and high fashion, a world financed by trade and embellished by precious things of gold and silver and ivory. But to Evans the most startling aspect of life at Knossos, as I mentioned earlier, was a hazardous acrobatic sport involving the animals sacred to Poseidon – bulls. Everywhere he found evidence that the Minoans had worshipped the bull beneath the ground, who tossed the earth on his angry horns and made it quake:

What a part these creatures play here! On the frescoes and reliefs, the chief design of the seals, on a steatite vase, above the gate, it may be, of the palace itself. . . . We know now that the old traditions were true. We have before our eyes a wondrous spectacle – the resurgence, namely, of a civilisation twice as old as that of Hellas. It is true that on the old Palace site what we see are only the ruins of ruins, but the whole is still inspired with Minos' spirit of order and organisation, and the free and natural art of the great architect Daedalus. The spectacle indeed that we have here before us is assuredly of world-wide significance.

But this bull-haunted world of the Minoans was quite unknown to Plato when he was recording the legend of Atlantis. By then, Crete had become an insignificant backwater in the Aegean. It was modern archaeology, through Sir Arthur Evans and then Professor Spyridon Marinatos of Greece, that first made the association between Atlantis and the Minoans possible.

It was at the ancient harbour-site of Amnisos, on the north coast of Crete, a few miles east of Knossos, that the trail to Atlantis really started. The Greek geographer Strabo had mentioned Amnisos as the harbour-town of King Minos, and Marinatos, who was Keeper (Ephor) of Antiquities in Crete in 1932, undertook the task of checking the reference archaeologically. At Amnisos, Marinatos found the remains of a number of important buildings and harbour installations, including a jetty that stretched out into the sea. But he found more than just the harbour from which Minos was said to have dominated Crete and the trade-routes of the Aegean with his invincible navy; he found indications that Amnisos had been destroyed by some natural catastrophe which he connected with the Santorini eruption of c. 1500 BC. The stoutly-built walls of solid limestone blocks had bulged outwards and collapsed. There was fire damage everywhere. Foundation stones had been grossly disturbed, and one basement was full of volcanic pumice.

Well, Professor Marinatos concluded that this destruction had been caused by tidal waves of appalling violence, perhaps some 600 feet high, that came raging in from the north over the exposed coasts of Crete. He had made a careful study of the catastrophic eruption of Krakatoa in the Dutch East Indies in 1883. Krakatoa,

Professor Marinatos

too, had been an island eruption. It, too, collapsed and formed a great caldera. It, too, has a young volcano growing up in the caldera again. In 1883, flood-waves, called *tsunamis*, had smashed the surrounding coasts of Java and Sumatra, killing 36,000 people. No volcanic eruption in the world since then has equalled it for destructive violence. Poisonous tephra clogged the sea for miles around. The noise of the explosions was heard 3000 miles away. The sun was blotted out for days. And yet, judging by the size of the Santorini caldera, the Santorini eruption may have been four times worse. The eruption of Krakatoa took only a hundred days, culminating in terrible paroxysms when the mountain exploded and collapsed in the final 24 hours – a single day and night.

And that seems to have been the way the Santorini volcano behaved, too. The devastation it wrought should therefore have been as bad as, if not worse than Krakatoa: flood-waves, perhaps, raging over neighbouring islands and low-lying coasts; searing shockwaves, flattening all walls in their path; a roaring darkness at noon; earthquakes and fires everywhere; great clouds of wind-born volcanic ash and pumice, poisoning and smothering all vegetation where it fell.

And in its wake, total desolation. Green fields and hillsides scorched and choked. No life left. No life possible. Just the stunned, awful aftermath of a holocaust.

The harbour-town of Amnisos was only one of many on Crete that suffered simultaneous destruction, Professor Marinatos concluded. All the great Minoan palaces excavated so far were found to have been wrecked at about the same time, as far as the archaeologists could tell, and all, except for Knossos itself, were abandoned and never rebuilt. The palace of Mallia was one: destroyed and burned, never rebuilt. The palace of Phaestos in the south was another: destroyed and burned, never rebuilt. And right out on the east coast, the most recently discovered palace, at Zakro, had been violently destroyed by fire, perhaps by earthquake and flood-waves as well, and abandoned so abruptly that the treasures lying in the ruins were never even looted.

This theory of a natural catastrophe of huge proportions was the first plausible explanation of the sudden and total collapse of Minoan civilisation and sea-power. Professor Marinatos published his theory in *Antiquity*, in December, 1939. The editors were politely sceptical, and noted that 'the main thesis of this article required additional support from further excavations on selected sites'. But what with the war and Greece's post-war troubles, it was several years before Marinatos could return to his theme. In 1962 he visited Thera to see what could be done.

Almost a century earlier, when large-scale quarrying had started at Santorini to make waterproof cement for the construction of the Suez Canal, the French geologist F. Fouqué had come across the first traces of prehistoric buildings buried under their mountains of volcanic tephra, on the smaller neighbouring island of Therasia, and in the region of Akrotiri (*Santorin et ses éruptions*, 1879). When Marinatos visited Thera, he was filled with despair:

The island is covered with a layer of volcanic ash as deep as 50 or 60 metres. It is impossible to reach the original surface, as it was prior to the eruption, by digging trenches. Not only would it be extremely expensive, but the sides would fall in upon the heads of the excavators . . .

It is a tragic irony that Professor Marinatos himself now lies buried in his site at Akrotiri. He died there in 1974 after a fall and his grave is now one of the houses he had excavated.

. . . Only if one knew exactly where to dig could such a dangerous venture be undertaken. It seemed then that the only possibility was to wait with patience till the quarries exploiting the volcanic ash for industrial purposes uncovered traces of the buried past, when reaching the surface of the island as it was before the eruption. (*Albert Reckitt Memorial Lecture*, 1971.)

In 1967 Marinatos got his chance. The Akrotiri district was tempting because water erosion had created a ravine some 400 metres inland. Marinatos decided to attack the side of an uncultivated field on the western bank of the *wadi*. He struck lucky in his very first trench. After a few hours, the first loose stones appeared, followed by recognisable walls.

Marinatos had a formidable reputation for almost intuitive digging. He was a man who seemed to be able to *feel* the configurations of a hidden site far beneath the surface. His first trench revealed the wall of a basement, about three metres high. The upper storey had collapsed, but the decomposed timber beams had left holes in the thick layer of tephra deposited by the eruption. It was the corner of a monumental building of hewn ashlar masonry. The fearful heat of the volcano – about 2000° – had left the stone so friable that it flaked at a touch. But inside he found three vases of unmistakable Minoan origin; and a hundred yards away he came across a store-room crammed with large jars (*amphorae*), wonderfully preserved, their colours still glowing. Marinatos, in 1967, had good reason to feel that his hunch about Santorini was going to prove correct.

When Julia Cave and I returned to Santorini in 1972, the site had become unrecognisable. Marinatos had been burrowing through the tephra for six seasons by then, working under a protective roof. The Minoan city at Akrotiri had lain at the roots of the volcano – and paradoxically it was the eruption of that volcano that helped to save the city for posterity; for after the initial damage the deep shroud of tephra preserved the remains intact – and all in much better condition than anything Evans had found at Knossos.

It is now an emormous site, and getting bigger every season. Since the tragic death of Marinatos, the excavation has been taken over by his assistant, Christos Doumas, who had been in charge of the day-to-day operations on the site. It was Christos Doumas who was my guide as I explored the site in 1972. In six years, the Greek archaeologists had uncovered a warren of meandering streets with underground sewerage, open squares, and mansions of beautifully dressed squared stones. The floors of the houses were paved with slate slabs – an indication of high prosperity.

But the most vivid evidence of wealth and sophistication was in the wall-paintings, or frescoes, that were found still adhering to the walls. The frescoes of Akrotiri are quite unbelievably beautiful. In one house, the so-called Western Building, the 'Priestess Fresco', about one metre high: a young girl clad in a yellow stole, wearing a blue wig, offering on a luxurious silver

(Left and above) *Excavations in progress beneath the protective roof;* (right) *Stamatis Perrakis uncovering the Fisherman Fresco.*

and gold vessel some kind of red cake which she is sprinkling with saffron. In the so-called 'Cult Room', the now-celebrated 'Young Boxers Fresco', depicting two boys aged about 8, wearing one boxing glove each, and naked except for red loin-cloths and blue wigs (the blueness may indicate divinity: Poseidon had blue hair, Zeus had blue eyebrows, Homeric heroes had blue beards. These may be Heavenly Twins). On the opposite wall, a splendid fresco of antelopes, painted in outline with red detail on the heads. It's a wonderfully compelling painting, all movement and strength and speed.

Next door there was a 'Monkey Fresco', which had disintegrated into hundreds of fragments, but has been painstakingly restored to show a group of monkeys fleeing and clambering up a tree, pursued by dogs, after raiding an orchard.

The frescoes were in the upper storeys, whose floors were supported by central wooden columns. In the lower floors were storage rooms crammed with ritual vases (*rhytons*) of superb quality, imported from Crete, as well as giant *pithoi* – storage jars that held olive oil and grain and flour, which were used as currency.

Ah, these frescoes! As we arrived at the site, we were lucky enough to find the archaeologists about to start uncovering a new wall-painting. For hour after hour, the chief restorer, Stamatis Perrakis, scraped and brushed to clear the volcanic ash from the surface. We were rewarded with the first sight for 3500 years of a glowing masterpiece, a full-length painting of a handsome young fisherman, naked, holding in each hand a generous catch of blue and yellow mackerel. It was a miracle that it had survived: the whole fresco was detached from the wall, perhaps loosened by water that disintegrated the plaster gypsum which had stuck it to the wall. But the falling tephra had filled up the cavity thus formed, and held it rigid in a free-standing position. Either that, or it was in fact a hanging picture – and therefore the first portable painting ever identified as such.

But to return to the Atlantis theme. In one tiny room, even the frescoes were overshadowed by another find. The frescoes were, in themselves,

The restored Fisherman Fresco

astoundingly beautiful: three walls covered with a depiction known as the 'Spring Fresco of the Lilies' – groups of yellow-stemmed, red lilies burgeoning against a background of green, blue, yellow and red volcanic rocks and mountain peaks, with swallows flirting gracefully in a ritual of courtship: a marvellous work of art. But also in that room the excavators found a bed – their first really human contact in Akrotiri – not so much a bed as a series of holes in the compacted ash; but by pouring plaster of Paris into the holes they managed to recreate the bed entire,

The Spring Fresco of the Lilies

lashings and all, with a mattress of barley-straw on top of a hide stretched across the bedstead.

The significance of this find lay in the fact that it seemed evidence of some sort of squatter-occupation after the city had been destroyed and abandoned. The bed had been brought there because the stout walls had kept the room intact. Along with the bed were found emergency supplies of storage jars and bronze cooking utensils, as if it were an air-raid shelter.

This question of possible squatters was rather puzzling, for a time. But in 1972, after six seasons of digging, Marinatos had pieced together what he was sure was the story of the catastrophe that overwhelmed the handsome and prosperous city of Minoan Akrotiri. No skeletons had been found, and few signs of panic-stricken abandonment, so Marinatos reasoned that the inhabitants had been given sufficient warning. The disaster had not been sudden.

It started with an earthquake, or rather a series of tremors, not particularly alarming in an area notoriously prone to earthquakes, but alarming enough to make the inhabitants hurriedly store their fragile

The pottery of the Santorini site is often wonderfully well preserved, for the inhabitants had time to store it safely in the lowest rooms of their houses (bottom left) before the city was engulfed by volcanic debris.

The city as its inhabitants saw it (above), and as it is now, re-emerging after nearly 3500 years underground.

Frescoes from Santorini: Sacred Procession;

Frescoe of the Monkeys;

pottery and vases in what they hoped (and they were proved right) would be the safest parts of their houses. But then the tremors started getting worse and worse. Soon the upper parts of the buildings started to collapse, and great chunks of masonry crashed down into the streets, to lie where Marinatos was later to find them. And now the inhabitants decided to evacuate the city. They fled, unhurt, taking with them all their personal belongings; but the once noble city they had built now lay in utter ruin, desolate and uninhabitable.

Soon afterwards, as always happens in the case of a disaster area, rescue teams started picking their way through the debris. They cleared one whole area, for instance, and piled all the debris into a kind of retaining wall; they cleared 'Telchinos Street' (the Street of Smiths), and made their headquarters in one of the buildings, where they blocked up broken doorways and tottering staircases, and made some makeshift dormitories. One of the rooms was converted into a

smithy for emergency repairs – the temporary forge was still there, with the scorch-marks on the plaster of the wall behind it, and a number of discarded hammers, as well as a stone bowl to hold the water for tempering the metal. And because the water system had been destroyed by the earthquake, they placed a salvaged stone bath on top of the ruins to collect rainwater.

It was ironic, speaking personally, that the following year a volcano erupted on Heimaey, in the Westmann Islands of Iceland, my homeland, on the outskirts of an inhabited town. I witnessed the eruption myself. No one, by a miracle, was killed. In a single night, the whole island was evacuated; but within hours, the first rescue squads were back, to start the work of salvage.

But Akrotiri was not so lucky as Heimaey. Today, Heimaey has been reoccupied and rebuilt, after its narrow escape from total destruction. But something happened to make Akrotiri beyond redemption.

The Boxers

A Priestess

Marinatos concluded that it was the volcanic eruption itself, at some unspecified time *after* the initial earthquakes, that forced the evacuation of the city. It started with a tremendous hailstorm of pumice which shot straight up out of the crater and fell back on to the island, burying the ruined city. Then the mountain began to blow up. A tremendous tidal wave of pulverised volcanic ash came bursting through fissures in the sides of the mountain, engulfing the city, forcing its way through doors and windows; and then in a final paroxysm the volcano collapsed in upon itself, leaving that great sea-filled caldera and the huge glistening walls of compacted tephra that were the rim of the crater. . . .

It's a very attractive theory, certainly, because it provides such a reasonable explanation for the archaeological picture of devastation of Crete. But there is a snag: one ugly little fact that seemingly wrecks the whole hypothesis. The Minoan civilisation on Crete was destroyed a full generation *after* the Minoan civ-

ilisation on Santorini came to an end. There can be no doubt about this whatsoever – the pottery styles prove it conclusively. Santorini 'died' *c.* 1500 BC, but Crete itself didn't 'die' until *c.* 1450 BC.

So how can this dating discrepancy be resolved? One simple answer would be to assume that Santorini erupted *twice* – the first time around 1500 BC when Akrotiri was buried, the second time a generation later when the caldera was created and Minoan Crete (apart from Knossos) was swamped or crushed. That's what everyone would like to believe. But the vulcanologists and geologists who attended an International Scientific Congress on Santorini in September 1969 were unanimous in their opinion that Santorini was a classic, one-phase eruption and that the whole thing would have been over in a year or less. So the generation gap remained. Recent research on Santorini now suggests that the time-lapse between the preliminary earthquakes and the volcanic eruption cannot have been very prolonged, certainly not more than a few months, because there is hardly any trace of erosion between the earthquake-effects and the first pumice-fall. This must throw doubt on the whole theory that the destruction of Minoan Crete was caused by the Santorini eruption. The dates will not match.

Even more recent research by the Graduate School of Oceanography, University of Rhode Island (*Nature*, Vol. 271, No. 5641), suggests that the tephra-fall from the Santorini eruption went east-south-east, and was probably not sufficient to account for the catastrophic decline in the civilisation of Minoan Crete *c*. 1450 BC, except perhaps in eastern Crete.

So, as with so many historical enigmas, scholars are not yet in a position where they can give an unqualified, definitive answer. It all depends on finding proof positive of what it was that destroyed Minoan Crete. Was it earthquake? Or tidal flood-waves? Or tephra-fall? Or fires? Or a combination of all four? Or was it a straightforward invasion from Mycenean Greece?

Professor Spyridon Marinatos died, still convinced of his theory that the Santorini catastrophe not only overwhelmed Crete as well, but lent to Crete the image of disaster that associated it with the legend of Atlantis in Egyptian folk-lore. Professor Luce, tackling the problem as one of source-criticism rather than geography, notes the correspondence of Plato's topographical description of Atlantis with Crete; he notes how Plato mentioned the sophisticated plumbing on Atlantis, which Evans also found at Knossos, and the remarkable fact that at certain times of the year the kings and princes of Atlantis had to go into the precinct of Poseidon, which was attached to the palace, and grapple with bulls without the aid of weapons – exactly the same set-up as Evans found in the frescoes at Knossos.

It would be a rash man who volunteered an adamant opinion to the effect that Santorini/Crete *was* the origin of the Atlantis legend. But somehow, when you are on Santorini itself, it all seems relatively uncomplicated. Legend has its own laws, untrammelled by the disciplines of history and science; and whether there was one cataclysm or two makes little difference, because memory always telescopes disaster. On Santorini, it's easy to assure oneself that the legend of Atlantis, that flawed paradise that died in a holocaust, really *was* born out of the memory of the awesome natural forces that tore the heart out of the island and destroyed the power and brilliant culture of the Bronze Age Minoans. And down the passing centuries the fable grew and grew, to become yet another aspect of man's incessant need for Utopia – for some distant, bygone never-never-land of perfect grace, somewhere far to the west of time itself.

Glozel

Paul Jordan

Fraud is ever fascinating – at bottom, perhaps, because we all sneakingly admire the daring of the rogues who perpetrate hoaxes, forgeries and frauds. These people are a bit outside the constraints that bind the rest of us. And then again we all rather enjoy the spectacle of the confounding of the experts who are taken in by the forgers – experts who have qualifications, reputations and salaries that are supposed to guarantee against their being deceived. Frauds and hoaxes, what is more, make rattling good yarns: it can be a pleasure to follow the ingenuities of their original perpetration and the detective work that finally unmasks them. For all these reasons, tales of frauds make good television programmes too, especially in areas of scientific and artistic subject-matter. Paul Johnstone always knew this and, back in 1954, he pioneered the theme of television investigation of archaeological frauds with a programme about the Piltdown Hoax, which Drs Kenneth Oakley and Joe Weiner had just exploded. That programme recorded the laboratory detective-work that conclusively proved the fraudulent nature of the whole bag of tricks from the Piltdown site. When we made a new film about the Piltdown affair in 1973, we were able to draw on bits of the original programme to illustrate the methods by which the forgers' work had been identified.

The Piltdown scandal highlights very vividly another of the satisfactions of examining frauds. For frauds of all sorts, and not just archaeological ones, are always made to order, made to fit a particular bill. They satisfy a need of the times and otherwise they would not succeed for ten minutes, however well contrived. Market forces operate upon them and the successful forger always serves up what people expect, what they want. So that years later, when the fraud has been thankfully exposed, a close study of how it fitted the bill at the time and how it got by can tell us a very great deal about the ideas and thinking of the time.

In the case of Piltdown Man, this is wonderfully clear. At the beginning of the century, people who were working on the problem of human evolution had very little physical evidence to go on. They had the Darwinian theory and some fossils, but not nearly enough to construct even an outline of the stages of human evolution. The theory was prevalent at the time that brain development was the leading factor in the evolution of man, and that our fossil ancestors, when found, would turn out to carry a noble human braincase on top of an otherwise simian frame. This is exactly what the forger or forgers – we still don't know who – of Piltdown obligingly provided: pieces of a recent, if unusually thick, human skull, associated with the deliberately damaged jaw of an orang-utan. And so, the unmasked Piltdown Hoax stands as a vivid realisation of the scientific theories of its time.

The same thing applies to the whole character of the material at the heart of the 'Great Glow-Curve Mystery', the finds from Glozel, near Vichy in France. Let it be said at once that not everybody regards this 'mystery' as a fraud. Some people, forty and more years after virtually all reliable archaeological opinion concluded that it was faced with clear-cut forgery, go on believing in the Glozel site. And they are not all cranks, though many of them are, and especially in France. A couple of them are physicists working with a well-established scientific method for dating pottery. And this is where the mystery comes in – for their results, unchallenged within the terms of the method they employ, conflict completely with the archaeological conviction that Glozel is one big fraud.

Glozel is a tiny hamlet a few miles outside Vichy in the foothills of the Auvergne mountains. In the early years of this century one of Glozel's farms came into the possession of the Fradin family. Now the previous owners are reported to have once found a strange old pot – that is as far as the story goes – in one of the fields on the farm and the Fradins themselves apparently turned up a couple more pieces around the time of the First World War. After the war, in 1924, the Fradins decided to recultivate a field that was by that time grown over with bushes. The field had once been called 'Duranthon', but was to go on now to become famous in the archaeological world as 'le Champ des Morts', the Field of the Dead. According to the Fradins' account, it was on the 1st of March 1924, in the course of clearing off the undergrowth, that a cow stumbled into a hole in the field, and new and altogether more exciting discoveries than before were made.

Along with the cow were the seventeen-year-old Emile Fradin and his grandfather, and they stopped work to have a look into the hole that the cow had opened up. When we visited his farm in 1975, Emile Fradin at the age of sixty-seven remembered for us what they saw: 'We found a kind of tomb. There were quite a few objects in there, pots and tablets. Unfortunately this tomb – well, we think it was a tomb – was destroyed the same night because we didn't know what it was at the time.'

In fact, Emile and his grandfather dug out the 'tomb' and carried off home up the hill to their farm the bricks and bits and pieces they found in it. It seems from sketches that were later made according to the Fradins' description that what they had found was an oval paving of bricks about eight feet long, with stones set around its edge. There were signs of very intense heat at work here, for a glassy vitrification was to be seen on some of the bricks, and there were some lumps of glass lying about. The next day, at more or less the same spot, Emile seems to have found a brick with strange marks inscribed on it. With hindsight, a professional archaeologist might well conclude that the Fradins had found a Roman or medieval glass kiln

– in fact one visitor, an amateur archaeologist, did come to that conclusion after a short visit to the site. But by that time the Fradins had absorbed a much more exciting notion of the nature of their find from a local schoolmistress who, for reasons best known to herself, plumped for the idea of a large cremation-grave. In this opinion she was subsequently supported by another schoolteacher from the neighbourhood.

To this second schoolteacher, at the end of 1924, Emile Fradin showed a stone ring which he said he had found in the hole that was inscribed with what looked like the letters STX. The schoolmaster, whose name was Clément, had been impressed by the native intelligence of the relatively unschooled Emile, and was by this time feeding his interest in the past by lending him various books on the subject. It turned out now that one of the original bricks from the hole could be seen – after cleaning – to carry some sort of inscription.

Early in 1925 the schoolteachers faded from the Glozel scene with the forceful appearance at the farm of a doctor from Vichy, that spa-town of thermal and hydropathic cures. His name was Morlet and he was a bit of an amateur archaeologist too. He died in the fifties, but his wife, who still lives in Vichy, told us that he arrived at Glozel fresh from an archaeological excavation in their own garden, where he too had found a tomb 'with big tiles and even a very well-preserved skeleton, and some very fine glass vases.' The Fradins had already been quietly hinting at the idea that they ought really to receive some money from the local historical society to defray their digging expenses and compensate them for the farming time lost in delving into their site. Morlet is reported to have told them, as soon as his connoisseur's eye lit upon their finds, that they possessed a most important piece of property and ought to put a fence up to guard it. He told them that they might make a good deal of money out of it and have scholars coming from the world over to look at their site. Now it is a well-known wrinkle in the archaeological trade that it is not a desirable practice to hold out the prospect of money to those who would come into it in return for making finds. In its most extreme form – that of payment per object recovered – it has led some archaeologists in the past into becoming the unwitting purchasers of stuff 'made to order' as it were: fakes. Morlet, out of his own pocket, quadrupled the sum sought by the Fradins and promised more if more finds were made.

Morlet and young Fradin in fact arrived at a deal that gave the doctor sole rights to excavate and publish the site and the two set to work to dig up the Field of the Dead together. They soon started to turn up that prodigious quantity of finds that to this day fill the shelves and display cabinets of the little museum on the Fradins' farm. The range of the material they brought forth is as astonishing as its sheer quantity. There is stuff very much in the manner of the celebrated cave-art from the famous Dordogne caves and elsewhere: little bone carvings of animal figures, including deer and horses, but not the typical animals of the ice-age like the mammoth and the rhino which the true palaeolithic cave-art shows, though there are bone carvings and drawings on stones of what appear to be reindeer. In a manner not seen in real palaeolithic examples, there are sometimes signs resembling letters and whole inscriptions on some of these pieces.

There are even representations of the men and women of old Glozel, grotesque little faces in bone about an inch high, and one small carving shows a human figure standing on the body of an animal in a way that recalls those reclining medieval knights with dogs curled up at their feet. Alongside this palaeolithic-inspired material, there is plenty more that would not belong at all in an ice-age context – masses of pottery, for example, which wasn't made on any palaeolithic site, but first appears in the archaeological record at around 8000 or 9000 BC in Japan, and didn't really catch on in the ancient world for several thousand years after that. The Glozel pottery often wears an extremely rough and amateurish look. There are scores of pots in the Glozel museum, frequently complete and intact (which is by no means always the case with pots recovered from archaeological sites), and many of them have not been properly washed since their time in the ground. Some of the pots resemble the so-called face-urns that come from

certain Bronze-Age sites in France: the Glozelian examples have various sorts of pinchy and owl-like faces upon them, again accompanied in many cases by the same sort of signs and inscriptions that decorate the animal carvings. In one case, a root sticks out of both ends of a hole that runs through the pot – an indication, according to Morlet, of the great age of the pot, or at least that it was not buried in the ground the day before it was dug up. One or two of the pottery productions from Glozel take off into rather bizarre anatomical expressions, like the three-times-life-size hand 'imprints', and the phallic and dual-sexed pieces.

The inscribed bricks, or tablets, are the most enigmatic feature of the Glozel collection. There are dozens of them, some apparently carved with whole texts. They vaguely resemble the sort of baked tablets found in the Middle Eastern river-valley civilisations, where writing made its first appearance in the world, about 3500 BC. The signs on the Glozel tablets were for a long time most often compared with Phoenician writing, though just about every language and script under the sun has been invoked in parallel. At all events, they have resisted every attempt at translation – and a good few attempts have been made. The collection also affords examples of things that look like neolithic polished axes – that is to say, belonging to the period called the New Stone Age, some time after 9000 BC, when flint-knapping had given way to stone-polishing, to the accompaniment of pottery making, and farming had taken the place of hunting and collecting food.

Indeed, when Morlet published his first account of the Glozel find, he called it 'A New Neolithic Site'. To appreciate why Glozel appealed to him in this light, it is necessary to recall how things stood with the conventional chronology of the past to which archaeologists subscribed in Morlet's time. Many very important discoveries had been made in various parts of the world, and a substantial picture of what had happened in the human past was beginning to emerge, but with gaping lacunae – rather in the way that a jigsaw may at a middle stage have a fully-finished bottom section and many details at the top of the picture

69

Dr Morlet examining an inscribed tablet

There was next to no art at all being created in Europe after the disappearance from the archaeological record of the old huntsmen, and what flint tools their successors were making were small and not very engaging. After the glories of the palaeolithic period, few specialists were very interested in this fag-end stuff.

Other scholars were meanwhile, in the Middle East, uncovering the impressive remains of the first civilisations of the ancient world, where settled life in towns and cities and the civilised arts of pottery-making, metal-working and writing put in their appearance. But the origins of these Middle Eastern civilisations were as yet quite obscure and their link, if any, with the palaeolithic sequence of Europe was quite invisible. Europe did, of course, go on in the course of time to display evidence of the arrival of farming, town-dwelling, pot-making, metal-working and writing. Many people assumed that all these good things had been brought to Europe from their oriental inventors but, in any case, there was a gap to all intents and purposes in the archaeological record between the old hunters and the first farmers. So powerfully did this gap exercise the minds of the archaeologists of the time that it was dignified with the title of 'the Hiatus': in French, 'le Hiatus'.

Morlet saw Glozel, with its mixture of palaeolithic-like objects and neolithic-like objects, to say nothing of the material reminiscent of even later periods, as heaven-sent to plug the Hiatus and reveal the origins of the neolithic period. Here, just as one might have imagined it, were those necessary indications of transition from the old to the new, taking place perhaps as long ago as 9000 BC. And, what was more, Dr Morlet's interpretation possessed the great advantage of making those inscribed tablets, found on a French site, quite the oldest writing in the world, a landmark in the process of civilisation to overshadow the efforts of the Middle East.

Morlet's claims were not met with widespread acceptance immediately: the great French archaeological authority Saloman Reinach, for instance, in company with other sceptical colleagues, did not at first receive the news with open arms. He was even inclined to doubt the authenticity of some of the material, and he

completely worked out, but with a yawning gap between top and bottom, and nothing to connect them.

The sequence of palaeolithic 'cultures' was very well known, particularly in France, which was the model for the world. This sequence stretched back to a remote time, for which a close date in years could not then be given, but which was certainly a very long time ago, to judge from the deep geological deposits with their long-vanished species of animals that contained the earliest traces of man and his stone handiwork. The sequence came on through more recent times with evidences for more and more refined tool-making until, in the last Ice Age, the artist-huntsmen of the Dordogne caves flourished and then disappeared. For at the end of the Ice Age, the traces of our ancestors became for the archaeologists of the first quarter of this century meagre and rather paltry.

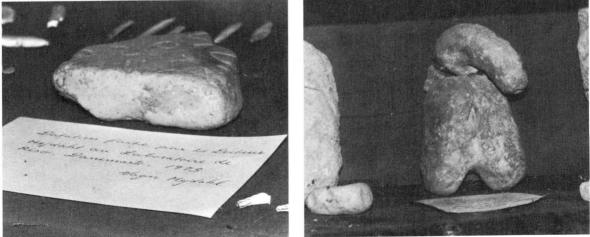

(Top) *The Fradin family (Emile is third from the right) standing before the farm building which they turned into a 'museum' to hold their finds* (below left and right).

was not alone in voicing such doubts. But when he was taken down to Glozel in person, there were some features of Morlet's claim that were bound to capture his enthusiasm. For Glozel — according-to-Morlet chimed in with two of Reinach's scholarly prejudices: one was that the reindeer had survived longer in France than everybody else thought — and here were pictures of it at neolithic Glozel and even what were claimed to be some of its bones; and the other was that the arts of civilisation had not in fact come from the Middle East as most people said, but had started up in France! So Reinach was soon converted to Morlet's Glozel and the doctor dedicated a later volume to his powerful ally in the academic establishment. With Reinach's advocacy behind it, Glozel became famous and the journalists flocked there to cry up the site, its romantic young discoverer Emile Fradin, and his wise mentor Dr Morlet. The place acquired the status of a tourist attraction: motor cars lined the roads leading to it, and a café operated there for a time.

But meanwhile the anti-Glozelians, as they came to be known, the doubters and downright decriers, were mounting their counter-attack. Both in France and England voices had been raised against Glozel. The distinguished pages of the British archaeological periodical *Antiquity* were graced with an article by its then editor O. G. S. Crawford in which he concluded that the vast majority of the stuff at Glozel was forged. The suspicions of the doubters had been raised for several reasons: there was the strikingly incongruent nature of the various finds, where palaeolithic and neolithic and God-knows-what were all mixed up together in a way that suggested to some, not Morlet's transition, but just eclectic forgery; there were those extraordinary tablets, with their untranslatable 'messages' written in what could be interpreted as a diverse jumble of signs copied and adapted from various examples in archaeological handbooks; there was the unusual state of preservation of the pots, a large percentage of which were unbroken in a highly unlikely way; there was the strange configuration of the site itself, where only a thin deposit on a rain-washed slope continued to pour forth amazing quantities of finds. The whole thing just looked and smelt wrong to

some archaeologists, as it still does to virtually every archaeologist today.

But the site went on being dug up and went on producing more and more objects. Everybody who was anybody at all could dig there, especially if introduced by Reinach. There was plenty to go round and you didn't have to be an archaeologist — at one time the King of Rumania had his own trench in operation at Glozel. In June of 1927 two new apparent 'graves' were found in the Field of the Dead, oval like the original one, but this time made of loose stone slabs. In a remarkable fashion, no earth had ever penetrated through the gaps in these roughly built tombs in all the years — thousands, according to Morlet — since they were constructed. There were more pots and pebbles and phallic idols and, in one case, a few human bones which are now displayed in the farm museum.

But reports were coming in from visiting archaeologists of suspicious disturbances in the soil of the site, and the claim was made that some of the bone and stone objects from Glozel could be seen to have been worked with modern metal tools. Worse still, a M. Vergne, who was curator of the museum of Villeneuve-sur-Lot, asserted that on the 25th of September 1927 he had been sheltering from a sudden storm in a stable at the Fradins' farm (after a visit to the little Museum) and had there come upon some half-finished artefacts of a Glozelian stamp and some inscribed, but as yet unbaked, clay-tablets.

Clearly some definitive investigation to settle the matter was called for, and the 1927 International Anthropological Congress sent a commission of archaeologists down to Vichy to examine the site. Among the distinguished archaeologists and scholars of that commission was a young Englishwoman named Dorothy Garrod, who was later to become Professor of Archaeology in Cambridge. When we came to make our Glozel film in 1975 we were able to draw on a long interview between Professor Garrod and Glyn Daniel, which Paul Johnstone had filmed in 1967 shortly before her death. Her account of the commission's work gives us a great deal of the circumstantial detail of their investigations.

Le Docteur Morlet vient de surprendre Miss Garrod, membre de la Commission Internationale, faisant avec le doigt un trou dans le front de taille des fouilles. De gauche à droite: le docteur Tricot-Royer; le docteur Morlet expliquant à la Commission ce qui vient de se passer; M. l'abbé Favret; M. Hamal-Nandrin; M. de Varigny; M. Bosch-Gimpera; Miss Garrod, baissant la tête; M. Vallat, avocat à Vichy.

The international commission (Dorothy Garrod second from right) is harangued on site by Dr Morlet (second from left)

She told us that they stayed in a posh Vichy hotel, and made daily sorties to Glozel to see the objects and do their own excavations, returning to the hotel each evening to confer behind locked doors. This was necessary because the French press were following their work with partisan eagerness. The commission, on their first afternoon's visit to the site, chose their digging spots quite randomly by throwing stones in the field and electing to dig where they fell – quite wisely, in fact, since they wanted their investigations to break new ground and not go on delving in ground already under suspicion. On their first day of digging in their chosen spots, they found absolutely nothing. Dorothy Garrod, anticipating at this stage of the story the conclusions that the commission finally arrived at, told us that, 'that was rather classic at Glozel, because of course people would start in a hole and there hadn't been time to furnish the hole with necessary finds. Well, on the second day we began to find Glozelian objects.'

In line with their growing conviction that skullduggery was afoot, Professor Garrod remembered that the members of the commission soon noticed that their first find, a Glozel tablet with inscription, was lying at the bottom of a pocket of disturbed earth inserted into the surrounding greyish deposit. 'That appeared to us suspect, to say the least of it.' This situation was repeated with other finds, so – to take precautions against any overnight tampering with their trench, for they suspected that objects were being introduced into the soil they were about to dig through long holes made with poles – the commission-members decided to powder the vertical face of their trench with plaster, and execute a complex pattern on the plaster whose disturbance would immediately give away any tampering. Next day Dorothy Garrod was elected to go on ahead and verify the survival of plaster and pattern, but as soon as she had started to do so she was hailed by Dr Morlet in high dudgeon, who accused her of being caught red-handed in the act of salting the site herself, in an effort to incriminate him. The row was eventually patched up, but by now the press had wind of the way the commission's opinion was moving. For its part, the International Commission was very clear, if polite, about its conclusions: 'Relying on our unanimous observations and discussions, we have decided that everything we were able to study in Glozel was of no very great age'.

The police now descended on Glozel and searched the premises. They took into custody a number of objects from the farm and museum and sent them crated up to Paris for forensic examination. The Morlet–Reinach party was incensed and issued a high-minded declaration: 'The admirable discovery of Glozel lacked only the highest blessing of all – that with which the Roman Inquisition honoured the genius of Galileo'. They got together a rival 'study committee' and set to work to dig up Glozel all over again.

They had 'forensic' experts of their own, for among the investigators in Reinach's team was a Swedish policeman called Soderman, who had become interested in the affair while seconded to the French police. He maintained a life-long advocacy of Glozel thereafter, and initiated a Scandinavian involvement in the controversy that remains to this day. Against the findings of the commission on which Dorothy Garrod served, Soderman was able to invoke the findings of a Stockholm laboratory to the effect that tested bone objects from Glozel had a lower organic content than modern bone and so should be older than recent specimens. It should be remembered, however, that the carvings on a bone may not be as old as the bone itself. Much was made in Reinach's camp of finds

Luncheon at Glozel for Reinach's study committee

which his team considered to have been excavated from quite undisturbed soil and attention was given to certain objects which appeared to have been totally enclosed in roots at the time of excavation. By May of 1928 Reinach's study committee was quite convinced that the site clearly belonged to the beginning of the New Stone Age, without any admixture of later objects.

But the police laboratory report on the objects taken away from the farm stated that the pottery was soft and would disintegrate in water in a matter of hours (there were photographs to prove it) so it couldn't, they thought, have lain in that rain-washed hillside for thousands of years; there were chlorophyll traces in some of the pots, deemed quite impossible in ancient fired clay (on this score, the report gave the pottery from Glozel no more than five years of age); there were unexpected foreign bodies in much of the clay, like mosses and bits of cotton; both bone and stone objects had been worked with metal tools, which didn't exist in any form in the New Stone Age (for example, a 'neolithic' polished axe-head showed signs of filing with a modern file).

On the combined evidence of the first commission

(Above) *Reinach being conveyed by bullock-cart to the site of the excavations* (left)

Emile Fradin stands between two lawyers after being cleared of fraud

and the police, an open accusation of fraud was made against the Fradin family, as being the likeliest perpetrators of the forgeries. The Fradins took the matter to court and the case went their way: they received in damages for libel the famous one franc which formalised their innocence of the fraud, but scarcely signalised it.

By the 1930s, with the exception of a few diehards like Morlet, the Glozel affair was over: most archaeologists had concluded with the commission and the police, and against the study committee, that Glozel was a patent fraud – whoever might or might not have done it. As to who the forger or forgers were, well – *pace* the court decision – there were some pretty obvious candidates. And to those who denied that an untutored farm boy or a thermal doctor could have

disposed of the necessary knowledge and expertise to fool some eminent scholars there was the reasonable reply (which applies in all such cases) that the scholars had in fact unwittingly guided their deceivers as to how best to go on deceiving them: by a sort of reward-and-punishment system which guaranteed that they went on getting more of what they liked and wanted and expected, and less of what aroused their doubts or puzzled them.

The circle of enthusiasts that centred upon Morlet and Fradin was always theorising about their finds and predicting what they would find next, making comparisons with known material from other sites at home and abroad, lending books with inspiring illustrations of other people's discoveries. The forger or forgers got to know what the experts wanted and gave it to them, said the sceptics. In another *Antiquity* article in 1930 the French archaeologist Vayson de Pradenne put this point of view very well: 'The hoax evolved itself gradually; it was unconsciously directed by the dupes themselves, and its course was guided by the criticisms of its opponents. It was the offspring of collaboration'.

Nothing remotely resembling the package of artefacts from Glozel had ever been found before and nothing like it was ever found afterwards. It was a sport and an irrelevance to the whole scheme of human development, as that scheme came to be better and better known with the progress of discovery all over the world. And that judgment stood whether Glozel was true or false, while all the signs were that it was false. Soon Glozel became a joke, and remaining enthusiasm for it increasingly wandered off into eccentricity. The mysterious tablets continued to exercise the ingenious minds of would-be translators. One such was a Colonel St Hillier – no one but himself was satisfied with his efforts, but one can see the direction in which his mind was working: 'Know yourself a woman. Come submissive and delightful. Hope for two cradles.'

Glozel passed into the byways of French chauvinism and popular crankery, and was lost in neglect and obscurity . . . until 1974, when out of the blue Emile Fradin was able to proclaim in *Paris Match*, under a large photograph of himself grinning over his collection: 'I was down for 50 years but I shall die happy. They've just written to me from Denmark: Glozel is authentic!'

This declaration, which certainly begs some questions, may turn out to have been quite premature. Whether Emile Fradin dies happy about Glozel remains to be seen – for he is happily still alive. And 'authentic' was a rather sweeping assessment of the import of the Danish findings. At that time, at the beginning of 1974, the archaeological grapevine was conducting the rumour that a fairly new but well-established and well-accepted method of dating anciently fired pottery – called thermoluminescence, or simply TL – had just been applied to a few objects from Glozel and had not, as every archaeologist might

have predicted, come up with a modern date for these Glozel 'fakes', but rather a date placing their last firing at some two thousand or more years ago. Interestingly enough, this date would have given no comfort to Dr Morlet had he lived to hear of it, for his 'neolithic' postulation required something like 8000 or 9000 BC as favourite.

'Thermoluminescence', as its Graeco-Latin formation suggests, means that this dating method has to do with light-glow engendered by heat. The scientists who invented it, and who practise it on behalf of archaeology, have themselves called it simple in principle. Pots and fired pottery-products of all kinds are made of clay, and most clays and soils contain very tiny quantities of radioactive impurities, including uranium, which give off a pretty constant flux of radiation. Clays and soils also contain grains of various minerals like quartz and feldspar and the radiations from the radioactive elements pass through these grains, losing some of their energy in the form of detached electrons.

A few of these detached electrons become trapped inside the mineral grains and will stay trapped for thousands and thousands of years, unless they are shaken free by thermal vibration of the crystal lattice of the mineral grains with the application of heat. When a man-made pot is first fired, at a temperature somewhere in the range from 300–500°C, the heat vibration shakes off all the trapped electrons in its mineral grains – setting the clock to zero, as it were. As the years roll by, the radioactive elements in the clay of the pot (and in the soil in which it may be buried, to some extent) continue to dispatch their alpha-particles, beta-particles and gamma-rays. These radiations again lose some of their energy as they pass through the mineral grains, and a new accumulation of trapped electrons is built up in the crystal lattices of those grains. If at any stage you can count how many electrons have been accumulated, and relate this number to the known propensity of the mineral grains to trap electrons and the known radiation level of the radioactive elements, then you can, roughly, know how long it is since the pot was last fired – in most cases, since some human being made that pot.

Counting those trapped electrons can be achieved thanks to the fact that a certain number of them, upon release, go to cause the emission of a glow of light from the heated sample. If you can measure this glow with sufficient accuracy, you arrive at a measure of the number of electrons that have got trapped since the pot was last fired. Having come up with your estimate of that number of electrons, you need to determine the glow-propensity of the particular clay you are testing, and how much radiation its radioactive impurities and those perhaps of its environment are sending forth. You can directly measure the latter, and you can arrive at the former by artificially dosing the sample with a standard amount of nuclear radiation. Armed with this information, you can proceed to interpret in terms of years-since-firing your estimate of the number of electrons that were trapped in your sample at the time when you heated it up and shook them loose.

We called our programme about the new evidence from Glozel 'The Great Glow-Curve Mystery' because in practice the scientists draw out a graph – a 'curve' – which plots the amount of light emitted against the temperature applied. This glow-curve is the basis for the estimate of age-since-firing. The mystery came in because, of course, the dates obtained were quite at variance with archaeological opinion and it was not clear immediately – nor later – why this should be. For, in terms of accepted TL dating techniques, there was nothing wrong with the method employed – while at the same time, as we have seen, there was otherwise every reason in the world to believe that Glozel was a bundle of forgeries.

For the British archaeological coterie, the first solid news of what had happened to justify Emile Fradin in his boast to *Paris Match* appeared in the lecture list of a scientific symposium held in Oxford in April 1974. The Symposium dealt in scientific methods of dating and identification for archaeological finds, and the lecture crucial for the resurrection of Glozel was announced in the name of two physicists, Dr Hugh McKerrell from the National Museum of Antiquities of Scotland, and Dr Vagn Mejdahl of the Danish Atomic Energy Commission. Both scientists had been invited, in different ways, to examine material from Glozel: in the case of Dr Mejdahl, his sample had come to him through a Swedish friend of Mme Morlet resident in France; Dr McKerrell's piece of Glozeliana had arrived in Edinburgh through the good offices of someone keen to nail the Glozel case to the final satisfaction of archaeology and science.

At the outset, the results of both the Danish and the Scottish determinations encouraged Dr McKerrell to tell us, when he was interviewed on our behalf by Professor Colin Renfrew, that dates of around the time of Christ could be assigned to the material so far tested. At this early stage of the game, Dr McKerrell warned that the TL determinations were pretty loosely bracketed, but something within the range of AD zero, plus-or-minus 500 years, could be relied upon. Going cautiously, Dr McKerrell told us that, 'it means that some of the tablets, the ones we've looked at, are genuine. It doesn't mean that all of the tablets are genuine, it doesn't necessarily mean that all the other material on the site is genuine, but some of the tablets are of the order of 2000 to 2500 years of age'. Colin Renfrew expressed, on behalf of the archaeological fraternity, his wonderment at the physicists' claim that some at least of the Glozel material was neither neolithic, as the old protagonists of the site had claimed, nor modern forgery, as all reputable archaeologists had long ago concluded.

Emile Fradin, when we visited him at Glozel late in 1974, was jubilant at his vindication by the boffins: 'It's official – this tablet is 3000 years old . . . about!' Fradin's interpretation of the TL findings was perhaps a little bit inclined to an early date for the tested material from his site, but at the time of our programme in early 1975 it lay only just beyond the outer margin of error of the determinations. Hugh McKerrell later quoted an average date of around 200 BC for the samples so far tested, ranging from perhaps 600 BC to about AD 200. He was sure that he was relating to us a real TL date for his samples and for the Danish ones, since he was able to demonstrate by a variety of experiments that the samples in question had really been fired in antiquity to a high enough temperature to set the TL clock to zero at that time. No other laboratory specialising in TL dating has ever faulted the method whereby Mejdahl and McKerrell arrived at their dates. And a carbon-14 date for an ox tooth 'found' inside one of the face-urns supported the TL estimations – it came out at around AD 0, a single independent check on the determinations by the TL method.

Hugh McKerrell was, moreover, prepared to go on to even bolder statements about the Glozeliana under his view. 'The thermoluminescence dating of course shows the tablets themselves are about 2000 years old, but does not necessarily date the inscriptions. . . . We have given a great deal of experimentation thought to this, and what we have been able to show is that a number of the tablets very fortunately . . . have been heated sufficiently for a vitrified layer to appear on the surface. Now this seals in effectively the letters underneath, and there is just no way that this sort of inscription could have been put on, other than in the original state.' In Roskilde, in Denmark, Dr Mejdahl concurred: 'We have now shown that at least 25 objects from Glozel are authentic. . . . We have been able to say that the date must be from AD 100 to about 700 BC. . . . There are at least a number of objects that are not faked, so we have a mystery that must be explained'.

The archaeological establishment was, to say the least, upset by these assertions. A certain non-meeting of minds ensued: to an outsider, it seemed clear that the archaeologists on the one hand and the physicists on the other were simply not remotely understanding one another's attitudes. The physicists stood by their graphs and measurements and their rather narrow faith in their technique in the face of all the circumstantially-persuasive evidence of fraud at Glozel. And they frequently seemed quite uninterested in the archaeologists' very real objections to the Glozel collection – its irrelevance to the known process of human development, its quite solecistic incongruity with all the well-documented finds of any time and place in the archaeological record. This lack of interest in the real substance of archaeological context did not stop the physicists from sometimes speculating outside their field about the possible meaning of Glozel in the light of their convictions about its valid dating to the period of, say, 600 BC to AD 100. Something was heard from them about Gauls and Greek influence and the like. For their part, the archaeologists were clearly rattled. If the preposterous rag-bag of Glozel (as they saw it) was indeed genuine, then a great deal of archaeology as they knew it went by the board: not just certain of its factual conclusions about bits of the past, but whole areas of its theoretical basis for proceeding to investigate the past.

In this thick atmosphere, *Chronicle* invited a party of leading British archaeologists to go and have a fresh look at Glozel, to see if the standard view of the site as a thumping fraud really did hold up in archaeological terms, now that the physicists had come up with these unexpected dates. We took along a leading authority in the Gallo-Roman field – the archaeology of France at the time that the TL dates now suggested for Glozel. Olwyn Brogan has worked in this field for many years, but she had never visited Glozel before. When she had inspected the finds in the little farmyard museum and taken a look at the site in the Champs des Morts, she reported to us on her feelings about the Glozel collection in the light of the TL dates. Her findings are quite crucial to the discussion and cannot be ignored for all the TL dates: 'What I can't understand is that, if we are to believe the TL dates, we should find Celtic and/or Gallo-Roman potsherds or other objects from the site. But in that museum *I could see no single Gallo-Roman or indeed Celtic object.*' Nothing, then, from Glozel, fits into the archaeological context to which the TL dates would consign the material from the Field of the Dead. Nothing: not just a few things, but nothing. Glozel, whatever else it may be, is archaeologically *sui generis*.

Professor Richard Atkinson of Cardiff began with some cautions – he told us that Glozel has patently never been excavated in a satisfactory way. He invoked Sir Mortimer Wheeler's famous derogation of certain styles of excavation: 'dug up like potatoes'. In Atkinson's view, Glozel did not even measure up to this deplorable standard: it was 'a dog's breakfast', so that what we were faced with was simply a collection of material in the museum. (It has, in fact, been suggested several times that a proper re-excavation of the site would go a long way to settling many – if not all – of the problems of Glozel. The French authorities seem loath to undertake any speedy new campaign and so we are denied this approach to a solution of the affair.) Professor Atkinson went on vividly to pose the problem of Glozel. It amounted to a 'balance of improbabilities'. On the one hand, there were the archaeologically unacceptable features of the site and of the material alleged to have come from it: 'It seems to me very improbable on a site where the soil is sandy and easily moved – if it had been occupied for that length of time (700 BC to AD 100) on a steep slope – that all this archaeological material should be in a layer . . . no more than about a foot thick, where there ought to be a very complex stratification. For all the fired clay material, there are no parallels at all, either at the dates in question in Central Gaul, or indeed in any other time or place. It's perfectly clear from examining both the soil and the vegetation growing on it that this is an acid soil, and it seems to me highly improbable that if these things had been buried in those conditions, for anything like up to 2000 years, this surface appearance could possibly have survived.' On the other hand, said Professor Atkinson, who knows his science, there was the 'improbability . . . of the thermoluminescent dates being wrong', and he was unwilling in our programme to predict any possible resolution of his balance of improbabilities.

Professor Glyn Daniel of Cambridge reminded us that the Glozel collection was simply not 'archaeologically possible as we know the archaeological record at the moment'. And, lest anyone underestimate our knowledge, let me add that we know that record pretty well for this time and place. And Glyn Daniel quoted a salutary observation of Sherlock Holmes's from 'A Study in Scarlet': 'When a fact appears opposed to a long train of deduction, it invariably proves to be capable of bearing some other interpretation'. Glyn Daniel admitted that, in the case of the TL dates from Glozel, he couldn't possibly tell us what that other interpretation might be, but he was certainly voicing at the end of our 1975 programme the archaeologists' trust in their judgment that something must be, however inscrutably, wrong with the TL dates.

A degree of interdisciplinary acrimony, fading with time like some radioactive source, has characterised the years since our programme was transmitted. No solution is in sight for the glow-curve mystery of Glozel, but some side-lights have been cast and some useful observations made by interested scholars.

A certain amount of light has, for instance, been shed on those baffling inscriptions on the Glozel tablets. Dr B. S. Isserlin of Manchester University had already told us, during the making of the programme, that he very much doubted the identification of certain signs on the Glozel tablets with Phoenician letters appearing in various known Phoenician inscriptions (it had been claimed by some anti-Glozelians that the forgers of these tablets had haphazardly copied Phoenician texts). He was inclined to compare the Glozel signs with, if anything, some ancient inscriptions from Spain, but beyond that he had been unable to do anything with them. In the July issue of *Antiquity*, a communication was relayed from Dr T. D. Crawford of University College, Cardiff, to the effect that, on the basis of statistical analysis, 'the corpus examined does not exhibit the characteristics to be expected of texts in a natural language, and linguistic methods are therefore not appropriate to the determination of the genuineness of the material'. On this view, the tablets from Glozel do not carry writing in any natural language, and all attempts to translate them as such are doomed.

At the Archaeometry Conference held in Philadelphia in Easter 1977, Dr Mejdahl reviewed the state of affairs with Glozel from the point of view of the physicists who stood by their TL determinations. He reported that, on the basis of a refinement of the TL technique, some ten dates had now been obtained that clustered more tightly around 100 BC, in only a slight change of emphasis away from the 700 BC to AD 200 spread hitherto revealed. On the other hand, TL dates on a glass fragment and on a glassy layer of vitrification on one of the tablets lay way away from the 100 BC group, at up to AD 1750, and could in fact be modern! – perhaps altered by reheating in mediaeval times. And, going greatly in the opposite chronological direction, a carbon-14 date on bone pieces from the museum had come out at 15,000 BC.

For the archaeologists, these results could only re-emphasise the inconsonance of the Glozel collection, suggesting, even if one accepted the TL dates, that what the champions of Glozel had declared to be the relics of a single and unique culture in fact did not belong together at all. Dr Mejdahl also revealed that fifty per cent of the tablets examined would disintegrate in water, reviving one of the findings of the French police report of the late Twenties. Archaeologists sceptical of the TL dates have speculated about the possible reshaping – without refiring or with only superficial refiring – of old, say Roman, pottery products. It seems possible on occasions for pottery to come intact but quite soggy from the ground after long periods of burial, though this is not a very usual circumstance. Could the Glozel 'frauds' have been manufactured with anciently-fired but rekneadable clay? So far no one has come up with a test for identifying such a latter-day piece of handiwork. Archaeologists have also wondered about the possibility of some special conditions in the soil and clay of Glozel – some high-radiation feature of the soil which could dose-up objects buried for only a short time in it, or some anomalous inclusions in the clay employed to make the Glozel pieces. No such simple, or indeed complicated, solutions to the problem have come to hand, and, purely from the standpoint of the TL method, the more-or-less BC date of most of the objects tested remains to be faulted.

But the sceptical archaeologists can draw some provisional comfort from another scientific test to which some of the Glozel material has been subjected. Writing in 1976 in the *Journal of Archaeological Science*, Mike Barbetti (of the Oxford Research Laboratory for Archaeology and the History of Art) and D. P. S. Peacock (of the Department of Archaeology at Southampton University) have shown between them that the tested pottery products of Glozel are indeed manufactured from the clay of the Glozel site and that measurements of the geomagnetic field obtaining at the time of their manufacture, and 'recorded' in their fabric, strongly suggest that these things were last heated up and cooled down in an earth's magnetic field very like the present day's. As far as it goes, this might make

any date between 500 BC and AD 1500 look pretty unlikely, though more work remains to be done. Dr Peacock remarks: 'if the anomaly lies in the TL dates, it is of the utmost importance to discover the cause, or the method may not continue to enjoy the widespread confidence among researchers which it has seemed to warrant until now'. That is a salutary, if rather fearful observation, when one remembers that it has sometimes been TL which has 'determined' the genuineness or fraudulence of some problematical objects from other collections than Glozel.

Something of a warning against the too-ready acceptance of all TL dates (or perhaps of all dates arrived at by the aid of physics) has recently been given in the case of some forgeries from a Mexican source. Though dates of a thousand or more years BC were published for these doubtful objects, recent work has shown that they were never actually suitable for TL dating, and their dates are worthless. These particular fakes had the anomalous property of acquiring a new TL age very rapidly after the test-heating that should have effectively put their clock back to zero for our lifetimes; and so the scientists were able to show that they were in fact manufactured in the 1940s at about the time of their 'discovery'. It must be firmly repeated that no similar solution applies to the Glozel problem, but at least caution is advised.

Certainly Dr Martin Aitken of the Oxford Laboratory thinks so. Writing with Mrs Joan Huxtable of the same laboratory in the Autumn 1975 issue of *Antiquity*, this founding father of TL declares: 'The Glozel tablets must have a message either for the archaeologists or for the TL-dating specialists, and, having been in business for only seven years, it behoves the latter to peer anxiously, in case the message is for them'. If and when that effect is discovered, the archaeologists will heave a sigh of relief; for what is to them a senseless hotch-potch of individually-doubtful and collectively-impossible 'finds' from an utterly implausible site, with no part to play in the known history of mankind, will trouble them no more. In the meantime, the physicists can glimpse no imaginable anomaly in their method to bring comfort to the archaeologists.

Bérenger Saunière, a poverty-stricken village priest of Southern France, discovered some old parchments hidden in his church. They appear to provide the clue to his sudden acquisition of vast wealth, but the traces are tantalisingly obscure – partly by Saunière's own agency. Even his apparently-casual purchase of a print of Poussin's Bergers d'Arcadie (above) *points an enigmatic finger towards the solution of the mystery.*

The Lost Treasure of Jerusalem . . . ?

Henry Lincoln

In a remote corner of Southern France, perched high on a hilltop is the tiny and isolated village of Rennes-le-Château. There is little to suggest to the casual visitor the drama of its hidden story. With its little church, its crumbling château, its handful of houses and few score inhabitants, it seems a typical and unprepossessing village with nothing to differentiate it from any other small rural community anywhere in the Languedoc. Nothing immediately obvious, that is, except for a crudely painted notice which greets the stranger at the entry to its one winding street: *Fouilles Interdites* – 'Excavating Prohibited'. The curious admonition seems to hang like a question-mark over the peaceful hamlet. The stranger, ignorant of the extraordinary history of the place, must wonder what on earth there could be that might be worth digging for on so lost and remote a mountain-top.

Such ignorant strangers, however, are few. Almost nobody arrives at Rennes-le-Château who has not come in search of the traces of a past curé of this parish, Bérenger Saunière, who arrived here penniless in 1885, and who died in 1917 having spent a huge fortune. His expenditure has been estimated at somewhere between one and two million pounds sterling . . . and the provenance of this fortune is shrouded in mystery. Today's visitors to Rennes-le-Château are all, in one way or another, treasure-hunters in search of 'the curé's gold'.

Saunière's first years in the village were a time of poverty and hardship. His account books demonstrate clearly his penniless condition. Over one sixteen-month period his expenses were a mere ninety francs, but his income brought him the even more impossibly low sum of twenty-five francs. Only his skill at hunting and fishing and the generosity of his parishioners enabled him to survive.

Of honest peasant stock, Saunière was able to accept his penurious lot with equanimity. His major concern was for his little church. For more than a thousand years the tiny building had heard the prayers of the village, but now, with centuries of grime upon its walls, the fabric was growing daily more dilapidated. Rain fell through gaps in the roof, forming puddles even on the altar stone, which was cracked and crumbling to powder. In desperation for this building which formed the centrepiece of his life and of his parish, the priest pleaded with the mayor, and the poverty-stricken community was able to scrape a tiny sum from its communal funds in order to carry out the most urgent repairs.

With no idea how the debt would ever be repaid, Saunière set to work. The damaged altar table was his first priority. He had it lifted from its two supporting pillars . . . and thus made the discovery which was to change his life and to begin the legend of the 'Golden Priest'. One of the two ornately-carved stone pillars was hollow. Inside, bedded in ferns which filled the hiding place, were some rolled parchments.

Copies of two of these parchments survive. They are curious documents. Both are written in Latin, each a carefully-penned passage from the Gospels. But in one of them there are scores of interpolated letters, while the briefer of the two documents is oddly arranged on the page with lines of uneven length and words seemingly arbitrarily broken, even where there is ample space for their completion. Saunière soon realised that they contained ciphers. He needed the advice of experts.

Borrowing the cost of the fare, he travelled to Paris.

He had obtained letters of introduction to the director of the seminary at the church of St Sulpice. The director's nephew was a young priest, a gifted linguist and palaeographer. With his help, Saunière was able to have the mysterious documents subjected to expert analysis.

During the week or so which it took the experts to complete their study, Saunière made the most of his unexpected holiday. There was much to see in the Paris of the 1890s, even for a penniless 'tourist', but Saunière did not apparently spend his time in aimless sightseeing. In some extraordinary way he was able to make the acquaintance of Emma Calvé. She was a world-famous opera singer who had just returned from a triumphal overseas tour. Wealthy, glamorous and famous, the Maria Callas of her day, she yet formed a close relationship with this obscure and penniless priest. His cloth was evidently no bar to their ripening friendship, which was to continue over the years to come, with Emma more than once visiting her friend's remote mountain-top parish. However, the palaeographer's report was soon ready and, presumably without being aware of the significance of their findings, the experts placed into Saunière's hands the key to a fortune.

His mission was accomplished and he was anxious to return to Rennes-le-Château, but before setting off he undertook one brief and significant errand. He went to the great museum of the Louvre where he bought a copy of Poussin's *Bergers d'Arcadie*. One of the great masterpieces of the seventeenth century, the painting depicts three shepherds and a shepherdess grouped around a simple tomb in an idyllic setting of trees and mountains. They are contemplating an inscription carved into the side of the tomb: 'Et in Arcadia Ego' – 'Even in Arcadia, I (Death) am present'. The purchase was not a whim on Saunière's part. *Les Bergers d'Arcadie* had assumed an unexpected significance for him. It was a part of the web of clues which were to lead Saunière into a new life.

Within a short space of time he was spending money at an extraordinary rate. He bought all the land to the west of the village church and there, on the very edge of the steeply-sloping mountainside, he began to build. A pleasure garden with fountains and shady walks was laid out. On one side of it he built what was for Rennes-le-Château an imposing house: the Villa Bethania. On the other side, to house his library, he built a battlemented gothic tower: La Tour Magdala – a rich man's folly which, perched on the very edge of the mountain-top, seems suspended in space against a backdrop of breathtakingly beautiful scenery. No expense was spared . . . indeed no expense seemed too much.

If Saunière's new-found wealth came simply through having in his possession the secret of the mysterious parchments, one must ask why the experts in Paris had so freely handed over the decipherments. Did they not realise the value of what they had found? A possible explanation might be that the indications in the parchments referred to local topographical features, and as such would have been meaningless to a stranger. A reference, for instance, to 'The Dead Man' would convey nothing to someone lacking precise local knowledge. Saunière, however, would have recognised it as the name of a tiny stream which flows down from the plateau beyond his village. References to 'The Circle', 'The Eagle's Nest' or 'The Holy Water Stoup' would all have seemed equally vague and cryptic. How could a stranger guess that these are the local names of a spring, a mountain and the confluence of two rivers, all of which are within a mile or so of Rennes-le-Château? Whatever may have been the nature of the clues, they certainly led Saunière to his 'crock of gold'.

His new-found wealth depended on a secret, and Saunière took pains to protect it. Some of the gravestones in his churchyard were evidently connected with the mystery. Saunière obliterated the inscriptions. Fortunately for followers of his trail, this labour of the village priest was wasted. The stones had already – and unknown to him – been recorded by a collector of tomb inscriptions. Like the parchments, these carved stones convey a hidden meaning . . . and Saunière was making sure that their message should no longer be in public view.

Naturally his behaviour, and especially his sudden wealth and lavish expenditure, caused much wagging

Bérenger Saunière

of tongues. His superiors demanded to know the source of his mysterious fortune, but Saunière, with self-assured arrogance, evaded their pressures. He was not at liberty to speak, he claimed coolly. The money was the gift of wealthy people, who had sealed Saunière's lips in the secrets of the confessional. And for a quarter of a century – until his death in 1917 – his secret remained inviolate . . . and his purse seemingly bottomless.

Could Saunière's explanation have been the true one? Or is it possible that this remote and insignificant hamlet could have been the hiding-place of some great treasure of antiquity?

A first hint of the richness of Rennes-le-Château's past is to be found on the hollow pillar which concealed the parchments. Saunière carved onto it the date of his discovery – 1891; but the pillar is in fact many centuries older. The style of its decorated carving belongs to the dark years of the Visigoths, one of the Germanic tribes who, in the fifth and sixth centuries, swept across Western Europe.

Saunière's village is all that remains of a mighty city. Spread below in the valley was once Aereda, a powerful fortified citadel. Boasting thirty thousand inhabitants, it was compared in strength to Carcassonne, and was one of the last great strongholds of the Visigothic Empire. Before the arrival of the Visigoths, the Romans had occupied the area, using the hot springs of the sister-village of Rennes-les-Bains, where they established a spa. The Romans also exploited mines of silver and gold which were to be found in the locality. Traces of these mines still exist, though the veins are now long exhausted.

Romans and Visigoths had crossed paths elsewhere than here, and it is this crossing of paths that provides one of the most dramatic clues to the mystery. In 410 AD the Visigoths sacked Rome. The historian Procopius records the event, and describes the booty taken. He tells us that this included, '. . . the treasures of Solomon, the king of the Hebrews, a sight most worthy to be seen. For they were adorned for the most part with emeralds, and in the olden time they had been taken from Jerusalem by the Romans.'

This is a reference to the sacking of the Holy City by

the Roman Emperor Titus in AD 70, and indeed Titus' Arch in Rome still shows the Temple Treasure with the great Menorah – the Seven-Branched Candlestick – clearly in evidence, as it was borne in the triumphal procession. This, then, is the treasure which Procopius tells us was snatched by the Visigoths, to become part of the booty from their many wars.

In the Fifth Century the Visigothic Kingdom straddled the Pyrenees. Their accumulated booty was well guarded. Part was used to finance the running of the State, and was held at Toulouse, their French capital. In AD 507 that 'state treasury' was captured by Clovis, king of the Franks. Some fifty miles away, however, at Carcassonne, was the more precious part of the Visigoths' Treasure. This was the 'ancient' or 'holy' treasure which – like the English crown jewels – was guarded as a symbol of the power, continuity and faith of the State. This, according to Procopius, was the treasure of which 'Solomon's' formed part. He relates how, after the capture of Toulouse, Clovis went on to besiege Carcassonne . . . 'for he well knew that the Holy Treasure was there. That treasure which aforetimes Alaric the Elder had taken as booty when Rome fell to his hand.' But at Carcassonne the Visigoths held firm and eventually Clovis abandoned the siege.

Part of the Holy Treasure was later taken from Carcassonne to Toledo, the Spanish Capital of the Visigoths. In 711, the Arabian Moors attacked Toledo and the treasure was hidden away for safety. In the ensuing period of conflict and unrest it was lost and forgotten. In the nineteenth century at Guarrazar near Toledo, the lost treasure was unearthed. But neither in that hoard, nor in the detailed accounts of booty captured by the Arabs and the Franks, is there any trace of the Jerusalem Treasure. The last records place it in Carcassonne, a mere twenty miles from Aereda – Rennes-le-Château. Finally, under the assaults of their enemies, the Visigothic Empire dwindled to a tiny area known as the Razès – of which Aereda was a principal city, and one of the few remaining strongholds of their fading power. It would seem not unreasonable to suppose that it was also the repository of their remaining wealth. Could it have been the final resting-place of the Holy Treasure?

The wealth of the Visigothic Empire is, however, not the only possibility which presents itself in the search for the source of Saunière's gold. A curious local legend provides the next link in the chain. In the year AD 679, one of the last kings of the Merovingian dynasty of France, Dagobert II – St Dagobert – was assassinated. According to some accounts, his infant son, Sigebert, was murdered at the same time. The legend, however, insists that Sigebert was rescued and carried off to the home of his mother, Dagobert's second wife. That home was Aereda. Dagobert's young heir grew to manhood and took the title 'count of Razès'. He founded a family and at his death was buried before the altar in the little church of Rennes-le-Château. Thus there is a second possible treasure – that of the descendants of the Merovingian king Dagobert.

What seems today to be a sleepy hamlet, lost to the world, does indeed have a colourful and dramatic history. It is perhaps after all not so unlikely that some rich traces of the past might have been hidden away over the centuries of Rennes-le-Château's quiet dwindling into obscurity. Something to which Saunière's lucky find could lead him.

There is to be seen in the village today a tangible link with this past of history and legend. When Saunière returned from his fateful trip to Paris, he had learned something which led him to dig at a particular spot before the altar of his church. He first raised a featureless stone slab from the floor, and the underside of this stone proved to be elaborately carved in the style of the Merovingian period. The stone is much worn and damaged, but the right-hand half of the design could be taken to depict a mounted knight riding off with a child on his saddle-bow. It has been suggested that the scene shows the rescue of Dagobert's infant son, Sigebert. Under the stone were two skeletons. The skulls bore the ritual incisions, intended to allow the escape of the soul, which were common to Merovingian burials.

Linked to this Merovingian find is a carved stone head which is embedded in the wall of the presbytery at nearby Rennes-les-Bains. This head was removed from a standing stone which was on the plateau be-

Copies of Parchment I (top) *and Parchment II*

tween the two villages. It bears an indentation which corresponds to the Merovingian burial custom – and is known as 'La Tête de Dagobert' – 'The Head of Dagobert'.

The foregoing accumulation of hints would make it not unreasonable to guess that the mysterious parchments discovered by Saunière might throw some light on the legend of Dagobert.

Parchment I is an account of the incident when Jesus went into the cornfields with the disciples on the Sabbath day 'and they did rub the ears of corn and did eat'. Although the Latin text is clear, it is noticeably curious in the way in which it is written on the page, with lines of seemingly haphazard length.

Parchment II is the text of John's Gospel, Chapter XII, verses 1–11, into the body of which have been interpolated 140 extra letters. More immediately noticeable than these, however, is the strangely 'untidy' device in the bottom right-hand corner. Superficially this could be a sort of ill-drawn direction-indicator, with the N at the top to denote North. The 'NO IS' seems without meaning, but at the bottom is an apparent 'arrow-head', which on examination can be seen to be the letter A written upside down. By simply inverting the document in order to turn this letter 'right way up', the 'NO IS' immediately assumes a meaning: SION – Jerusalem. With this hint, it is not now difficult to spot the SION keyword again, this time on Parchment I, where the block of four lines in the bottom left can be seen to end with those same four letters aligned one under the other – S I O N. Further, the 'helpful' inverted A of Parchment II helps to draw the eye to the letter 'a' at the end of line 2 in Parchment I. This is the only letter which is isolated in the text. On examination this isolated 'a' proves to be written slightly higher than the adjacent letters. A simple hunt for further raised letters reveals that a total of 45 have been similarly written above the lines of the remainder of the text. Taken in sequence they spell out a clear message: A DAGOBERT II ET A SION EST CE TRESOR ET IL EST LA MORT. 'This treasure belongs to Dagobert II, King, and to Sion and . . .'

The last phrase: IL EST LA MORT is open to two

different interpretations. 'Il est la Mort' means 'It is Death!' 'Il est là mort' means 'He is there, dead'. Can the second interpretation refer to Dagobert? Were the two bodies which Saunière found before the altar those of St Dagobert and his son Sigebert? Whichever interpretation of the phrase may be the correct one, the message has certainly conjured up both the treasure possibilities: Sion/Jerusalem/Visigothic, and Dagobert/Merovingian. There is of course much more to the parchments than just this simple, one might almost say, childish code. But, being easy to find, the code is in effect saying: 'There *are* hidden messages. Now look further'. Saunière evidently did . . . and found his crock of gold.

Whatever it was that he had found, he was certainly jealous of the secret – but by no means selfish in his distribution of the benefits. In his new and comfortable home, he entertained lavishly. He made many charitable gifts. Impoverished local families received open-handed help. For Rennes-le-Château he built a water tower, so that every house might enjoy the luxury of piped water; and he had the three-mile-long dirt-track down into the valley made over into a good modern road. Other examples of his generosity may perhaps be indicative of the nature of his find. To a fellow-priest, for example, he gave an ancient and beautiful chalice. To another he gave a magnificent collection of ancient coins – some dating from the time of Dagobert.

Above all, there was his lavish expenditure on the little village church which had been the scene of his discovery. It was repaired, restored and redecorated. Statues, paintings and stained glass create a sense of almost vulgar splendour. But this act of generosity on Saunière's part is not as simple as it seems. It was his contribution to the pattern of mystery surrounding his treasure. The first hint of this is overhead as one approaches the church door. There, carved above the portal is the daunting phrase: TERRIBILIS EST LOCUS ISTE – 'This place is terrible'. True, the words are not out of place: the House of God should indeed be an awesome place. But here the meaning seems to take a jolting shift, as one opens the door to find a hideous and

The crouching devil Asmodeus by the church door

deformed devil crouching in wait. And this hunched, club-footed and winged devil represents Asmodeus – who was the legendary guardian of Solomon's Treasure.

The interior of the church is a strange, phantasmagoric mass of imagery and colour. The more one looks, the stranger it becomes, and the more uncomfortable one begins to feel. One senses that there is more to this florid clash of detail than meets the eye. Certainly, Saunière's bishop was disturbed when he came to bless the restorations. Thereafter, it seems, he paid the church no further pastoral visits. But what is Saunière trying to say in this mass of imagery? Like his predecessors who had created their cryptic parchments and tomb inscriptions, Saunière felt compelled to pass on his secret in some way. But in typical flamboyant fashion, his cipher was on a grand scale. Saunière's clue to the treasure was to be the church itself! A few of the features will give an insight into his methods.

Filling the whole of the upper half of the west wall of the church is a huge and brightly-coloured sculptured group. It represents Christ succouring the afflicted. Jesus stands on a little pointed hill, his arms stretched out in a gesture of welcome. Beneath, Saunière has written the fitting quotation: 'Come unto me all ye who labour and are heavy laden and I will give you rest'. The normal rendering in French of this phrase is 'Venez à moi vous tous qui souffrez et qui êtes affligés et je vous soulagerai'. Saunière has changed the word 'affligés' to 'accablés'. The sense is unaltered, but the knowing eye has been attracted by the alteration. At once a further oddity presents itself. The first two letters AC – are written smaller than the rest of the word, and a faint line links them to the s of the preceding word ETES . . . SACCABLES. The sound of the indicated part of the text is identical with SAC A BLES, which means bag of corn – and 'corn' is a French slang word for gold!

Now the eye is immediately drawn to the strangely irrelevant feature which is prominent in the foreground of the sculptured scene. Lying at the foot of the pointed hill is a money bag, so full that it has burst open. The hill is sprinkled with flowers: in French, it is 'un terrain fleuri'. And Fleuri was the name of one of the local noble families! To the right of the little hill on which Christ stands is a castle ruin; to the left, a hilltop village. Saunière has made his statement. If one stands in the valley below Rennes-le-Château, one can see the village on its hilltop to the left, while to the right is the shattered ruin of the castle of Coustaussa. Between them is a little pointed hill . . . which was part of the Fleuri lands! Is the purse not intended to indicate a spot on that little hill?

But this is not the only place to be indicated in Saunière's cryptic imagery. The devil who crouches by the door is hunched in a curious and twisted pose almost as if he were sitting. But where is his chair? In fact, it is on a hillside to the south of the village. There, an enormous boulder has been carved to the shape of a great throne. To the locals, this stone is known as 'Le Fauteuil du Diable' – 'The Devil's Armchair'. Additionally, the right hand of the devil-figure makes a precise gesture, the thumb and forefinger curving into a neat circle. Beside the 'Devil's Armchair' rock, a spring seeps from the hillside into a small basin. It is known as 'La Source du Cercle' – 'The Spring of the Circle'. Saunière's devil does indeed seem to be indicating this precise location.

Imagery everywhere in the church seems to be trying to impart some sort of message, though the voice is muffled. The Stations of the Cross – common to all Catholic churches – have many strange and perhaps significant details. Station I depicts – as it should – Pilate washing his hands. But why is there a figure in the background who turns his back on the scene and raises his hand which seems to be clasping a golden egg? Why does Pilate wear a veil? He washes his hands in a white dish – in French 'un plateau blanc' – which is held by a negro. Close to Rennes-le-Château, Blanchefort – The White Castle – is perched on a plateau beside Roco Negro – The Black Rock. Is this location, too, significant? In Station II, the most prominent foreground feature is the seeming irrelevance of a young man picking up a stick. In Station VI, a soldier turns his back and holds up his shield against the sky. The gesture is meaningless in terms of the story of Christ's journey to Calvary.

But it is too easy to become buried in the mass of confused and confusing imagery. In fact it is possible to demonstrate how very precise Saunière's indications can be, once his language is understood. As convention demands, Station VI shows the incident when St Veronica wiped the face of Jesus. As composed by Saunière, the principal elements of this picture, when defined in simple terms, convey a clear instruction. Firstly, there is the 'irrelevant' soldier, who has already been noted as holding up his shield. This element can be simply described as 'High Shield' – in French, 'Haut Bouclier'. The shield partially obscures a tower, of which half is visible: 'Half Tower' – 'Demi Tour'. The next element is Simon of Cyrene, who is noticeably staring upwards and out of the picture: 'Simon is looking' – 'Simon regarde'. Finally, there is the principal figure of 'Veronica with the cloth' – 'Veronica au lin'.

The above four definitions convey Saunière's message. In Station VI he is playing with the sounds of words. HAUT BOUCLIER spoken aloud is saying equally clearly AU BOUT CLIER, which means 'at the bottom of the enclosure'. DEMI TOUR means not only a 'half tower', but also 'a half-turn'. SIMON REGARDE says exactly CIME ON REGARDE, which means 'the crest one is looking at'. VERONICA AU LIN is also the sound of VERS HAUT NID KAOLIN. This means 'towards the High Nest . . .' (Cardou, the dominant mountain in the landscape, is called The Eagle's Nest); and kaolin is chinaclay. Cardou is composed of this substance! Hence the phrase implies clearly: 'towards the high china-clay peak'. Station VI therefore conveys the instruction that one should go 'to the bottom of the enclosure, make a half-turn towards Cardou' – and the crest one can then see is the important thing.

In Rennes-le-Château there is only one enclosure. This is the cemetery. To go to the bottom of the cemetery and make a half-turn does indeed face one towards Cardou: and in confirmation of the instruction, a crest is clearly visible in the middle distance. It is the crest on which stand the ruins of the Castle of Blanchefort! Where is one to go from there? There are, after all, thirteen more Stations of the Cross, any or all of which may convey additional in-

The hollow pillar which had contained the parchments was set up by Saunière to support a statue of the Virgin

structions or information. With much ingenuity – and perhaps some luck – someone may follow Saunière's trail to its end. But will there now be anything left to find? It would seem possible. Only two days before suffering a fatal stroke in 1917, Saunière had signed the contract for new major building works to the tune of eight million francs. There is no reason to doubt that he would have been able to foot the bill.

Naturally, the will of so wealthy a man was read with interest. But even from beyond the grave Saunière could continue his game of secrecy. His will showed that in fact he owned nothing. His houses, his land, all his goods and chattels proved to have been in the name of his housekeeper, Marie Desnarnaud. She had been Saunière's faithful servant since the days of his poverty. Could she also have possessed his secret? It seems likely that she did. She certainly lacked for nothing after Saunière's death, living in discreet comfort for another thirty years. She had promised to pass on 'a secret' before she died, but in 1953 she was struck down by a cerebral haemorrhage. Paralysed and speechless, she carried her secret – whatever it was – to the grave.

There have been many attempts to discover the source of Saunière's wealth – to unravel the secret of Aereda. People have dug in and around the church and the village, both officially and unofficially. Such indeed became the extent of the clandestine activity that at last the community was forced to pass the bye-law which forbade any further excavations. But has anyone else succeeded in following Saunière's path to the crock of gold? There is one great handicap for those who make the attempt. Saunière discovered four parchments which gave him the key. Of these, copies of only two survive. Nevertheless, one more door can be opened for the searcher by Parchment II. The 140 letters which have been interpolated into the text of this document contain an extremely complicated cipher. The message when finally unravelled is vague and ambiguous, but it contains one illuminating phrase: 'Poussin holds the key'.

Suddenly a tiny light begins to illuminate one of Saunière's actions. When he was given the decipher-

ments in Paris, he bought a copy of Poussin's painting *Les Bergers d'Arcadie* – 'The Arcadian Shepherds.' Painted in Rome in about 1640, it has been so far held by art historians to be the pure product of Poussin's imagination. The shepherds are studying an inscription on the tomb 'Et in Arcadia Ego' – 'Even in Arcadia, I (Death) am present'. In some way this must help to pierce the fog of mystery which surrounds Saunière's story. He is known to have concerned himself with tomb inscriptions. He obliterated the words

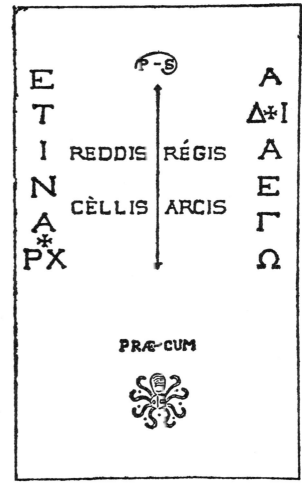

The tombstone of the Countess of Blanchefort (see page 92)

on certain gravestones in his churchyard, in particular the tombstone of the Countess of Blanchefort. And on this stone – obvious and yet disguised – is a link with the Poussin painting.

The two outer columns of letters – apparently part-Latin and part-Greek – seem to be meaningless. They make sense, however, when it is realised that both columns in fact form a Latin phrase, but written in a form of the Greek alphabet. It is necessary to transpose the letters from one alphabet to the other in order to arrive at the simple 'sense' – 'Et in Arcadia Ego'. Even so – why should this link have led Saunière to obliterate the inscription? There must be more to be gleaned from the stone than just this simple phrase.

The central block of text REDDIS REGIS CELLIS ARCIS is ambiguous Latin which can be 'interpreted' in a number of ways, one of which is: 'At Royal Reddis in the caves of the fortress'. Certainly 'Reddis' is one of the early names of Aereda – Rennes-le-Château. At the top of the stone are the letters P S enclosed within a loop. A vertical line with an arrow-head at each end links these letters with the word PRAE-CUM. As one word, this has no meaning, but PRAE means 'before' or 'preceding' and CUM means 'with'.

Seeking for a significance in the first element PRAE (before), it can be noticed that the looped line around the letters P S begins *before* the P and ends *before* the S. A meaning can now be elicited simply by taking the letters which come *before* P and S in the alphabet. P is preceded by O and S by R. The two 'hidden' letters therefore spell OR, which is the French word for gold. This word must now evidently be put CUM – 'together with' something . . . and all that remains is the curious 'spider' at the base of the stone. The French word for 'spider' is 'ARAIGNEE'. Saunière in his Stations of the Cross has already demonstrated a 'game' which can be played with the sounds of words. And in the thick local accent of Rennes-le-Château, OR ARAIGNEE is almost exactly OR A RENNES – 'the gold at Rennes'.

Thus far then, the stone has yielded the message that 'The gold is at Rennes – at Royal Reddis in the caves of the fortress'. But a significance yet remains to be found in 'Et in Arcadia Ego'. As this phrase is written in two separate halves, it may be considered permissible to deal with each half separately. Research has so far shed no light on the second half: ADIA EGO, but ET IN ARC has led in a startling and unexpected direction. The phrase means simply 'and in Arc', and added to the message already deciphered gives the information that the gold is 'At Rennes . . . and in Arc'. This might be considered as nothing more than an attempt to force a meaning where perhaps none is intended, if it were not for one surprising fact. Some few miles to the east of Rennes-le-Château is a castle: its name is ARQUES. And close by the Château of Arques is a tomb and landscape which reproduces with astonishing accuracy the tomb and landscape depicted in Poussin's 'Bergers d'Arcadie'. All the principal features of the painting – and even some of the minor ones – can be identified. The towering rock pinnacle behind the tomb – the Peak of Cardou just to the right of the trees . . . and, most striking of all, the insignificant bump on the horizon to the far right of Poussin's picture proves to be the hill-top of Rennes-le-Château itself!

The Shepherd to the right rests his foot on a round stone. Incorporated into the ledge which now runs along the front of the tomb is just such a stone. The larger of the two trees which Poussin has painted close behind the tomb was thought by botanical experts to be possibly Quercus Ilex, the holly oak. In precisely the same spot, a large and ancient Quercus Ilex is growing. Between the mountain which represents Cardou in the painting and the distant hilltop of Rennes-le-Château, Poussin has placed another mountain. Its outline faithfully captures that of the mountain crest which is there in actuality. It is the crest to which Saunière pointed in his cryptic message in the Sixth Station of the Cross – the crest of Blanchefort. And it was the tombstone of the Countess of Blanchefort which led to the tomb!

Art historians insist that Poussin never came to this part of France. Can they be right? The tomb of Arques is impressive evidence to the contrary. But is there any reason to suppose that Poussin was involved in a secret which might later have been stumbled upon by Bérenger Saunière? There is a letter, addressed to Nicolas Fouquet who was Superintendent of Finances to the Court of Louis XIV. It was sent by Fouquet's brother who had just paid a visit to Poussin in Rome, and is dated 17 April 1656. The letter has never been fully understood, but in part it says:

... He and I discussed certain things, which I shall with ease be able to explain to you in detail. Things which will give you through M. Poussin advantages which even Kings would have great pains to draw from him, and which it is possible that nobody else will ever rediscover in the centuries to come. And what is more, these are things so difficult to discover that nothing now on this earth can prove of better fortune nor be its equal. ...

An art historian's commentary on this letter asked: '... What marvellous enterprise was in Poussin's mind? What secret could he have had that even kings would have pains to draw from him?' It has been suggested that it could have been an important archaeological find somewhere in or near Rome. Could it not equally well have been in or near Rennes-le-Château?

The hunt for Saunière's gold is still very much alive. All the answers have not yet been found. While the film of 'The Lost Treasure of Jerusalem?' was being shot, somebody attempted to break into the 'Poussin Tomb' – and the effaced gravestone of the Countess of Blanchefort was shattered in someone's attempts to move it. There are obviously still those who would give much to discover the source of Saunière's wealth, to decipher the clues. Many have tried to unravel the secret of Aereda. Someone may succeed – but the trail is a difficult one. Fictional treasure hunts follow a logical progression to their final solution – but this trail is not fictional. It is all too real, and nothing is as simple as it seems. In many ways the mystery seems to be a disturbing one ... something more important than the mere discovery of a hoard of gold. Saunière seems to have felt a compulsion to pass it on – as did his predecessors with their strange ciphers.

There is a parallel in the legend of King Midas whose touch turned everything to gold. When the barber discovered that the King had ass's ears, he felt compelled to pass on the secret, and so he dug a hole in the ground and whispered it there. Saunière felt the same compulsion, and so he created his curious church. But that was not enough. Something seemed to burden his conscience still. On his death bed he made a confession. The priest who heard it was deeply disturbed. It is said that he left Saunière's beside, white and shaken, and for many months remained withdrawn and unsmiling. What terrible confidence had he been given? Must it not have been more than the mere fact that Saunière had cashed in on a lucky find of gold? Something extraordinary is waiting to be discovered on the hill-top of Rennes-le-Château. Only the future can reveal what that secret may be.

Eric Thompson at Tikal in 1972

The Lost World of the Maya

David Collison

Had the late Sir Eric Thompson used Cambridge University as the base from which to pursue his life's work among the ruins of the Maya civilisation, it would have come as no surprise to find him in 1971 living in active retirement in the Essex countryside. However, in 1925 Cambridge, in the formidable person of the great anthropologist Dr Alfred C. Haddon, took a dim view of New World archaeology and so the young Eric Thompson, eager to study the mysterious Maya, was obliged to head for the United States, and there he was to remain with the Field Museum of Chicago and the Carnegie Institution for the next thirty-five years. Would-be students of the Maya on this side of the Atlantic knew of Dr J. Eric S. Thompson only from his learned publications on Maya hieroglyphic writing and his *Rise and Fall of Maya Civilisation*, a popular textbook of such grace and humour that one wanted to meet the author face to face.

In 1971 Paul Johnstone decided that *Chronicle* had for too long neglected Maya archaeology. Research began at the Museum of Mankind, the British Museum's ethnographic department, where it was very tactfully suggested that since the world's foremost authority on the Maya civilisation had been back in England for the past fourteen years – indeed had visited the Museum only the day before – we should pay him a visit.

No Maya temple hidden in the depths of the Guatemalan rain forest was ever rediscovered with quite the respect and amazement that attended *Chronicle*'s 'discovery' of the eminent Maya archaeologist tending his broccoli, musing on East Anglian parish churches, and turning out a steady stream of papers on the decipherment of the baffling Maya hieroglyphs from a modern bungalow on the outskirts

of Saffron Walden. Surrounded by books – Trollope and Kipling as well as a library of scholarship – and a few personal mementoes of his years in the Maya area, Eric Thompson was enjoying an amiable, scholarly existence, the constant companionship of his wife Florence, and, from his study window, the view of a field of ripening barley. With cheerful enthusiasm, at the age of seventy-three, he allowed *Chronicle* rudely to interrupt that quiet scene and to return with him to the world of the Maya to relive some of that life of excavation and original research which began in the Yucatan peninsula of Mexico in 1926.

John Eric Sidney Thompson (invoking our three brief years of friendship I shall hereafter call him Eric) was born in England on the last day of 1898, but his family background lay in Argentina; his great grandfather settled there at the beginning of the nineteenth century and part of his grandfather's ranch, La Primera Estancia, is still worked by a member of the family. After schooling at Winchester and distinguished service in the Great War – wounded at Vimy Ridge and later commissioned into the Coldstream Guards – Eric returned to Argentina to try his hand at ranching. This episode lasted four years, long enough to convince him he did not want to spend the rest of his life on a ranch, but long enough also to make him fluent in Spanish and give him what he called 'a kind of Latin American background' which was to dictate the course of his life.

By 1922 Eric was back in England with a place at Cambridge University. 'My teacher was Dr Haddon – a very famous man who specialised entirely in New Guinea and the Pacific. He told me not to waste my time on "those damned Maya" as he called them. I only got one reference to the Maya all the time I was

95

there, and that was a wrong one.' At University Eric had taught himself to read the Maya hieroglyphic script – or at least that small part of it that was understood in 1925 – and he had heard reports (false) that there were representations of elephants on some of the Maya monuments in Central America. Egypt, Syria, even the Solomon Islands, where Haddon wanted to send all his graduates, seemed tame, unromantic, by comparison; moreover in 1925 the great Alfred Maudslay, most brilliant and most revered of the nineteenth-century explorers of Mexico and Guatemala, came to Cambridge to receive an honorary degree. This was the archaeologist who first cleared the forest from the ruins of Tikal in 1881 and 'whose five published volumes of photographs and archaeological reports', Eric wrote later 'set a scientific approach which the twentieth century was to follow and amplify'. Maudslay's appearance in the flesh can only have confirmed Eric's determination to pursue his chosen course along those same paths of scholarship and exploration that Maudslay himself had taken.

Almost fifty years later we sat in a Soho restaurant planning our *Chronicle* film. It was to introduce Eric Thompson to millions of television viewers in Britain and America and would attempt to recapture some of the sense of wonder and admiration which any student of the Maya must possess. Another professional student of the Maya was present, the British archaeologist Ian Graham. Like Eric he worked from an American academic base, in this case the Peabody Museum at Harvard, and spent half of each year in the field seeking out and recording the stone monuments of the Maya civilisation. He would be working at Yaxchilan in Southern Mexico during our location and would be showing Eric his latest discoveries.

The tyros at this meeting were Magnus Magnusson, who was to be Eric's companion on our film journey, John Hooper our cameraman, and myself. Our combined experience of Mexico and Guatemala was strictly limited, confined as it was to a visit to the British Museum, a study of *The Rise and Fall of Maya Civilisation* by J. Eric S. Thompson, and a mutual distrust, not to say fear, of those winged and crawling creatures that were said to inhabit the rain forests. Eric gave us crisp instructions as to footwear – leather or canvas boots which could lace around the calf to prevent ticks and worse from attacking the nether regions. Ian told us to be prepared for two or three nights in the open and recommended we secure the full-time assistance of Joya Hairs who ran a photographic and expedition service from Guatemala City. She would plan our five-week schedule, provide light aircraft, camping equipment, drivers, etc., and was generally deemed to be a fairy godmother, as indeed she turned out to be.

So for five weeks in the spring of 1972 a party of six of us, skilfully organised by Joya Hairs, flew, drove or tramped around Southern Mexico, the Yucatan Peninsula and the forests and mountains of Guatemala, ostensibly in search of the Maya, but really in search of Eric Thompson. He gave us Spanish nicknames, mine was 'Jefecito' – Little Chief – to be used amicably or ironically according to the success or otherwise of the day's filming. But Eric, armed with stick, sporting beret or straw hat and red cummerbund (canvas boots carefully laced to set a good example), we called the *Halach Uinic*, the Maya term for the temporal ruler of a Maya city state. Never did ruler command such admiration or affection. In the account that follows I have tried, by borrowing from transcriptions of the hours of conversation that we enjoyed in Central America and at his home, to retain the authentic tone of Eric's voice, the colloquial style with which he communicated his great scholarship.

A very cursory daily diary I kept at the time must serve to set the scene along our route, described here not in order of filming but as each location relates to the chronology of Maya Civilisation. Archaeology divides this civilisation into various periods. The 'Formative' period began around 1500 BC when developed agricultural societies began to emerge throughout Middle America. The first pyramids seem to have been built during this phase and the cultural foundations laid down for the rise of the high Maya civilisation which, by AD 200, was established right across the tropical forest region of present day Guatemala (The Department of Peten), Belize and Southern Mex-

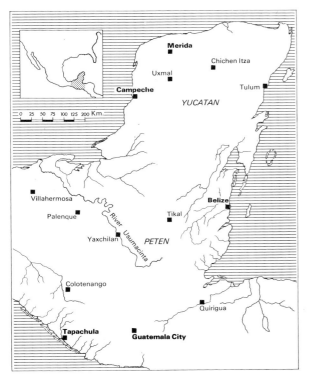

The Maya area

ico. This so-called 'Classic' period collapsed in the early tenth century AD, to be succeeded by three hundred years of Mexican influence in the huge Yucatan peninsula to the North; this was the Mexican, or post-Classic period. Here too the Maya culture lost its impetus so that it was totally dominated by groups from Central Mexico from 1200 till the year 1541 when Cortés and a mere handful of Spanish soldiers finally occupied the Yucatan and founded a very different empire in Central America.

Tikal, *Guatemala: Classic Period*

Fly to Tikal from Guatemala City by scheduled DC3. Burnt out remains of two aircraft left by Tikal landing strip 'pour encourager les autres'. Astonishing first view of peaks of pyramids (temples) pushing up out of forest. Filming first day at dawn we meet wild turkeys among the ruins. Toucans, small green parrots and huge macaws are the only other occupants till a few tourists arrive mid-morning. Start by examining the wooden beam to which Eric fixed his hammock 44 years ago!

Although it may now be reached by plane and visitors can stay overnight at the nearby hacienda, Tikal still has an air of remoteness and mystery befitting a lost city, though in the Maya context the term 'city' is a misnomer: these are the ruins of huge centres for administration and ceremony, not primarily dwelling sites. Superb restoration work carried out since the 1950s by the University of Pennsylvania Museum and the Guatemalan government, on the most dramatic section of the six-square-mile site, including the great plaza (central court) and the pyramids, gives today's visitor a real sense of the achievement of the Maya builders and a clear impression of how the centre of Tikal must have looked in its prime around AD 700. On the other hand, who, in his heart of hearts, would not wish to have arrived there, as Alfred Maudslay did in 1881, to find the ruins silent and deserted, drowning in the forests that had covered them since the tenth century AD? In spite of Maudslay's attentions to the vegetation this is how Eric Thompson himself first saw Tikal in 1928 after a journey which included a long trip up the Belize river and five days on muleback across the Santa Fe swamps. 'The mules staggered along here. In a way it was like a kind of pilgrimage; we might have been coming to Rome or Rheims or Canterbury – coming to see one of the great shrines of religion.' As in all Eric's conversation or writing, similes abound – cross references between the remote images and concepts of Maya culture and the more comfortable familiar events of European history or English literature: 'On that occasion we had a lady archaeologist with us making her pilgrimage on muleback. I thought of her as the Wife of Bath, but she was a lady of impeccable morals and might not have

Tikal: (above) *before restoration;* (opposite, left and right) *during and after restoration*

enjoyed the comparison very much! Incidentally, there was no water here in those days so we could only stay for thirty-six hours. The place was completely covered with forest and to all intents and purposes there wasn't another person living within fifty miles.'

Here at Tikal we talked for the first time, but not for the last, about human sacrifice: about the real paradox to European minds, that human endeavour and great mental and artistic skill have existed alongside, even depended upon, the ritual killing of other human beings. Although the evidence for large-scale sacrifice in the Classic Maya period is scanty (it certainly never reached the savage proportions of Aztec bloodshed centuries later), nevertheless human sacrifice certainly played its part in ritual – something with which Eric could quite easily come to terms.

'The best time to visit the ruins of course is first thing in the morning – the sun has no strength at all. Of course we Maya know perfectly well why he hasn't any strength, and the reason is this: at sunset the sun goes into the underworld, he steps into a litter and is carried through that underworld. He stops at midnight, deep under the centre of the earth, gets out of his litter and is allowed a little snack – maybe a tortilla or two and some black beans – then he resumes his journey right up to the moment of rising in the East. But the trouble is that this underworld is the land of the Dead and the sun becomes as the inhabitants of that land – nothing but skin and bones, so when he rises he is very weak. That is why people are sacrificed to him, to give him flesh and blood.'

Thus runs one explanation of blood sacrifice culled by Eric from a Maya storyteller and used with innumerable other stories as an adjunct to his archaeology, as a means of illuminating the intractable messages of the hieroglyphs or understanding the motives of ancient priests and rulers. Eric Thompson spent months living in Maya Indian villages on his field trips to the Peten forests or the highlands of northwestern Guatemala, where, more than anywhere else, the Maya spirit lives on.

Over a period of forty years labourers and locally-recruited excavation foremen became Eric's friends and confidants. 'If you are going to spend your life with a people you *must* develop a great feeling for them. You have to relate to them, as that terrible modern expression goes; and I would say that for me it has been much more than "relating". It's been a kind of marriage bed, my way of looking at things.'

Standing in the Great Plaza of Tikal at sunrise,

dwarfed by the pyramids at either end, Eric contemplated the inscribed stelae (vertical stone slabs, usually covered with hieroglyphs and symbols of kingship) and began to conjure up the scene on the morning of a great ceremony a thousand years ago as priests, princes and peasants (some archaeologists have estimated a population of 40,000 living around the ceremonial centre of Tikal, though Eric Thompson thought the figure nearer 20,000) gathered to hear the proclamations of the astronomers, attend the markets and gaze at the processions. 'You might say this was like the enclosure of one of the great English cathedrals, a religious centre but also for courts of justice and administration; Salzburg is probably a better analogy. People living in the surrounding area came in for the ceremonies. You get the same thing happening today in the Guatemala highlands.'

Colotenango, N.W. Guatemala:
Maya village 9000 ft above sea level

Drive via Quetzaltenango and Huehuetenango to Chiantla, where we stay with Father Quinn at the Mission House. Then drive to Colotenango (The Fortified Place of the Scorpion) arriving at the start of the Feast of St John. Save for Father Fox, who is missionary, doctor, agricultural adviser and social worker rolled into one, we are the only non-Maya. Film the deer-dance and another dance which mocks the Spanish conquistadors and later the procession of the statues of St John and the Virgin. Hard to detect where Catholicism ends and Maya tradition takes over. Ripe corn cobs laid between feet of statue of the Virgin in the church. Eric in his element, gossiping with the market women and joking in broken Maya dialect with the men. At nightfall the sound of the marimbas gives way to ocarinas, flutes and drums. Film the candle-lit procession round the village and many dangerous-looking sky rockets – by the light of two butane gas lamps!

Some of the high, remote villages have been left more or less to their own devices by all but the Catholic church, whose tough, hospitable Fathers have a relationship with the old Maya beliefs which is hard to define. These men are the spiritual descendants of the Conquistadors who tried to eradicate the abominated Maya religion with its, to them, barbaric ritual. Yet we were aware of a deep sympathy for the Maya Indians

Eric Thompson with group of Lacandón Maya, c. 1930

and for their dilemma – an understanding from the Fathers of the confused, hybrid set of beliefs that occupied the minds of the people of Colotenango and similar villages. Father Fox stated the case: 'Should I tell the people of Colotenango that they must put all thoughts of their ancient beliefs out of their minds? All over the world in the nature of things, traditions and old cultural habits are eradicated by government action or by the young peoples' drift to the cities. I don't think it's any part of my role to hasten that process.'

Francisco Ortiz Gomez, chief Mayan helper to Father Fox, spoke and wrote some English. He and I have corresponded twice a year since 1972; his latest letter reports that his 10-year-old son will soon begin high school in Huehuetenango and his wife, Reyna, is studying third-grade high school too. One day Colotenango will be transformed and Francisco Ortiz Gomez will no longer live in a one-roomed adobe

The family of Francisco Ortiz Gomez of Colotenango

house with his wife and six children. But on Monday 24 April 1972, the Feast of St John, the Fortified Place of the Scorpion was wearing its Maya heart on its sleeve. That evening, as the candlelit procession wound its way through the village, it was easy to overlook the four hundred years that had passed since Cortés and his successors came this way, and to see in the faces of these villagers the living image of the lost Maya civilisation.

Eric Thompson was always ready and able to make such imaginative leaps between archaeology and living anthropology – a practice frowned upon by purists twenty years ago as being unscientific, but now coming back into favour. 'To me', said Eric when we had left Colotenango, 'the really nice thing about Maya archaeology is being able to bring the past into the present and to use the present to interpret the past. In Egypt there's no connection between the "fellahin" and the ancient Egyptian gods, but the Maya *live*.

Take off that veneer of Christianity and Spanish culture, and there underneath is all the surviving Maya culture. For instance, in ancient times the colour yellow was associated with the south (red with the east, white with the north, black with the west) and the south was the land of the dead. Today the Maya put yellow flowers on family graves on the day of All Souls and we have the explanation – it goes back in history a thousand years or more. The past and the present – that's the whole story.'

This is true not only of religious observance but of everyday life too. In some isolated pockets of the highlands can be found people who live entirely by the original Maya calendar. The ancient priests and scribes were obsessed by Time and Eric Thompson devoted most of his working life to the study and understanding of that obsession and of the way in which it was set down.

Quirigua, *E. Guatemala: Classic period*

There's a recent history of hold-ups, banditry and border tension in this part of the lowlands. Glance at map convinces some of us Quirigua too close to Belize and Honduras for comfort! Why couldn't Guatemala City officials say *no chance* of incidents this week? Why is United Fruit Company HQ, where we are staying (a place called Bananeras, where you can't get a banana for love nor money), defended like Fort Knox? Woke 5 am convinced United Fruit Co. being invaded by guerrillas armed with FLNs and machine guns. Wonder how to save Eric – a good prize – from abduction. Would BBC pay ransom? Fully awake, discover gunfire effect is produced by small frogs. Magnus and film crew very scathing. Feel better on visiting Quirigua – magnificent sandstone stelae and altars crawling with hieroglyphs and images – all hemmed in by the forest.

At Quirigua we were to tackle the question of Maya hieroglyphic writing – an almost impossible task. One of Eric's own books on the subject runs to 500 folio pages and he calls that an 'introduction'!

The 'glyphs' appear on everything the Maya touched – on the stelae, or stone columns, which grace the plazas of the ceremonial centres, on the wooden or stone lintels of doorways, on flights of steps, on the stone or plaster walls of rooms, on pottery, on jade ornaments, and in the pages of the three surviving Maya codices (books). The story the glyphs tell is one of Time: Time in the abstract; Time measured by the movement of stars and planets; Time expressed in relation to the reign of a particular ruler, the genealogy of a dynasty or the influence of a god. The purpose of this preoccupation is obscure; the need for priestly divination certainly, but perhaps also a deep concern with simply keeping track of the passage of Time. The emphasis that scholars place on the hieroglyphs is constantly shifting. A number of years ago Eric Thompson was convinced that the glyphs dealt only with calendric or religious matters, 'then a colleague of mine was able to show that there was material there giving names of members of dynasties and elements like that. Well, that meant a complete reversal of one's attitude. Nobody likes to be proved wrong, but the terrible sin is to persist in error. It's no good digging your heels in!'

Eric Thompson's first contribution to the decipher-

Stela F at Quirigua photographed by Maudslay in 1912.

ment of the hieroglyphs was made in 1925 and his last published work was *A Commentary on the Dresden Codex* (1972). For almost fifty years he was one of a mere handful of scholars who might devote months to the unravelling of a single glyph. 'The system is extremely complex. There were probably about 850 of these pictorial signs of which 370 were main signs and the rest affixes. The glyph for sun KIN (1 opposite) was called in Maya (it also meant day, festival and grasshopper). The numerical component was affixed by means of a bar, meaning 'five', with or without the dots which represent single units; so that three dots meant three, a bar and four dots meant nine, etc. So if they wanted to say 'eight days' they put a bar and three dots in front of the sign KIN (3). Likewise the picture of a hand meant 'end'; affixed to the KIN sign (day or sun) it meant 'end of sun', or in other words 'the west' (4).

Eric Thompson it was who discovered that later Maya scribes would sometimes use rebus writing – signs whose description provided their meaning, as in 'I can see Aunt Rose'. It occurred in the case of the all-important word 'count', in Maya XOC. XOC meant 'count' but it was also the word for a mythical fish (5). 'It's a lot of trouble having to carve a fish every time you want to indicate 'count', and the Maya were so hipped on numbers they were counting all the time, so they got round it like this: the fish lives in water so let's use water as the symbol (6); but there were difficulties there because the symbol for water is jade (both being green). So finally they used the symbol for jade = water = mythical fish = XOC = "count" (7).'

These were the ideas we explored at Quirigua. Maya scholars will long continue to wrestle with them, for although most of the dates and calendrical calculations can now be read, some texts remain utterly impenetrable.

On top of a twenty-foot stela at Quirigua was carved the bland face of a king: unknown, perhaps unknowable, even to Eric Thompson. 'I don't feel I will ever know him, frankly. I would feel, if anything, a bit closer to the person who is not represented here, the high priest himself, busy with his calculations.

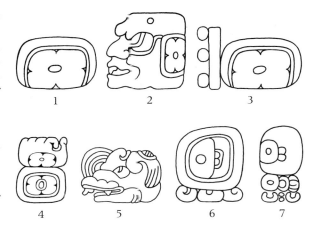

(Above) *Maya glyphs: 1 (of which 2 is a more elaborate variant) the KIN sign; 3 'eight days'; 4 'end of sun' (= the west); 5 XOC (fish sign); 6 water sign; 7 jade sign.*

(Below) *Zoomorphic boulder at Quirigua photographed by Maudslay.*

That's because, above all I think, I admire the astronomical success of the Maya. They were able to measure the synodical revolution of Venus with incredible accuracy – I mean a one-day error in 6000 years. They made long calculations many millions of years into the past, at a time when our ancestors thought the world began in 4004 BC. And remember another thing: the writings of the peoples of the Old World were built up by a great interchange of ideas – one group learning from another – but the Maya had to develop their ideas and their writing *without the help of any other culture.'*

In his book *The Rise and Fall* Eric Thompson makes one small concession to the idea, prevalent in some quarters, anathema in others, that Maya civilisation *did* owe something to outside influences. The suggestion that reed boats from North Africa brought the ideas of ancient Egypt to the ignorant natives of Central America he found insulting, as he did the idea that Chinese or Japanese 'torch-bearers' crossed the Pacific Ocean to hand over Civilisation. Archaeology shows that the New World was populated by a steady stream of peoples moving out of Asia across the Bering Straits from around 20,000 BC. If this movement continued right up to the start of our Christian era then it might, says Eric Thompson, account for some extraordinary parallels between Maya and Asian thought. For example, the Maya associated colours and celestial dragons with the four quarters of the world and similar beliefs are held to this day among the Hindu population of Eastern Asia.

However, if one thing made Professor J. Eric S. Thompson see red it was the suggestion that Maya achievement was really the work of spacemen.

Palenque, *Mexico: Classic period*

Fly to Villahermosa, a hot, sticky town which evokes Graham Greene and *The Power and the Glory*. Then drive all day through flat landscape towards the Chiapas foothills and Palenque. Tall trees with bright yellow blossom dotted over the plain. At Palenque village the ticks get a grip on us at last but the ruins next morning are magnificent. Again the rewards of dawn filming – slanting light and no visitors.

Palenque must by now be known to millions, from the

(Opposite) *The Temple of the Inscriptions, Palenque, and the carved sarcophagus lid* (above) *which was found deep under it.*

attempts of Mr Eric von Daniken to see the representation of an astronaut and space vehicle on the sarcophagus of a great chief deep inside the Temple of the Inscriptions pyramid.

After some ironic observations on the huge disparity between the sales of books which attempt at least to illuminate and comprehend the Maya world and those which invoke Other Worlds and Strange Flights of Fantasy, Eric explained the complex design on the sarcophagus lid as an archaeologist sees it. A figure reclines on the head of a highly-stylised monster. Behind rises the great ceiba or silk-cotton tree which stood at the centre of the Maya universe and which, assisted by the four world-directional trees, one at each corner of the earth, held up the sky. Although the design, including the languid pose of the central figure, is mirrored in other Maya carvings and can clearly be related piece by piece to highly-conventionalised Maya iconography, von Daniken finds this interpretation amusing, and says, 'It seems intolerant of them [the archaeologists] to reject my version' (*The Gold of the Gods*), and calls the rejection of his theories 'stupidity' (*In Search of Ancient Gods*).

The sarcophagus is dated from the glyphs on its side to AD 692. Inside was the skeleton of a chief decked with jade and wearing over his face a magnificent mask of jade mosaic. Dr Alberto Ruz, who excavated the tomb in 1952, believes that the magnificent Temple of the Inscriptions pyramid was raised to cover the burial of the man who lay in the tomb. This quickly attracted the attention of those who wanted to prove a connection between Central America and the Ancient World; did not the Egyptians too raise great pyramids over their dead rulers? Magnus Magnusson,

Palace area and tower at Palenque

our devil's advocate, put this to Eric as they climbed the steep steps of the temple pyramid. The Professor conceded that the discovery had 'put the cat among the pigeons', but then dismissed the idea of any connection and pointed to the known tradition of mound and pyramid building in North and Central America which has a long archaeological record of its own. Maya pyramids were designed for ceremony, their flat tops were crowned with temples and the great staircases leading to these temples were put to a particular use. 'They used to send the sacrificial victims down from the top, you know, and they must have gone down with one heck of a bump. Then certain members of the congregation down below had the right to cut the victim up and take part of the flesh as a kind of communion service.'

When talking to us Eric always took a philosophical view of such matters; but he was always at pains to point out the more delicate aspects of Maya society too. Standing on top of the pyramid, gazing out over

the ruins of Palenque and the green sea of rain forest that stretched away to the horizon, he remarked, 'Oh boy, what a marvellous view. That's another of the nice things about the Maya, I think the high priests must have had a good aesthetic sense.' Entering the tomb after a long descent into the bowels of the pyramid, he used a phrase which spoke volumes for his own vision of the Maya as people of discrimination. He said, 'Of course, Alberto Ruz didn't find any gold down here but he found plenty of jade, which after all for the Maya was more valuable. *Not so vulgar either!*'

On our last night at Palenque the superintendent of the ruins lit a small brazier for us in the uppermost story of the Palenque palace tower, the only such tower in the entire Maya area, giving Eric an image for the coming end of the Classic Maya period – a tiny light twinkling in the dusk high above the treetops. 'The Maya had a special ceremony at the end of every fifty-two years when there was a possibility the world would come to an end. They extinguished all their fires and then a light would be rekindled and the new fire was carried all over the country. You can imagine that ceremony taking place up there; the light would be visible for miles around and people would know they were all right for another fifty-two years.'

At our next location we would discover not only echoes of the militarism which first disturbed the Classic Maya world but also evidence of the despoliation which now threatens its superb archaeological remains.

Yaxchilan, *Mexico: Classic period*

Hair-raising flight from Palenque to Yaxchilan with one-eared, gold-toothed pilot looking like refugee from 'Treasure of Sierra Madre'. Three light planes, Roger (sound recordist) in ours and Dave (assistant cameraman) in Eric's as they each have a pilot's licence. The gear takes care of itself in the third Cessna. But the pilots are marvellous, like airborne cabbies. Ian and Maya helpers have prepared a large palm-thatched shelter with three open sides. Our home for three days and nights. Usamacinta River is flowing twenty-five yards away through banks of mud and sand. On the far side is Guatemala. First evening is an odd mixture of poetry recitals, tape-recorded Bach and the constant sound of the forest – howler monkeys, frogs, cicadas. Visited at dawn by our first scorpion and immense bird-eating spider which Ian casually picks up between the halves of a grapefruit (legs sticking out all around) and returns to the undergrowth. Joya announces, rightly, that it is 'hotter than the hinges of hell' and produces wild pig sandwiches. Water tastes terrible, so start to drink the river. Eric and Ian perfectly at home.

Ian Graham, director of the Maya Hieroglyphic Study Project at the Peabody Museum, Harvard, was engaged in the task of tracking down and recording by drawing and photography the inscribed stelae that were still lying undiscovered or neglected in the forests of the Peten and Southern Mexico, vital data for all scholars working on the riddle of the hieroglyphs. Sadly these stelae are no longer neglected by a network of looters for whom the carved stones are valuable prizes to be sold to the highest bidder, in some cases the less-scrupulous museums of Europe and America, but more often private collectors and dealers who would happily part with 50,000 US dollars for a good specimen. Joya Hairs was a founder

member of *Operacion Rescate*, a Guatemalan organisation created to save known treasures from the attentions of the looters. From her we heard tales of stones being lifted from the forest by helicopter and despatched to the United States in crates marked 'Heavy Machinery'. Only recently Ian Graham's Maya guide had been gunned down by looters surprised in the act of removing a choice piece of carving from a remote site.

The Guatemalan and Mexican governments have now (1978) increased the force of guardians at large sites like Yaxchilan, but the problem remains and will continue so long as there is a market for illicit treasures. The chain saws (to slice the carved façade from a bulky stone), helicopters and shot guns will never be

Carved lintel from Yaxchilan

far away until world scholarship lends a practical hand. 'It wouldn't cost a great deal of money to put guardians in all the important sites,' Eric observed. 'Not a tenth of what it cost to save Abu Simbel.' But are the treasures comparable? 'Well, if looters come in and steal them we might never know. I'd say they are of course, but then I'm prejudiced.'

The fairly recent threat to the Maya monuments is sinister and highly organised, but Eric Thompson's own fieldwork was often dogged by destructiveness of a different kind. His field notes, now lodged, together with his library, in the archives of the Museum of Mankind in London, record (1942): 'We learned there had been a number of sculptures at the nearby village of S. Magdalene but these had been buried by the present owner because the Indians had been burning candles to them.' One way or another twentieth-century greed and prejudice have taken their toll of the ancient Maya.

In the eighth century AD Yaxchilan was ruled by a chief named Shield Jaguar, the first of a series of militant Yucatec rulers whose names are recorded on the stone door-lintels of Yaxchilan. An offshoot of the Classic Maya, the Yucatec gradually moved up into northern Peten and the Yucatan Peninsula. Boastful military prowess had had little part to play in the Maya world we had visited on our journey so far but, in any case, the great days of that world – the Classic Maya civilisation – were over by the mid-tenth century AD.

Why did this civilisation collapse, or appear to do so from the archaeological record? There are innumerable theories, just as there are to account for the 'sudden' disappearance of the dinosaurs seventy million years ago. Military conquest? There seems little evidence. Exhausted land? Many Classic sites continued to be fertilised regularly by the silt of flooding rivers long after they were abandoned. One lady scholar suggested the collapse was brought about by a shortage of women, girl babies being neglected in favour of sons. Eric Thompson always favoured a straightforwardly human explanation: 'The theory that I myself like best of all is that it was due to a revolt of the peasants against their rulers, because the rulers

were losing that old attitude of co-operation – "we'll supply the rain provided you build the pyramids". In Old Testament terms they went whoring after other gods, gods like the planet Venus and war gods, which didn't help the peasant at all. So, I think, the peasants threw out the ruling group. There is some evidence for this – broken and defaced monuments set up again, upside down, by people who didn't understand them. We also find late pottery among the ruined ceremonial centres. In other words, the old idea that people moved out and left a vacuum is perfectly untrue.'

A Maya peasant family had made its home in one of the ruined courtyards of Yaxchilan – a thatched, wattle cabin providing midday shade for an assortment of dogs, children, chickens and piglets. Is this how the Maya continued to live at Tikal or Palenque, in and around the magnificent ruins of palace and temple after the princes and priests had fled? Up in the Yucatan, at Uxmal, there is evidence that this was so.

Uxmal, *Yucatan Peninsula, Mexico:*
Late Classic Period

Fly to Merida, capital of Yucatan Province. Eric and I pay visit to the Gran Hotel where he stayed in 1926. A moment of nostalgia among the dusty potted palms and lazy fans, then drive to Uxmal. The governor of Yucatan wants to give a reception for Eric in the palace quadrangle. Everywhere we go our man is awaited, then fêted! At the Hacienda there are queues of American students with copies of *Rise and Fall* to be autographed.

Eric Thompson first came to Uxmal as a visitor in 1926. There being no road in those days it was usual to arrive on muleback, but Eric took some delight in relating how he and four friends lurched there in a Model T Ford; the first car ever to reach Uxmal!

The standing structures at Uxmal are among the most magnificent achievements of Maya architecture. Some buildings incorporate façades of delicate limestone veneer, a style called 'Puuc', after the nearby range of hills. The Temple of the Magician (so named by the Spaniards), the 'Governor's Palace' and the 'Nunnery' are all dated to the later Classic period, but in common with their southern counterparts they too

Temple of the Warriors, Chichen Itza

were abandoned in the tenth century AD. In 1951 Mexican archaeologists discovered the stone foundations of a simple house, its wooden walls and thatched roof long disappeared, in the quadrangle of the 'Nunnery'. From pottery found in the floor it was dated to the eleventh–twelfth centuries AD. Another hut of similar date was found in the forecourt of the 'Governor's Palace'. 'In terms of our own culture', Eric Thompson has written, 'imagine Rome in ruins and the discovery of a squalid tenement building set in St Peter's piazza, with its back to the fallen basilica of St Peter and with fragments of Michelangelo's dome incorporated in its walls.'

By the time these rude homes had been built, Maya power was centred eighty miles to the East.

Chichen Itza, *Yucatan Peninsula, Mexico:*
Classic and post-Classic period

Only by more dawn filming can we avoid terrific crowds; American, German and French tourists as well as Mexican. By 11.30 the heat is intense but Magnus and Eric gallantly leap up and down the pyramids. On first morning a visit from Eugenio Mai, who worked here for Eric forty-six years ago, now come to see his old boss. If anything needed to

demonstrate the rapport which exists between Eric and the Maya then their moment of greeting says all.

This is the site Eric came to first in 1926, fresh from Cambridge. He worked at Chichen for the Carnegie Institution, sweating over the animal frieze around the Temple of the Warriors which he and his Maya labourers had to reconstruct. 'If you look very carefully there are one or two *small* mistakes, but nobody so far as I know has ever written to complain about them.' Four years later, Eric brought his new bride to Chichen Itza for a working honeymoon. 'My old boss Sylvanus Morley used to bring his old hand-wound gramophone down here with a mixture of boogie-woogie and *Swan Lake*. Florence and I danced on top of the Castillo.' But the honeymoon was not all dancing and moonlight, it included a muleback expedition to Coba, seventy miles away – 'a pretty tough spot for a honeymoon' is Eric's laconic comment (*Maya Archaeologist*).

The Castillo, which is the name given to the central temple-pyramid of Chichen, the Temple of the Warriors, the huge court where the Maya men met to play their curious and combative ball game, and many of the outlying buildings on this massive site are

Tulum

decorated with feathered serpents, skulls, or representations of armed warriors, a style quite foreign to the Classic sites of the south, and one which betrays the influence of the Toltec. This warlike people from north of Mexico City fought their way into the Yucatan around AD 1000 and rebuilt or remodelled Chichen Itza. This was to be the last great centre of Maya civilisation, a civilisation that now had more in common with the neighbouring Aztec than with its own roots in the rain forests of the Peten. So had the Maya themselves been brutalised? What about those scholar-priests with their aesthetic outlook? 'Well, there is some evidence for thinking that civilisations become more brutal, the older they get. The Maya himself is a rather moderate individual, but here we had a warlike element coming in and imposing their

ideas – and a growing cult of taking prisoners in order to sacrifice them to the sun.'

By AD 1200 Chichen Itza too had fallen into decay, the power centre having moved to Mayapan where, said Eric, 'the architecture's bad, the pottery's useless and the sculpture's even worse. They were going very rapidly downhill by the time the Spaniards arrived.'

Tulum, *Yucatan Peninsula, Mexico: Mexican period*

Sadness of Tulum made up for by its setting. Deep blue Caribbean sea – pelicans flying offshore. With sea breaking at the foot of the small cliff and ruins above it looks for all the world like Tintagel.

110

Tulum may well have been the first Maya site that Cortés saw in 1519 on his journey to conquer Mexico. His ships are known to have made landfall this far south and he reported seeing a town 'the size of Seville', which may just have been a hero's exaggeration, for Tulum is a small site by comparison with the others we visited. In any case Cortés sailed north, round the Yucatan peninsula, and set about the conquest of Mexico. Not until Montezuma and the Aztec empire were destroyed did the Spaniards turn their attention to the Maya. By 1541, or, as Eric put it, 'a year or two after poor old Anne Boleyn lost her head', the demoralised Maya were overthrown, unable to withstand the Spanish muskets and horses. Spanish sources relate that one isolated group of Maya, descended from the one-time inhabitants of Chichen Itza, founded the 'city' of Tayasal on an island in the middle of Lake Peten (where modern Flores stands today) and survived, amazingly, till 1697, when they too fell to the conquistadors.

And so at the bedraggled little site of Tulum we ended our search for the Maya and returned to London. For Eric Thompson the next three years were full of incident. He was further honoured by the governments of Mexico and Guatemala for his contribution to the understanding of their past; when we met in London he wore the insignia of the Aztec Eagle in his lapel – an honour rarely bestowed outside Mexico. On 6 December 1974, he wrote to me, 'I have received an invitation from Sr Loret de Mola, governor of Yucatan . . . to return to Uxmal to be present at the supper he is offering the Queen and the Duke of Edinburgh in February.' In the New Year honours of 1975 Eric received his knighthood, in February he accompanied Her Majesty to Uxmal, and in September of that same year to our great sorrow, he died.

In 1973, shortly after our return from Central America, Eric Thompson had received an honour which gave him particular pleasure. He was summoned to his old university, Cambridge, to receive the degree of Doctor of Letters (honoris causa) from the Chancellor of the University. It was a strange case of history repeating itself as the University Orator was not slow to realise:

'Almost fifty years ago, when our University admitted to an honorary degree Mr Alfred Maudslay, a man for his time very learned in Maya antiquities, that same month there left Cambridge with the award of a diploma the man who now stands here to be honoured. If we can today omit the task the Orator had then, of explaining briefly who the Maya were, it is to him that we owe it. . . . Recently he was elected an honorary fellow of his College; he has also been seen on television, disguising his years (as of old) to clamber up Maya pyramids far more nimbly than his juniors. Among Maya scholars he is everywhere reckoned the greatest. I present to you John Eric Sidney Thompson, Fellow of the British Academy.'

A break in filming, Colotenango

111

(Left) *Stonehenge and* (right) *the Easter Island statues though separated by thousands of miles and ages of time, have raised almost identical questions as to how they were built;* (below) *map of Pacific with inset of Easter Island, showing tribal divisions (see page 122).*

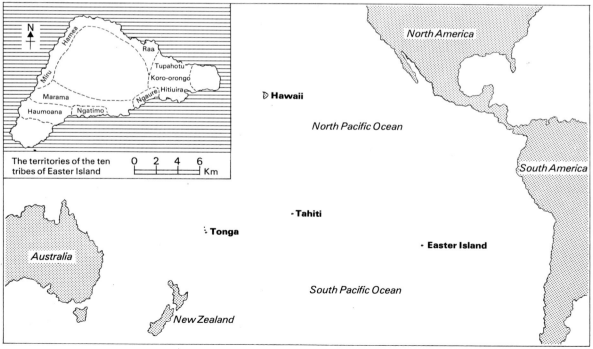

The territories of the ten tribes of Easter Island

0 2 4 6 Km

Islands Out of Time

Colin Renfrew

In the year 1722, a vessel captained by the Dutch explorer Jacob Roggeveen sailed round the tip of South America, through the Straits of Magellan, and into the Pacific Ocean looking for a lost island, reportedly sighted by a British explorer and privateer fifty years earlier, and called after him the 'Isle of Davis'. The Dutch expedition never found this legendary land, but instead on 5 April (Easter Day) they sighted a small island. They called this tiny and remote landfall 'Easter Island'.

Remarkably it proved to have a human population. They lived what seemed to the Dutch sailors a simple life, with yams, bananas and fowls for food. But one thing was extraordinary: the large stone statues with which many of their ceremonial places were decorated. These striking monuments were apparently built by the inhabitants of this small island on the easternmost fringe of Polynesia, 1500 miles from the nearest land.

At first sight it may not be obvious what bearing that discovery has upon our own great prehistoric monuments in the British Isles – stone circles such as Avebury or Stonehenge, or megalithic tombs such as the West Kennet long barrow. Certainly it would be nonsensical to think of any direct link between them. Yet we can learn from 'the mystery of Easter Island', the paradoxical occurrence of major building works in a tiny and remote area, with a small population entirely lacking the advanced technology of urban civilisation. For in a sense this is the same problem which has perplexed antiquaries and archaeologists who have tried to explain our own great European prehistoric monuments. How did they do it? Could they have done it without some assistance, if only indirect, from some more advanced technology? The best way

to answer these questions, I believe, is for the archaeologists to look across the world to Polynesia, where some of the answers are beginning to emerge.

The Problem of the Monuments

For centuries the prehistoric monuments of Britain have puzzled and teased the imagination of scholars. Already in the twelfth century Geoffrey of Monmouth mentions Stonehenge in his *Chronicle*, and relates that the stones had been transported from Ireland and erected at Stonehenge by the magic arts of the wizard Merlin. The great architect Inigo Jones visited Stonehenge during the reign of James the First and pronounced it to be of Roman construction, and in the seventeenth and eighteenth centuries scholarly opinion came to favour the Druids, the Celtic priests whom Julius Caesar encountered on his expedition to Britain. But in truth very little was known of such monuments, or of the collective burial chambers, the megalithic tombs, which are common in the British Isles and in other areas of north-western Europe. So it was that the British antiquary Sir Richard Colt Hoare, writing in 1807, could say of the Irish megalithic tomb Newgrange and of these other monuments:

I shall not unnecessarily trespass upon the time and patience of my readers in endeavouring to ascertain what tribes first peopled this country, nor to what nation the construction of this singular monument may reasonably be attributed, for, I fear, both its authors and its original destination will ever remain unknown. Conjecture may wander over its wild and spacious domains but will never bring home with it either truth or conviction. Alike will the histories of those stupendous temples at Avebury and Stonehenge which grace my native county remain involved in obscurity and oblivion.

Fortunately Colt-Hoare was too pessimistic, and gradually archaeology was able to establish a series of facts about these monuments. It soon emerged that they belong to the neolithic period, built that is by the early farming population of Britain, at a time before copper or bronze tools were used.

For many years, indeed until just ten years ago, it was believed that the megalithic tombs of Europe were the result of a movement of colonisation, or at least a wave of influence, from the more civilised lands of the eastern Mediterranean. There monumental stone tombs were being constructed from around 2500 BC. So it seemed likely that the first European megalithic tombs were those of Spain, built perhaps just a little after 2500 BC, and that the techniques of construction, the practice of collective burial, and perhaps the religion which went with them, gradually spread across Europe, reaching the British Isles around 2000 BC or a few centuries after.

This clear picture has been completely disrupted, however, first by the application of radiocarbon dating, and then by the use of tree-ring dates to correct and modify the radiocarbon dates further. It now seems clear that the megalithic tombs of north-western Europe were being built earlier than anything comparable in the east Mediterranean: the earliest of them, in Brittany, before 4000 BC.

So the old idea of the 'diffusion' of culture from the more civilised lands of the Near East can no longer be used to explain the megalithic tomb architecture of Britain. Nor can it explain for us the construction of the even larger and greater monuments, the so-called henges, of which Stonehenge and Avebury are the most famous examples. Until a decade ago it could reasonably be argued that they were the result of some influences from the more civilised cultures of Mycenaean Greece. As one distinguished writer put it: 'Is it then any more incredible that the architect of Stonehenge should himself have been a Mycenaean than that the monument should have been designed and erected, with all its unique and sophisticated detail, by mere barbarians?'

Today, however, the barbarians have it. The new dating makes entirely clear that the megalithic tombs are a European phenomenon, built by 'barbarians' – if by that term one means a population with a fairly low level of technology, lacking the use of metal, without writing, and without urban centres. Likewise the great henge monuments, from Mount Pleasant in the south right up to the Ring of Brogar in the Orkney Islands, must be seen as the work of the descendants of the early megalith builders, descendants who at 2000 BC were still (in the same sense) 'barbarians'.

How then did they do it? What special skills did they have? What forces impelled them to invest so many man-hours in such monuments? How could these simple societies marshall the skills and co-ordinate the manpower for such massive undertakings, which represent in some cases millions of man-hours? Perhaps, faced with these difficult questions, it is not surprising that a few writers with uncontrolled imaginations and an eye for the lurid have written of flying saucers, of intelligence from outer space, and of lost and secret lore. But that is the easy explanation, and one without a single shred of sound evidence to sustain it.

The right explanation, demanding the exercise of a more controlled imagination, implies greater respect for the abilities of the human species. It involves the acceptance that 'natives' – whether in neolithic Britain or in Polynesia of just a century or two ago – are not idiots, and that, on the contrary, 'barbarians' differ from us mainly in their lack of advanced technology. It is here that the Polynesian experience has so much to teach us. And we are fortunate that the greatest of all the Pacific explorers, active just two centuries ago, was a man of humane intelligence and curiosity: the 'Great Circumnavigator', Captain Cook.

The Concept of Chiefdom Society

When Captain Cook visited the Pacific, he found in some of the island groups societies which were highly structured, highly organised. Social relations were ordered by rules of conduct as rigorous (and as courteous) as any in contemporary Europe. And in the Friendly Islands (the modern kingdom of Tonga), in the Society Islands (the modern Tahiti) and in Hawaii (which he himself first discovered for the western world) he described communities with a very coherent system of government. In each the ruler was a chief of very high status, whose person was regarded as sacred and surrounded by taboos as elaborate as in any European monarchy.

Much of this did not, I think, greatly astonish him, for he was of course accustomed to the England of King George III. But it fascinates me, for here we have a direct insight into the working of a society with the simplest of technologies – none of the Polynesian communities knew the use of metal (they were amazed by metal axes, and Cook's sailors could obtain all manner of goods and services in exchange for just a few iron nails).

Cook described for us what modern anthropologists sometimes term a 'chiefdom' society. Societies with a similar structure and social organisation have been described from other parts of the world, including Africa, and they share a number of common features which, I believe, can be of real help to us in understanding those rather remote and mysterious communities of prehistoric Britain which were responsible for the erection of our great monuments. The key to the problem lies in social organisation, in what I like to call Social Archaeology. Unless we can begin to reconstruct the basic features of a prehistoric society – not just its technology (what tools they used, what food they ate), but social aspects too – we shall have no understanding of its capabilities. We need to know how large social groups were. Did they have a central organisation, central leadership? What were their relations with neighbouring communities? How much energy did they invest in religious activities? The Chiefdom Model gives us a very general picture of one kind of structure, which it is profitable to apply to prehistoric Europe.

In chiefdom societies, kinship is a dominating principle. Who you are – your place in life – depends on who you are born, on the status of the parents. But this status is not simply a question of 'class', or of hereditary wealth, as in most state societies. It depends upon kinship in a more subtle way – each individual, whether of high or low rank, is a member of a group, and the groups themselves are ranked and regulated

kinship. Those whose heredity links them most closely to the chief are of the highest status.

One such arrangement has been termed by the anthropologist Marshal Sahlins the 'conical clan' – conical because the lineage lines all lead back to the founding ancestor at the apex, whose direct descendant (usually in the male line) is the paramount chief. The hereditary lineage organisation in such a society is reflected in the territorial organisation – in the lands which the different groups occupy.

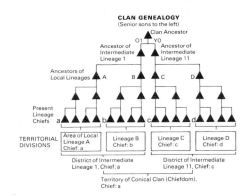

This kind of analysis was not of course carried out by Captain Cook: it has been set out by anthropologists using Cook's observations among many others. But Cook observed also other features of chiefdom society. The first of these is its harmonious unity. Individuals serve the chief not through repression but because they want to: social respect and prestige comes from correct behaviour. And while the chiefs exercised powers of life and death over their subjects, a more common sanction was the general contempt and disapproval which disrespectful or deviant behaviour would incur.

A second feature of chiefdom society is redistribution: goods and services are offered to the chief. They flow into his hands, and he assigns them, some for his personal use, and others for the common good. This makes possible a third feature: a measure of craft specialisation. The economic device of redistribution allows some craftsmen to specialise in their calling – whether it be boat-building, or carving, or religious practice, or the occupation of chief itself. All are possible because they are supported by society, and more specifically by the chief personally. He in turn assigns their produce in a way which works for the good of society as a whole.

From our point of view this is an important feature of chiefdom society, and so is another: mobilisation. The chief has at his call the entire manpower resources of the community. When some major endeavour is projected, he can ensure that there is the workforce to carry it out.

These then are some of the features of chiefdom society, which make it possible, I think, for us to understand Stonehenge and our other monuments without recourse to beings from outer space or other flights of fancy. I have deliberately stated them in a general form, since there is no suggestion whatever that the specific features of any Pacific society can tell us just what happened at Stonehenge. I shall argue below that some of these general features must have been present in neolithic society in south Britain.

But Tonga and Easter Island today offer more than these rather cold and academic generalisations. The Kingdom of Tonga, while a modern state, a member of the United Nations, offering to the visitor all the comforts of the twentieth century, still retains many of those features of a traditional chiefdom society which were encountered by Captain Cook. Easter Island, although its traditions have sadly decayed, still shows in its great monuments the achievements of which such a society is capable. It is still possible, then, to *experience* at first hand some of the features of chiefdom society. And while the details are different, in escaping from the preoccupations of the western world with its aggressively market economy and its mass production, one is able to see more clearly just how a chiefdom society can work.

Traditional Tonga

Captain Cook spent several weeks in Tonga during his Third Voyage to the Pacific, arriving in May 1777. His published account, and the detailed journals which he and some of his officers kept, are a precious document of the functioning of a chiefdom society before it was extensively influenced by European culture, indeed the earliest full account of such a society in existence. (Some would claim that the descriptions by Caesar and Tacitus of the iron-age Britons and Gauls could be so designated, but Cook's sympathetic curiosity about the lives and customs of the natives far exceeded theirs.)

Soon after his arrival Cook was entertained by dancing, and he and his colleagues have left detailed descriptions of these occasions, one of which ends with the assessment: 'The dance was musical and harmonious and all their motions were performed with such justness that the whole party moved and acted as one man. It was the opinion of every one of us that such a performance would have met with universal applause on a European theatre.'

Even more valuable than these descriptions are the drawings which Cook's illustrators made, many of which were engraved and published at the end of the Voyage. The finest of these draughtsmen was Webber, who was responsible for most of the illustrations accompanying the account of Cook's Third Voyage. Some of Cook's illustrators have been criticised for romanticising, for drawing what they imagined rather than what they saw, and there is some truth in these accusations. Yet these engravings surpass in quality any earlier ethnographic illustration. Webber's views of the night dances on the island of Ha'apai contain many authentic touches of detail – any European who has had to sit cross-legged for several hours on such an occasion will recognise the rather uncomfortable attitudes of the Europeans in the front row (including Cook himself) with their 'backs to the camera'.

The Christian missionaries who succeeded Cook in Tonga worked consistently to extinguish most that was original and traditional in Tongan life, forcing the natives to conform to European conventions about what what was good and moral. Dancing, conceived as a pagan activity, was stopped altogether for a while, until the natives 'invented' some new dances which, lacking the pagan associations of the earlier ones, were seen as acceptable. Happily the newly-invented dances seem in fact to have much in common with those seen by Cook, with the same emphasis on a whole line of figures moving together in harmony and

(Above) *Performance of a night dance before Captain Cook and his party on Ha'apai (engraving after J. Webber);* (below) *modern dancers in Makave perform the lakalaka.*

the same exquisitely graceful movements of the hands. The modern *lakalaka*, where the dancers sing in harmony as they move, still gives the observer an authentic glimpse of the harmony and perfection of traditional Tongan song and dance, a reminder of the consummate artistry of which technologically simple societies are capable.

The same sense of continuity, of the old not fundamentally changed beneath the surface of the new, is seen in other aspects of Tongan society. The King of Tonga today, His Majesty King Taufa'ahau Tupou IV receives much the same traditional respect as did his ancestors who held the office of Tu'i Tonga, traditional head of Tongan society. As he remarked to Magnus Magnusson and myself: 'When you consider the changes that have taken place in Tonga over the last 150 years, they have been very big changes, and yet it hasn't really affected village life all that much, particularly in the smaller more affluent villages.'

It was such a village, Makave on the northern island of Vava'u, which we visited at the King's suggestion. On our arrival we were at once greeted by the chief, the Honourable Tu'i'afitu, one of the hereditary nobles of Tonga, and conducted to the village hall for a ceremony of welcome. This is the ceremony of the *kava*, a drink made from the *kava* root, and its interest is great, since nothing shows more clearly the formalism of traditional Tongan society. Webber has left a beautiful engraving of a *kava* ceremony two centuries ago, which incidentally illustrates well the sophistication of Tongan building using wood and matting. Today, just as two centuries ago (and no

The Honourable Tu'i'afitu at the kava ceremony in the village of Makave.

Engraving after Webber of the Tongan kava ceremony.

doubt for centuries before that), the chief sits cross-legged flanked on each side by his retainers and guests.

In front there is an open space, and opposite is the man who will make the *kava* drink, seated behind a three-legged wooden bowl. On the Chief's right and left are his two *matapules* – 'talking chiefs' or heralds: the herald of the right and the herald of the left. The chief himself says nothing throughout, and it is his *matapule* who pronounces the instructions to grind the root and put it in the bowl, to pour in water, to remove the root after soaking, and then to serve the drink (in a coconut cup) to each of those present, in an order as strictly prescribed by etiquette as the seating of a banquet in Buckingham Palace.

I found participation in this ceremony an altogether remarkable experience. Not only was it a great honour to be the guest of the Honourable Tu'i'afitu on such an occasion, but as an archaeologist I could not help remarking on how little of all that went on would find any direct trace in the archaeological record. The most formal *kava* ceremony held during our stay, which involved the presentation of a pig, was held outdoors on the village green. Apart from the stone used to pound the *kava* root, most of the artefacts used were of perishable materials and would not survive in the archaeological record. Even the fine hall depicted in Webber's drawing would leave little for the archaeologist beyond a few post-holes in the earth, very like those which have in fact been found at the henge monument at Durrington Walls in Wiltshire. But above all, the traditional formality and strictness of etiquette was impressive. As Cook put it: 'There is a decorum observed in the presence of their great men that is truly admirable. Whenever he sits down, all those with him seat themselves at the same time in a semi-circle before him, leaving always an open convenient space between him and them.' No one who has participated in such a ceremony could doubt the powers of organisation or the social complexity of a

Engraving after Webber of the inasi *ceremony before a burial mound*

society which, if technology were the only criterion, might have to be regarded as composed of 'mere barbarians'.

The ceremony of the presentation of the pig was interesting in many ways. Once again it was conducted with a formulaic elaboration, according to precise rules. It was presented to the chief, the Honourable Tu'i'afitu, and he, in accordance with convention, in turn sent it on to be presented to the man senior to him in the hierarchy, the Governor of Vava'u. Here in fact is a last vestige of the traditional system of redistribution, a feature of most chiefdom societies.

Redistribution, or at least one component of it, was most strikingly seen by Captain Cook in Tonga at the great *inasi* ceremony, the ceremony of the first fruits, usually held in October. It took place at Mu'a on Tongatapu, the main island of the Tonga group. Mu'a was the traditional home and centre of the Tu'i Tonga, the head of Tongan society, as well as the burial place of his ancestors. Their great burial mounds or *langi* are

seen in the background of Webber's drawing. At the ceremony it was usual for the chiefs and population of the area to bring their first fruits and offer them to the Tu'i Tonga. Much of the ceremonial was complicated, and little understood by Cook, who was only allowed to be present on condition that he removed his shirt and loosed his hair. One of his officers wrote:

We who were on the outside were not a little suprised at seeing Captain Cook in the procession of the Chiefs with his hair hanging loose and his body naked down to the waist, no person being admitted covered above the waist or with his hair tied. I do not pretend to dispute the propriety of Captain Cook's conduct, but I cannot help thinking he rather let himself down.

Today the verdict is reversed and nothing could more effectively document the value of Cook as an observer than his respect for the community which he was visiting.

Such ceremonies in many societies have a religious as well as a social significance, indeed the two cannot be distinguished, and Cook's colleague Anderson

Burial mound or langi *of the Tu'i Tonga*

rightly observed: 'This ceremony which is call'd Natche has so much mystery running through the whole that it is hard to tell whether it is most of the religious or political kind.'

There is much more about Tongan society today which recalls that of two centuries ago – the yam plantations, the manufacture of bark cloth, the language itself are little changed. And there is much in both which is perplexing and thought-provoking to an archaeologist asking himself how many of the activities of a sophisticated and complex society, where many of the artefacts are of wood, will be preserved in the archaeological record. But let us leave Tonga with the words of Cook himself:

I must notwithstanding conclude by observing that the natives of Tonga and the isles around it are upon the whole arrived at as much perfection in their manual works, as much regularity in their government, at as high a pitch in the agriculture and some other things as any nation whatever under the same circumstances: and that exclusive of the helps obtained from learning the use of metals and communication with nations who have these advantages, they are in every respect almost as perfectly civilis'd as it is possible for mankind to be. They seem to have been long at their ultimum, and at least by what we may judge from the general description of them given by Tasman they have been so for above these hundred and thirty years, and had they not been visited by Europeans would probably ever have remained the same.

The Easter Island Monuments

In the previous section I have not attempted to draw many conclusions from those observations on traditional Tongan society. But they are already of great value when we come to Easter Island, at the extreme eastern end of Polynesia, for the society there was in effect destroyed by the terrible Peruvian slave raid of 1862. It was only after that time that the remarkable wooden inscriptions in the *rongo rongo* script came to light. We have little first-hand knowledge about this Easter Island writing, or about the use of the great monuments, the *ahu*, surmounted by those extraordinary statues.

Indeed, it is not surprising that some writers should

121

Easter Island rongo rongo *tablet*

speak of a 'mystery' of Easter Island. For there is no doubt that one of the most remarkable sights in the world is at the volcanic crater of Rano Raraku, where the statues were quarried. Evidently they were carved before being transported, with only the fine details incomplete, and for reasons which may never be clear, a great many statues were hewn from the rock, presumably well in advance of requirements. There they still stand in their dozens and hundreds, gazing enigmatically across the Pacific.

At the same time the element of mystery should not be exaggerated. The language of Easter Island survives today and it is a Polynesian language. Archaeology has helped to clarify the prehistory of the area, and Easter Island was probably settled by Polynesians coming from the west (perhaps from the Marquesas Islands) around the time of Christ. There seems no need for the theories of Thor Heyerdahl, proposing contact with South America. The custom of building ceremonial monuments is quite common elsewhere in Polynesia, for instance in Tahiti, and statues not unlike those of Easter Island (although smaller in size) are also known.

What is special about Easter Island is the intensity of the *ahu*-building activity. They are dotted along the coast, imposing platforms with one or several statues looking inland, dominating the plaza behind the *ahu*.

Their significance was appreciated by Cook and his colleagues, who visited Easter Island in 1774 (although on account of illness Cook did not himself go ashore):

Stone images whose names we got from the natives, and by what I could understand from them they were erected to the memory of their chiefs, for they all had different names and they always called them *ariki* which I understand to be the king or chief, and they do not appear to pay the respect to them that I should think they would to a deity.

It seems fairly clear that Easter Island at this time was divided into territories, and that each territory was the home of a tribe or lineage (see page 112). The approximate territorial division was recorded in 1914 and it may be reasonable to regard each of the main image *ahu* as the focal centre for the lineage territory. Easter Island society does not seem to have been welded into a single coherent polity with a single political leader, as Tonga was. So there is no single political centre to compare with the seat of the Tu'i Tonga at Mu'a, with its great series of burial monuments. Certainly Easter Island did have a ritual centre at Orongo, but through much of its history there may have been an element of competition among the various lineages, which is perhaps reflected in the grandiloquent monumentality of their focal *ahu*.

Uncompleted statues on the slopes of the Rano Raraku volcano, Easter Island

With some knowledge of Polynesian social organisation, it is possible to see how the society of Easter Island, despite its special features, does not stand apart. The *ahu* of Easter Island may be compared with the *langi* of Tonga or with the *marae* of Tahiti. Perhaps their very isolation led to the great florescence in the statue building which accompanied them.

Even the *rongo rongo* tablets can begin to fall into position when we recall that they were apparently used exclusively in conjunction with religious chants. They may have acted as mnemonic devices, like the string figures traditionally made on some other Polynesian islands. Indeed for me the most exciting experience on Easter Island was to meet Amalia Tepano, an old lady who remembers not only how to make some of the traditional string figures but also some of the chants that go with them. I think there is little doubt that some of these are real *rongo rongo* chants, which the wise men of Easter Island society used to sing using not string figures but *rongo rongo* tablets as their *aide mémoire*. Listening to the chant of Amalia Tepano is as close as we shall ever get to the lost secret of the *rongo rongo* writing.

Stonehenge Revisited

I have deliberately avoided referring to Stonehenge directly in the two preceding sections. But anyone who has really puzzled over the problem of our neolithic monuments in south Britain will already see something of what I am getting at. It is my belief that the major henge monuments of Britain – great sites such as Durrington Walls, or Avebury or Stonehenge itself – could only have been built by some centralised and coordinated society, of the kind which we can today call a chiefdom society.

Clearly a degree of mobilisation was needed to provide the manpower for these great works, and the economic device which made all of this possible must have been redistribution. It is likely, although not certain, that this was still a kin-based society – there is no need to suggest the clear-cut division into separate social classes characteristic of state societies. It is likely that there was indeed a paramount chief behind the construction of Stonehenge and Silbury Hill. Yet I

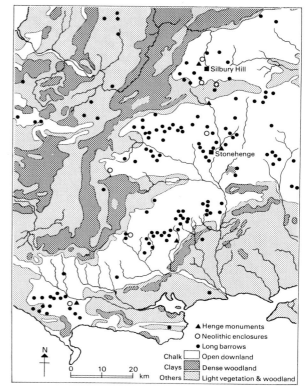

Henge monuments ▲
Neolithic enclosures ○
Long barrows ●

Chalk — Open downland
Clays ▓ Dense woodland
Others ░ Light vegetation & woodland

believe that in the Salisbury Plain it is possible to distinguish traces of the same kind of territorial division suggested for Easter Island. In the early neolithic period long barrows are seen, burial mounds which may have been the focal points for very small communities. But soon larger and more widely-spaced focal points emerge – the causewayed camps. In the late neolithic period these are superseded by the major henges, which in territorial terms may be regarded as the equivalent of the great image *ahu* of the ten tribal territories of Easter Island. That is to say, they may have been the focal point of the tribal territory, the main home of the tribal chief, and the site of both social and religious ceremonies; as Cook's colleague observed, the religious and the political cannot always be separated. Then at the end of the period, neolithic monument-building in Britain culminates in the erection of Stonehenge and Silbury Hill.

Of course there can be no doubt that Stonehenge represents also a close experience and interest in astronomy: Stonehenge was a solar observatory. Yet here again Polynesia can offer us parallels – although they need be no more than that. The present King of Tonga has claimed that the remarkable trilithon, the Ha'amonga a Maui was used for solar observations, and there can be no doubt that the economic system there allowed for much craft specialisation. There is no reason why the society of Stonehenge should not have allowed for men as erudite as the *rongo rongo* chanters of Easter Island, as steeped in traditional lore as the *matapule* of Tonga, and as skilled in astronomical observation as we know were the Polynesian navigators.

There is no need then to argue that the builders of Stonehenge must have been possessed of some special skills derived from the Near East. Nor do I see much virtue in recent attempts that have been made to suggest that this must have been a state society of the kind represented by the Ancient Maya of Mesoamerica. The Polynesian experience does not tell us

Tonga trilithon: the Ha'amonga a Maui.

what happened in England around 2000 BC, but it does show us the potential of chiefdom societies, with a low level of technology and the complete absence of urban centres, in achieving remarkable works of communal endeavour and traditional specialised skill.

Let me stress again, therefore, that my argument here does not depend upon any supposed one-to-one correspondence between traditional Polynesian society and British society of four thousand years ago. There is no cause for the traditional pedantic complaints about the dangers of 'ethnographic analogy', with which academics like to restrict the range of dicussion. My claim is that both the Salisbury Plain of 4000 years ago and Tonga of two centuries ago may be seen as examples, different examples, of a recurrent social form, namely chiefdom society. Many of the resemblances which occur are structural resemblances arising from this underlying regularity: others come from ecological constraints such as the use of wood for domestic architecture.

In conclusion I shall quote once again Cook's colleague Anderson who knew and understood traditional Tongan society as well as any modern anthropologist has done. His remarks apply to many chiefdom

Amalia Tepano with one of the traditional string figures of Easter Island.

125

Magnus Magnusson and Colin Renfrew with HM the King of Tonga

Acknowledgements

My experience of modern Polynesian society is based on a voyage made in the agreeable company of Messrs David Collison, Ray Henman, Magnus Magnusson, David South and John Tellick, which also owed much to the encouragement of the late Paul Johnstone. In Tonga we were aided by the personal interest of HM King Taufa'ahau Tupou IV, and in Makave I am much indebted to the hospitality and friendship of the Hon. Tu'i'afitu, his wife Luisa and son Niulala and to the help of Mr Epeli Kauvaka. I should like to acknowledge the assistance and advice on Easter Island of Mr Sergio Rapu and Professor and Mrs William Ayres.

societies, and *for this reason* and not through any superficial similarity between the two cases, they are relevant to prehistoric Britain:

> In several respects the Government resembles the old feudal states of Europe, where though all acknowledge the Sovereignty of the Prince there are many who seem to exercise their authority with no less restraint in their several provinces, and are in some respects wholly independent unless in the single circumstance of paying homage due to the Lord of all. The island is divided into many districts, each of which has a chief who may be considered as Lords or Barons. . . . The immediate dependents of these Chiefs who are very numerous assume the names of their masters (besides their own proper name) and use it as was customary amongst the Scottish clans.
>
> Each of these no doubt decides differences and distributes justice in their several districts. . . . Whether it be from that mode of government or some other policy to which we are strangers, it does not appear that any civilis'd nations have as yet exceeded them in the great order they observe on all occasions and ready compliance with the commands of their chiefs, nor in the harmony that subsists throughout all ranks and unites them as if one man inform'd with and directed by the same principle.

This, then, is the essential clue to the understanding of chiefdom society and through it to an explanation of the early monuments of Britain. Human originality, and the creative capacity of human societies, albeit with a simple technology, should never be underrated, whether they border the Atlantic or lie in the Pacific.

Girl in bark-cloth dress dancing the ta'olunga.

Chronicle and the Industrial Archaeology Dilemma   Kenneth Hudson

Paul Johnstone could never quite make up his mind about industrial archaeology. Although he was much too kind and diplomatic to put the point in such blunt terms, one could feel him trying to decide if this strange arrival on the cultural scene was a new subject, a fun-subject or a non-subject. For someone who had earned the trust of Bronze Age archaeologists, medieval archaeologists and maritime archaeologists, was it safe or prudent to be seen in the company of people calling themselves industrial archaeologists? What did the term mean? Was 'industrial archaeology' – the inverted commas were faintly noticeable – ever likely to make the academic grade? Could one ever imagine a Professor of Industrial Archaeology? If he existed, what would he profess?

This was in 1970, when industrial archaeology was officially seven years old, the first book with those two words in the title, *Industrial Archaeology: an introduction*, having appeared in 1963. Since then, missionaries had been hard at work up and down the country, preaching the new gospel, visiting and blessing Ironbridge, the Great Laxey Wheel, Kidderminster Gasworks and other holy places, and generally doing their best to make their somewhat apathetic and disbelieving fellow-citizens aware of Britain's industrial monuments and the perils to which they were exposed. We were, they told us, unbelievably rich in eighteenth- and early nineteenth-century factories, in pioneering railways, locks and canals, in cast-iron aqueducts and bridges and, through sheer ignorance and folly, we were allowing them to be knocked down, filled in and disposed of before our very eyes.

The point had begun to go home. The Council for British Archaeology had set up committees, the Min-istry of Works, as it then was, had appointed what amounted to a surveyor of industrial monuments, the beginnings had been made with an extension of the official definition of historic buildings to include industrial structures of one kind and another. But the doubters and scoffers remained, many of them in fairly high places, such as university common rooms and the Board of British Railways. 'To the objectors,' reported *Industrial Archaeology: an introduction*, 'industrial archaeology is an impossible mongrel, the ugly offspring of two parents who should never have been allowed to breed. "Industry", they say, is by common agreement a recent growth, a phenomenon no more than two hundred years old. "Archaeology", also by common agreement, deals with the more distant past. How then, they demand, is it reasonable or decent to speak of industry and archaeology in the same breath?'

All these considerations must have been in Paul Johnstone's thoughts as he was trying to decide whether to lead *Chronicle* towards industrial archaeology or firmly but tactfully away from it and into more adequately charted seas. But there were other factors. The BBC was, after all, a broadcasting organisation, not an academic body or a government department. It was supposed, rightly or wrongly, to thrive on novelty and innovation, on the fresh approach. If it failed to experiment, it was certain to wither away and die. It had to pay attention to new movements and new opinions, always being careful not to lead from too far out in front. In the particular instance of industrial archaeology, a further point which no representative of the media could afford to disregard was that the campaign to hunt out, record and preserve old woollen mills, railway stations and iron-framed department stores seemed to have struck deep roots. Local industrial archaeology groups had sprung up all over the country, as a symbol of the amateur effort on which the 'subject' depended for its success. Paul Johnstone decided that, from every point of view, the wisest and most constructive course for *Chronicle* to follow, at least for the time being, was to put television's spotlight on the private soldiers of the industrial archaeology army and to leave the generals and colonels to their own devices for a while.

The result was a competition. Local groups were invited to send in details of themselves and of the projects on which they had been working, and *Chronicle* promised a prize of £250 to the one that seemed to come out best, 'the most deserving project going on in the country at present'. 60 entries were received, a short-list of 8 was eventually drawn up from them, and those on the short-list were filmed in action. On March 14 'Chronicle' showed the results in a programme pleasantly entitled, *Win a Second-hand Crane*. It was introduced by Magnus Magnusson, and in the studio with him were the three judges – Neil Cossons, Kenneth Hawley and myself – and an audience made up of members of the groups that had entered for the competition. The 8 projects and the people responsible for them provided a very reasonable illustration of the kind of work which was going on at that time, and of the spirit behind it.

Redditch had been restoring an old needle-making mill to full working order. The Sussex group was highly organised and busy with a range of tasks, from restoring Kipling's electric generator at Burwash to preserving a series of eighteenth-century milestones that run from the Surrey border to Hailsham, and recording details of all 147 railway stations in the county. 'The group's strength', said Magnusson, 'lies in its ability to attract the help of bodies like the National Trust and local councils', a comment which seemed fully justified. The programme passed along, film by film, from the Peak Forest Canal to Helmshore and the Higher Mill Museum Trust, where an old woollen mill was being used as a means of helping schoolchildren to find out about social history, and then on to Pembrokeshire, where the group was based

on the County Museum. The Manx Mines Research Group was devoting its attentions to the lead mines on the island, the Northern Mill Engine Society was salvaging and restoring superannuated steam-engines from the cotton-mills, and the Berkshire Group was anxious to draw attention to its survey of animal-powered wheels for bringing water up from wells.

The three judges gave their views on what the films had shown and explained why they proposed to give the prize to the Northern Mill Engine Society. The Society had an unusually wide social base, it was doing a much-needed practical job, all its members seemed to be taking an active part in what was going on, and it had produced evidence of an excellent intelligence system and a realistic public relations policy. The Controller of BBC 2, Robin Scott, handed over the cheque in front of the cameras and, from the public point of view, industrial archaeology had unmistakably arrived. It had had 40 minutes of television all to itself. *Chronicle*, and by inference the BBC, had taken it seriously. Equally important, the viewing public showed signs of having rather liked the people and what they were doing.

The experiment was considered sufficiently promising to justify a further programme in the following year. This time Skipton had been restoring a water-driven cornmill, Faversham a gunpowder mill and Sittingbourne an old boat-builder's yard. The East Lothian County Council had helped and encouraged the conservation of a beam pumping-engine at Prestongrange Colliery. The Great Western Society, with its base at Didcot, in Berkshire, was rehabilitating veteran locomotives and coaches, with the ultimate aim of collecting a cross-section of everything the GWR ever owned, from main line engines to coffee-pots. Then there was the South Yorkshire Industrial Museum at Cusworth Hall, near Doncaster – a piece of municipal enterprise – and after that a piece of enterprise in London, which Magnusson introduced in these terms: 'There are some societies in Britain that deserve a prize right outside the terms of reference of this competition – a prize for sheer nerve. The Greater London Industrial Archaeology Society – GLIAS for short – was set up to record the past of the largest built-up area in the world: Greater London – a mere seven hundred and twenty square miles.'

The last of the eight finalists was in the Potteries, the Cheddleton Flint Mill Preservation Trust, where the guiding spirit was Robert Copeland, director of a modern pottery factory at Stoke-on-Trent. The three judges deliberated in private, put the Greater London Society in first place and gave their reasons to the studio audience. The cheque was handed over to the Society's secretary, a London train driver, who promised to put the money to good use, and the competition was over for another year. In 1972 *Chronicle* and the local groups were at it again, with no apparent falling off in enthusiasm, and industrial archaeology seemed to have found a regular annual television slot.

But at that point Paul Johnstone called a halt. It was a sound instinct. This method of drawing attention to the existence and achievements of industrial archaeology had accomplished everything that might have been expected of it. The right moment to stop, as every showman knows, is when the public is still asking for more. The well-proved formula can all too easily become automatic, and with this particular formula few radical changes were possible. One could have tinkered with it, changed the judges or the presenter, had six finalists instead of eight, made each film four minutes 10 seconds long instead of three minutes 10 seconds, given two prizes, not one, but the result would still have been a competition for industrial archaeology societies. By 1972 the novelty had worn off and the judges at least were coming to look not unlike a stage army. *Chronicle* had to look for something different and in a moment we shall consider what took the place of *Win a Second-hand Crane* and its successors. Meanwhile, it may be useful to mention one or two unpublicised benefits of the competition, which occurred as spin-offs.

After each programme had been recorded, everyone – BBC staff, audience and judges – migrated to the Television Centre restaurant, partly to take advantage of a little of the BBC's simpler type of hospitality but also to carry out a post-mortem on the programme. This must have been some of the cheapest and most effective research the BBC has ever carried out. By encouraging the visitors to unburden themselves of their complaints, suggestions and misgivings, the *Chronicle* producers were able to feel their way inside the shell of industrial archaeology, to sort out the genuine characters from the mountebanks and confidence tricksters, and to judge where the future television opportunities were in this curiously speckled subject. These annual coffee-and-sandwich meetings developed into what are best described as loose seminars. The restaurant in which they took place was broken up by thick pillars, so that often one could hear, but not see the person whose point one was trying to pick up and develop. Some of the contributions to the discussion were quite violent in tone, especially when an academic nerve had been accidentally or perhaps deliberately touched, but a thick pillar turneth away wrath. It is unsatisfactory to curse a person if one cannot see him. One cannot judge how he is responding. He may even be asleep.

It would be an exaggeration, perhaps, to suggest that the knockabout hour after the programme was as interesting and valuable as the programme itself, but it was a wonderful way of becoming sensitive to the jealousies, clashes of personality, and warring sects which existed within the brotherhood of industrial archaeologists. After one particularly sharp exchange of views, Paul Johnstone, safely hidden behind his pillar, was heard to whisper to his neighbour, 'Industrial archaeology has arrived. These people are behaving like real archaeologists now.' These restaurant-debates were, of course, private and off the record, but how interesting it would be to have a recording of them.

The second bonus was of a quite different kind. Administratively, the competitions caused little difficulty. An advertisement, followed by application forms, brought in the entries, the judges met to draw up a short-list, film was shot and edited, and the framework of the programme was complete. But the actual filming was not as simple as it seemed. *Chronicle* producers and directors were always hard-pressed with other and more ambitious projects and work on these short films about waterwheels and brass-foundries somehow had to be fitted into the schedule.

This meant that almost everybody lent a hand. One likes to think they educated themselves in the process. It is far from easy to make an interesting film about machinery or technical processes, at least for a general audience, and there is always a temptation to take the soft option of going for some not always relevant human angle on the story. What *Chronicle* needed on this occasion was a special blend of people, history and technology, and that – with varying amounts of pain and suffering – is what it nearly always got. Some producers inevitably showed greater interest and aptitude than others; but there was a lot of cross-fertilisation and inter-office discussion, and after three years a recognisably *Chronicle* style of presenting industrial archaeology on film had emerged, a style which came to full maturity in the subsequent *Industrial Grand Tour* series.

When one looks back at the scripts of the competition programmes, one is astonished to find what a vast amount of technical information was put across with the help of film and film commentary. Viewers were instructed in the art and history of needle-making:

'Redditch had been a centre of the needle-making craft before the Industrial Revolution. The application of water-power to hand-operated devices has given Forge Mill a uniquely hybrid technology. The heavy ''wee-waws'', as they were called, were originally swung to and fro by hand to keep up the momentum of the machinery; but they were incorporated into the water-powered design. Levers bring the power from the ''wee-waws'' to the scouring-tables, where the needles, wrapped in long linen sausages, were polished repeatedly with pumice powder. Forge Mill had its own stone-crushing department to supply the pumice.'

The working of Tower Bridge was explained:

'How many Londoners know that Tower Bridge is raised and lowered by steam power, or that a staff of seventy is required to keep it on standby round the clock?'

Then there was 'the incredible building, out on the marshes beyond Woolwich':

'Crossness pumping station, was built with loving care in 1865 to cope with the sewage of South London: a great monument of British pumping. This place was the pride of the Empire one day in 1865, when the Prince of Wales was pleased to start the first of the four massive beam engines and name it after his mother.'

Porthgain, in Pembrokeshire:

'A derelict slate quarry with its own tiny harbour and deserted brickworks, and a long-forgotten railway line. Today's photo survey will make a sad contrast with other photographs collected by the Group, taken in braver days almost a hundred years ago. Now the abandoned quarry with its towering sea wall and its dilapidated outbuildings has all the remoteness of a Gothic ruin. But in the good days there was a fleet of ships to take the slate as far as France and Germany. It's only 40 years since the last sailing ship left Porthgain.'

One knows very well, of course, that in any film the words can be no more than the handmaiden of the pictures. *Chronicle* was not writing a textbook of industrial archaeology. It was trying to awaken interest, not to teach, and how much of the information in the commentary registered with viewers is, as always, impossible to say. The competition framework for the programme can be seen as a dramatic method of stimulating public interest, a good showman's trick. The message to be put across was something like this: 'All over Britain there are groups of people who have got together in order to spend their spare time ferreting out and studying the remains of industrial history. We want to show you what kind of people they are, how they work at this new kind of hobby and the kind of things they feel are important. Some of them seem to be going about the job more successfully than others and we reckon that if you watch this programme carefully you'll finish up by understanding why this or that group got the prize.'

There can be no doubt at all that the plan succeeded. Industrial archaeologists as a whole were enormously encouraged by the BBC's patronage of their efforts and the discussions during and after the programme helped many of them to clarify their ideas. After these three programmes, the situation was never

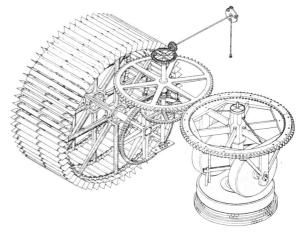

Two British industrial archaeology projects. The Chart Gunpowder Mills at Faversham, seen (top right) *in a derelict state, were restored by Faversham Society* (top left); *the diagram above shows the mechanism.* (Left) *Members of the Northern Mill Engine Society prepare to remove, through a narrow window, the flywheel of a Musgrave non-dead-centre engine in Radcliffe, Lancashire.*

quite the same again. Paul Johnstone could certainly feel that he had not been wasting either his producers' time or the BBC's money. This was not to say, of course, that everyone was happy with the choice of finalists, the arrangement of the programmes, or the idea of a competition at all. But the series certainly made more friends than enemies, and broadened the outlook of many people who were not industrial archaeologists at all. *Chronicle* had every reason to be proud of its achievement.

In the following year, it embarked on the much more difficult task of investigating the progress of industrial archaeology on the Continent. There was no thought of a competition or a prize. The aim was simply to see and hear what other countries had been doing, in the hope that such a programme would encourage ideas to cross national boundaries and that it might just possibly prevent British industrial archaeologists from becoming too complacent and parochial.

The programme was eventually called *For Love or Money*. The choice of title and the organisation of the filming and the studio discussion were explained by Magnus Magnusson at the outset. 'For Love or Money', he said, was 'the most vital question facing the science of industrial archaeology in Britain today.' 'For three years now', he went on, 'we've offered a cash prize for effort or enthusiasm or practical success in the field of industrial archaeology. This year there's no prize. All our films have been made in Europe – in Belgium, Germany, Denmark, Sweden and Poland – to see how they tackle this whole business of preserving or simply expressing admiration for the great monuments and achievements of the Industrial Revolution.'

The five films all had the same director, who brought to the work the great advantage of having been born and partly brought up on the Continent and the same interviewer, whose researches for a recently published book on the industrial archaeology of Europe had made him familiar with the ground to be covered. In each country an attempt, not always completely successful, was made to find an expert who spoke English, to add colour to the item, and to concentrate on some aspect of industrial archaeology in

which the country concerned had shown particular strength.

In the case of Denmark, there was no doubt that the subject had to be wind and watermills. The team went to the island of Fyn, where they had the good luck to come across a miller who spoke English, in charge of one of the few working windmills left in Denmark. The mill had been well maintained and it provided the kind of pictures that cameramen dream of – an overfondness for windmills and watermills is something of an occupational disease among television people dealing with industrial archaeology. Anders Jespersen, one of the world's leading molinologists and the man in charge of the Mill Preservation Board at the National Museum in Copenhagen, was interviewed on Fyn at his watermill-home, which he bought when the last miller died. A filming visit was also made to the Board's workshop base and training centre at Lumby Mill, also on the island of Fyn.

Belgium provided Henri Guchez and a remarkable story to go with him. Guchez is a very successful architect. He was born in the small mining town of Le Grand Hornu, not far from Mons, in the Borinage. Le Grand Hornu was a model industrial town of the early nineteenth century, created by an elightened coalowner, Henri de Gorge Le Grand. It included a majestic complex of workshops and offices for the mines, built around a vast oval courtyard, possibly the grandest industrial monument in the whole of Europe. In 1967, with exhaustion of the coal reserves, the Government issued a decree ordering the removal of all evidence of the industry. Henri Guchez, the local boy made good, stood up to bureaucracy, said, in effect, 'the bulldozers shall not pass', and bought the workshop area lock, stock and barrel. He restored it at his own cost and installed his architectural practice there. Asked why he had done it, he provided, perhaps unknowingly, a perfect justification for industrial archaeology, a creed.

'I do it in the first place', he said, as the camera followed his walk into the great courtyard, 'in homage to Henri de Gorge, the son of a poor and simple peasant, who launched himself into industry in about 1800. He built not only an industrial empire, but

(Above) *Le Grand Hornu, near Mons, Belgium, an enormous complex of workshops and offices for the local coalmine, build around an oval courtyard,* (left) *Lillemølle, on the island of Fyn, the watermill home of Anders Jespersen, built in 1827 and restored by him in 1961.*

achieved a work of genius in creating an urban environment which showed great social responsibility. This is why I want to rebuild this historic witness to the past, which at the same time is a great page in the history of the civilisation of man.

'To me this place holds extraordinary echoes of the past. These walls speak to me, as I think they will also speak to others, and they must be restored to give absolute calm and peace for a better understanding between all peoples. It is a memorial to the men who left their agricultural way of life and entered the realm of industry, where they had to learn the rhythm of factory work, which cradles the new Trade Unionism. These people went six hundred metres underground, they started at the age of nine, undernourished, girls and boys, and they had to work for eighteen hours a day. Therefore, I believe that this is more than an industrial site. It is a monument to men.'

The translation does not, of course, do full justice to the passion, the eloquence and the charm that M. Guchez poured into the film recordist's microphone on this occasion but it is fair to say, even so, that no British enthusiast for industrial archaeology would have expressed his feelings in quite this way. *For Love or Money* revealed, in fact, both the strength and the weakness of the situation in the mother-country of industrial archaeology. The previous three programmes, the competitions, had reflected the good side, the activity and enthusiasm; the fourth programme, which looked at industrial archaeology through continental eyes, showed that the practical-minded British had not given a great deal of thought to the philosophical implications of what they were doing. They felt what had to be done but, at that stage, they saw no particular reason for asking themselves why they were doing it. This typically English way of proceeding always baffles and frequently annoys people on the Continent, just as the English are apt to become infuriated by what they regard as the over-intellectualism of the French, Germans, Russians or whoever: mental gymnastics which inhibit action.

At which point one begins with hindsight to understand Paul Johnstone's predicament rather better. In the early '70s the academics, and especially the archaeologists, sensed that industrial archaeology was strong on enthusiasm, weak on theory. It was in its first acquisitive, collecting phase, sweeping steam engines and fulling mills into its net in much the same spirit as the early Hellenists and Egyptologists had gone into raptures over gold ornaments and statues. The third and fourth generation of archaeologists with which 'Chronicle' was normally concerned found it impossible to identify themselves with this strange new breed of collectors of industrial birds' eggs. One day, when the tree-climbers had grown up, perhaps, but not just at the moment.

British industrial archaeology was beginning to mature at about the time when *For Love or Money* was broadcast. But the process brought problems of its own. So long as it remained immature, piling up one discovery on another for the sheer joy of it, the amateur not only had a place: he was king, he was needed. During the period of primary accumulation, there were simply not enough professionals to do the job, and one was not sure, in any case, what an industrial archaeology professional looked like. One certainly had no idea what an industrial archaeology professor looked like. There was none then and there is none today.

The Golden Age of industrial archaeology, which lasted from the mid '60s to about 1972 or 1973, was characterised by an interest in quantity, rather than quality. In a country like Britain, which was one huge industrial museum and junk-yard, it could hardly have been otherwise. An embarrassment of riches rarely makes for discrimination. Sweden, Poland and Germany were not so embarrassed in this respect as Britain was and still is. They had more time and energy to spend on theory, and their traditions would have led them along this path in any case.

If *Chronicle* were making its first contacts with industrial archaeology today, instead of in 1970, it would be meeting a different kind of person and proceeding quite differently. The most significant people today, the people Paul Johnstone would have wanted to recruit for his programmes, are the synthesisers, the model-builders, the environmentalists, the experts who are trying to fit industrial archaeology into the broad pattern of human history and to use it as a tool, rather than as an end in itself. It would be too much to say that the professionals have finally arrived, but at least we can begin to get an impression of their shape and motivation. *Win a Second-hand Crane* and its successors would not be possible today, but they performed an immensely useful service in their day. They encouraged, if not compelled, industrial archaeologists to take an objective look at themselves, which was something that had hardly happened previously.

The European programme carried this process a stage further. The Danes, Belgians, Swedes, Poles and Germans all saw the tasks and the possibilities in a slightly different way and, although some British industrial archaeologists resented the suggestion that the Ark of the Covenant was not in their sole keeping, the comparison was both salutary and stimulating. The Swedish item was particularly illuminating. It was centred on Surahammar, a company town in Västmanland, where, in the course of a hundred years, a small iron-forge had developed into a large modern steelworks. Swedish industrialists have shown an exceptional degree of public responsibility in preserving industrial monuments and it was felt that Surahammar, where this attitude had been particularly marked, was a good place to film. The Good Swedish Industrialist, in other words, might shame the Bad French Industrialist or the Bad Italian Industrialist into doing something similar. The Swedish item was to be a kind of parable, a moral tale.

It did not turn out exactly like this, mainly because the steel company did not realise all the implications of its special kind of historical interest. The old nineteenth-century forge, which had been especially concerned with making railway wheels, had been converted into a museum as it stood and other exhibits relating to the firm's past were preserved in its archives building. The film showed all this, offered pictures of the elegant Victorian mansions built for the directors, and dealt to some extent with the way steel is produced today at the modern works. The company, it was agreed, 'has obviously gone to a lot of trouble to preserve the evidence of its own past', but, the film commentary added, 'there's a growing body of opinion in Sweden that's become irritated by the paternalism that's traditional in Swedish industry. These people want industrial museums to reflect something wider than just the achievements of the owners and the board of directors.'

At that point, viewers saw and heard a young architect, very influential in Swedish industrial archaeological circles. He was interviewed in the main shopping street and he said this: 'The workers should really feel that the work of their parents has been of cultural value, and that the work they are doing will be of cultural value for tomorrow. Modern industry is a hard place to work in. Human feelings and people are kept down. Workers have contributed much to the welfare of our society, and we should honour them. I think that we should stress a little more in modern museums, in new museums, the workers' culture. Perhaps the workers should build the museums themselves.'

With these words, *Chronicle*, intentionally or not, showed that industrial archaeology could not exist in a political vacuum. It was not a neutral subject. Industrial monuments could be presented and interpreted either from the point of view of the owners and managers or from that of the workers. Instinctively and almost certainly without any deliberate intention, the history of Surahammar had been sifted, organised and offered to the public as it appeared through board-room eyes, so that what was preserved was being made to yield only half its potential meaning. What the BBC's Surahammar film was showing was a special kind of industrial archaeology, the archaeology of paternalism. In objecting to this, the street interview made a perfectly valid point. If an industrial monument is to be regarded as part of the national or international heritage, it must belong to the people as a whole, it must be seen to reflect the part it has played among all levels and sections of the community. The re-interpretation of historic monuments along these lines is still in its infancy, but the pressure to undertake it becomes stronger each year. In 1973 industrial archaeology in Britain was only just beginning to emerge from its primitive stage of naive innocence. The three prize-programmes could be not unfairly described as politically illiterate, and it is this more than anything else which gives them period flavour and charm today. They belong to a departed world, the world of industrial archaeology's childhood, when steam-engines and canals provided a marvellous escape from reality. They showed the places where the industrial proletariat had worked and lived, but they did so rather in the spirit of the owner of a large country house making the kitchens and stables available for public inspection, presenting these features as quaint and in their minor-key way interesting, but secondary to the main business of drawing-rooms, ballrooms and picture galleries. If a factory, like a mansion, is, so to speak, turned back to front, so that one regards the workers' entrance as the front door, the whole enterprise begins to look different. But to insist that this should be done, as a matter of both social justice and professional integrity, is a conscious political act and it is bound to meet with great suspicion and hostility. The comparison is with an old-type Women's Institute meeting, where there was supposed to be no mention of politics or religion, subjects which might cause civil war among the membership. It is a peculiarly British attitude and *For Love or Money* planted a small bomb underneath it. How many people heard the explosion is difficult to say. But it was an indication of bigger changes to come.

Chronicle passed on from Surahammar, paternalism on the small scale, to Dortmund-Bövinghausen in the Ruhr, paternalism of mammoth proportions. Here was a great complex of early twentieth-century coal-mining buildings, built around lawns, trees and quadrangles to produce an effect not at all unlike that of a major English public school. Why had these hard-headed coal-owners gone to so much trouble? Why had they engaged a fashionable and expensive architect for the job? Why such a thick, luxurious icing on such a workaday cake? The attempt to discover the answers was another piece of *Chronicle*'s public pioneering in the industrial archaeology field, and, for those with ears and eyes to understand, it threw considerable light on the nature of German capitalism and German industrial society.

Here was one of the most advanced coal-mines of its day, the first to install electrically-operated winding gear, made by Siemens and miraculously preserved in a huge machinery hall, complete to the last marble switchboard. With its steel and glass structure, its Egyptian-style carvings and its stained glass ornamentation, the Machinery Hall – it has to have the capitals – is a shrine for both art historians and industrial historians. It represents a great mining concern telling the world in general and its fellow German industrialists in particular that it was technically advanced and, equally important, that it was run by very

(Opposite) *Machinery Hall at Dortmund-Bövinghausen.* (Above) *Original Siemens winding gear still preserved inside.*

cultured people. Everything here is Art Nouveau, Jugendstil, the pit-head baths, the apprentice school and the mortuary included. And the lawns and trees in front of the baths and locker-rooms – 'A totally new idea', said the head of the Regional Department of Historic Monuments, 'based on social reasons, to give the workers some green, to contrast with most other factories which were dirty and dreary. In this building, the worker could change and wash himself before going home across the green.' And just outside the mine area was the new workers' Garden City, built in the English style, 'sturdy individual family houses, rather like some of London's garden suburbs, official

compensation for the hard life that the miners had underground'.

This was the 'why' as well as the 'what' of industrial archaeology. It was an unpopular approach in 1973 but much more widely accepted today. Once again, one has to pose an unanswerable question. Paul Johnstone had the ultimate responsibility for these programmes and without his support and confidence and his persuasiveness in high places, they could never have been financed, made or screened. Did he, however, realise the implications and the cultural importance of what he was doing? Was he backing the programmes on the basis of journalistic instinct or of considered judgement? One cannot, alas, put this problem to him, but one can be sure that he would have enjoyed discussing it. Nobody is ever fully aware of what one is doing at the time when one is actually doing it. If a television programme has any merit, it has something useful and interesting to say to its viewers there and then, but it also contains the seeds of future attitudes and ideas, a fact which is not likely to become apparent until several years later.

There is, in this sense, no such thing as a 'safe' programme. It may seem safe enough when it is broadcast, but to someone who studies it 10 or 20 years afterwards, it may suggest possibilities which are far from safe. The last item in *For Love or Money* illustrates this. It referred to the comprehensive catalogue of Poland's technological monuments which had recently been completed, in which each watermill, ironworks and limekiln was meticulously described and illustrated, an achievement unequalled in any other country. It drew attention to the 300 monuments scheduled for conservation, taking two early nineteenth century sites, the iron furnaces at Bobrza and the iron works at Sielpia as examples. What the programme did not say is something which has only become apparent more recently, that the Communist countries keep industrial archaeology on a very tight rein. In Britain, the United States or Sweden the industrial archaeologist is free to carry out his researches and take his photographs pretty well where he pleases, but in Poland, Romania or East Germany any attempt to interview old workers, visit factories or take pictures of bridges, railway stations or industrial premises will be viewed with the greatest suspicion and may very well lead to arrest and punishment. One is wise to confine one's attentions to rural blast-furnaces and cornmills built a century ago or more, and of no conceivable interest to the intelligence organisation of any potential enemy. Industrial archaeology, as the British understand it, cannot be practised under a totalitarian system.

By promoting these four programmes, three dealing with Britain and one with the Continent, *Chronicle*, under Paul Johnstone's leadership, grasped the industrial archaeology nettle while it was still young and soft and before its capacity to sting had developed. If such programmes were to be made today, it is most interesting to wonder what form they would take and what the public response would be.

Maximilian

John Julius Norwich

Early in the morning of 19 June 1867, the Emperor Maximilian of Mexico, younger brother of the Austrian Emperor Franz Josef, was executed by a firing squad. Sixty years later his widow, hopelessly insane, died quietly in a moated castle a few miles outside Brussels. These two deaths, over half a century apart, marked the culmination of a single tragedy, one of the most poignant in modern political history and perhaps the last to be played out as Sophocles or Shakespeare might have written it – in personal terms.

The question of how this young, idealistic Austrian Archduke – he was only thirty-four when he died – found himself in Mexico in the first place introduces yet another Emperor into the story: Napoleon III of France. Napoleon had always been fascinated by the New World, and had somehow resented the fact that his country had enjoyed so much less influence there than his English and Spanish neighbours. Mexico, with its fabulous mineral wealth which had already made it the producer of the world's silver, attracted him most of all; and in 1861 an unexpected turn of events in that country provided him with precisely the opportunity he needed.

The history of Mexico had been a sad one. By now it was a little over three centuries since a party of some four hundred Spanish conquistadors under Hernan Cortés had defeated and destroyed the Aztec Empire of Montezuma and transformed its whole vast territory into a colony of Spain. Those Spaniards, and the succeeding generations of their countrymen who followed them, did much for the land and its people. They bestowed on it their magnificent language, their art and architecture and their cultural traditions, and they introduced the Christian faith which, despite the repressive tendencies of Spanish Catholicism and the worst atrocities of the Inquisition, constituted none the less an incomparable improvement on the old pre-Hispanic religion whose only liturgy was that of human sacrifice. (It is recorded that only a few years before Cortés' arrival the consecration of the new temple in the Aztec capital of Tenochtitlan had required the sacrifice, within four days, of 80,000 victims, all of whom met their deaths in the traditional manner – the blood-soaked priests tearing out the still-beating hearts from the bodies and offering them up for the appeasement of the insatiable gods.) Politically, however, they allowed their Mexican subjects no rights of any kind or any experience of government, with the obvious result that when, in 1810, the latter at last managed to free themselves of Spanish domination, what followed was chaos. For fifty years the young Republic of Mexico was torn apart by one civil war after another – until, in January 1861, there rode triumphantly into Mexico City a President unlike any that had gone before: a left-wing liberal of pure Indian stock named Benito Juarez.

No national leader ever had humbler origins. Born of illiterate peasant parents in a remote village in the province of Oaxaca and almost entirely self-educated, he spoke nothing but the local Indian dialect until the age of twelve; his swarthy complexion was further accentuated by the jet-black suit and high collar that he always wore, even through the savage heat of the Mexican summer. Yet within that tiny frame – he was barely five feet tall – and behind that dark, expressionless face there burned a passionate love of his country and an inflexible determination to cast Mexico in the mould that he himself had conceived. In that mould there was no room for the *haciendas*, the vast properties and estates of the old Spanish aristocracy, nor even for the Roman Catholic church, whose immense power and wealth – to say nothing of the lifestyles of several leading members of the hierarchy – had indeed become something of a public scandal. Mexico, proclaimed Juarez, must be for the Mexicans; foreign influences, from whatever quarter they might come, must be mercilessly eliminated.

Unfortunately, after its half-century of internal strife, the country was left virtually bankrupt and heavily in debt to several European governments. Juarez himself, who had earlier spent prolonged periods of exile in the United States, had been obliged to compromise his principles to the extent of accepting American subventions – undesirable perhaps, but preferable to those from elsewhere – to carry him through the first difficult years; but within a few months of his assuming office he saw America herself plunged into a paralysing civil war. With his one source of financial support gone, he had no choice but to suspend all payments on European loans. The three European nations most seriously affected by this decision – Britain, France and Spain – reacted at once and with vigour to what the British Minister in Mexico City described as 'barefaced robbery', and on 30 October 1861 signed a convention agreeing on the joint occupation of the port of Vera Cruz. The real measure of their agreement, however, was a good deal less complete than it appeared; for while Britain was careful to disclaim any territorial ambitions, Spain was largely impelled by dreams of re-establishing herself in her former colony – and Napoleon too was out for everything he could get.

But how was he to get it? A limited occupying force shared with two potential rivals could not possibly produce the sort of results the French Emperor had in mind; diplomatic and political offensives would also be necessary. Napoleon was pondering the question when he was approached, through his Spanish wife, the Empress Eugénie, by a powerful group of right-wing Mexican émigrés in Paris. These men, representing the dispossessed Catholic landowners of the old régime, were determined to oust Juarez once and for all and to replace the Republic with a properly autocratic monarchy under which they could return to

Benito Juarez

their former prosperity. Naturally they could count on the full backing of the Church, whose lands and properties Juarez had confiscated wholesale to pay his soldiers' salaries. Their problem now was to find a suitable sovereign – young, able, energetic, irreproachably Catholic, and of birth and breeding such as to enable him to treat as an equal with the noblest princes of Europe.

They did not have to look far; the Archduke Maximilian of Austria seemed the ideal candidate. Appointed while still in his early twenties to the command of the Imperial navy, he had reorganised it on English lines and within a very few years had completely transformed it as a fighting force. Later, as Governor and Viceroy of Venetia-Lombardy – in those days still a province of the Austrian Empire – he had done much to overcome the resentment felt by the Italian popu-

The right-wing émigrés who offered the Mexican throne to Maximilian

lation against its foreign masters, and would have done more if the Emperor, jealous of his brother's dazzling success, had not goaded him into resignation. He was now living with his wife Charlotte – daughter of King Leopold I of Belgium and first cousin of Queen Victoria – in the castle of Miramar, just outside Trieste, which he had finished building only the year before. He was twenty-nine, out of a job, and bored stiff.

It was thus scarcely surprising that when Maximilian received the formal offer of the imperial throne of Mexico he should have accepted it with enthusiasm. 'It gives me the chance,' he wrote in his diary, 'to free myself once and for all from the pitfalls and oppressions of a life devoid of action. Who, in my position, in youth and health, with a devoted and energetic wife spurring me on, would do otherwise?'

There was, admittedly, the problem of Juarez to be considered; but Napoleon, as principal sponsor of the enterprise, brushed all such objections aside. The emigrés had assured him that Juarez was already tottering, and had no support among the people. Even before Maximilian landed in Mexico the whole country would have rallied to the imperial flag. Besides, the French expeditionary force was now to be considerably increased in size; with the navy firmly established at Vera Cruz, a military force would march the 300-odd miles to Mexico City and proclaim the new Empire. Maximilian would enter his capital not as a hated conqueror, but to the cheers and rejoicings of his ecstatic subjects.

So wrote Napoleon. Within a few months, however, reports began to arrive from Mexico which suggested that the situation there was not quite what he had

(Above) *Empress Charlotte and Emperor Maximilian;* (below) *the imperial couple being conveyed by barge to the Novara, 14 April 1864 (painting by Cesare dell'Acqua).*

The ceremonious leave-taking at Miramar (painting by dell 'Acqua)

been led to expect. The French, British and Spanish forces in Vera Cruz had been met not with cheers but with cold hostility and fear – scarcely surprising since Juarez had decreed that any Mexican offering them help or co-operation was to be executed on the spot – and had been obliged not only to recognise but also to negotiate with the Republican Government. They had then begun to quarrel among themselves, and early in 1862 the British and Spanish had sailed off, leaving the French alone to pursue an adventure which was looking increasingly perilous with every day that passed. Malaria and yellow fever, endemic along one of the unhealthiest coasts in the world, were taking such a hideous toll that out of seven thousand men less than six thousand were fit to take part in the march to the capital. And there was worse news to come: on 5 May – a date ever afterwards to be celebrated in

Mexico – 4000 Mexicans, armed with obsolete rifles left over from Waterloo and sold off cheaply to them by the British government years before, inflicted a pulverising defeat on the French invaders at the city of Puebla.

By now the Archduke was being advised on all sides to withdraw from the affair while there was still time; but he remained firm. Encouraged as always by the determined Charlotte, he refused, as he put it, 'to let Napoleon down'. The French Emperor for his part, though his letters to Maximilian never betrayed a hint of anxiety, had come to understand that he had been hopelessly misinformed about the real state of affairs in Mexico and had allowed himself to be manoeuvred into an impossible situation. But he also knew that there could be no backing out now. 'In France,' as he privately confessed, 'it is no longer possible to be mistaken.' All he could do was to send major reinforcements to his troops in the field, with orders to smash their way through to the capital whatever the cost might be.

Ultimately, 30,000 men succeeded where 6000 had failed. After a two-month siege Puebla surrendered and Juarez, several of whose best commanders had been captured, was forced to abandon the capital and withdraw to the little town of San Luis Potosi 300 miles away to the north. Nevertheless, it was only on 7 June 1863 that the conquering French were able to make their triumphal entry into Mexico City and have Maximilian proclaimed Emperor; and not until ten months after that that the young couple were ready to sail to their new dominion. By now all Maximilian's early optimism had deserted him; he wrote to a friend: 'I am about to leave for many years to engage on a dangerous task, for the throne of Mexico is, unquestionably, a dangerous one. . . . If I were to hear that the whole Mexican project had come to nothing, I assure you I should jump for joy – but then, what about Charlotte?'

Indeed, to anyone reading the diaries and correspondence of the time, it is clear that Charlotte had from the beginning been far more enthusiastic about Mexico than her husband; and in the weeks leading up to their departure, when all Europe knew that the two of them were sailing quite possibly to their deaths, she was the only one untroubled by fear or doubts. A pious blue-stocking, without a ray of humour, she may already have been showing early signs of the mental instability that was to overshadow the greater part of her life. On her wedding day one of those present had commented on 'her rather strange look, and her total lack of charm or grace', and we now find her writing to her grandmother, the exiled Queen Marie-Amélie of France: 'To take upon oneself the immense responsibility of refusing a throne would be failing in one's duty towards God, for when one is called upon to reign it becomes a vocation.'

Whether her husband would have expressed himself in such terms is doubtful – particularly since, only a fortnight before his departure, he received a further shock which caused him such anger and bitterness that he actually announced his decision to abandon the whole venture. This was the result of a message from Franz Josef, giving his consent only on condition that his brother renounced all rights to the Austrian inheritance for himself, his heirs and successors. To Maximilian, this was the final betrayal. Franz Josef had been aware of the preparations for two and a half years; why had he thus waited till the eleventh hour before imposing these savage terms? It took frantic telegrams between Paris and Vienna, and a personal visit by the Austrian Emperor to Miramar, to persuade the Archduke to receive the delegation of émigrés already waiting in Trieste and formally to accept from them the imperial crown of Mexico. But the strain had told on him. The evening before they were due to sail, his doctor found him alone in the summer-house, in a state of nervous collapse. At that night's farewell banquet Charlotte, calm and confident as ever, presided alone while her husband lay sobbing uncontrollably and the doctor struggled to save him from a complete breakdown. For four days he kept to his bed, while his flagship, the Austrian frigate *Novara*, rode at anchor off the coast. Then at last, in the afternoon of 14 April 1864, the imperial couple embarked, the *Novara* spread her sails for Mexico, and Maximilian gazed back on his homeland for the last time.

He is said to have spent the greater part of the six-week voyage planning the details of the ceremonial and protocol to be followed at his new court. But the reception accorded to Charlotte and himself when they finally reached Vera Cruz was far from imperial. The population of the town, republican to a man, were sullen and unwelcoming; the French Admiral who came on board was furious at the *Novara's* choice of anchorage and warned them that the whole party would almost certainly be captured by bandits on their way through the mountains to the capital – for, as he put it, 'General Bazaine had no time to ensure their protection'. During the night a great storm blew down most of the makeshift decorations and when Maximilian and Charlotte disembarked the next morning to begin the long journey to Mexico City their spirits must have been low indeed.

As they progressed, however, the situation began

to improve. The Indians in the villages came out to greet them, and at Puebla of all places – the very city which had put up such a desperate resistance to the French only a year before – a cheering population lined the streets and the French garrison gave a magnificent ball to celebrate Charlotte's twenty-fourth birthday. Mexico City, into which they made their state entry on 11 June, gave them a still more rapturous welcome as they drove in their new state coach (ordered months before in Trieste and shipped out with them) through the flag-bedecked capital to the *Zocalo* – the great central square dominated by the Cathedral and the State Palace. The Mexicans have always loved colour and sumptuous parade; this procession, and the service of Consecration which followed it, provided them with the most brilliant display of pomp and circumstance that they had ever seen – an irresistible contrast to the sombre-suited, stony-faced Juarez, now travelling ceaselessly through the deserts of the north in a sinister black coach as the French army pursued him from one city to another. Throughout this 'wandering Presidency' as it came to be called, his courage and determination continued as strong as ever; but few people in Mexico City spared him much thought that evening, as the imperial couple appeared again and again on the palace balcony to acknowledge the cheers of their new subjects – least of all Maximilian and Charlotte themselves. For them, Mexico was at last fulfilling its every promise; they were not to know that within an hour or two they were to be driven out of their beds by vermin, and that the Emperor was to spend much of his first night in his new capital curled up on a billiard-table.

Not far off, however, on a wooded hill known to the locals as Chapultepec – the Hill of the Grasshoppers – which had once harboured the summer residence of Montezuma, the Spanish viceroys had built themselves another palace. It was derelict and dilapidated; but within a week the imperial couple were camping in one wing, and before long Maximilian – never happier than when he was supervising building operations – had transformed it into their principal home. 'The Schönbrunn of Mexico' he somewhat optimistically described it, while Charlotte wrote to the Empress Eugénie: 'The view is perhaps one of the finest in the world; I think it surpasses Naples. The air is excellent and suits us well. All this offers ample compensation for the patience we have to exercise in other respects.'

Patience was indeed at a premium. Maximilian and Charlotte did their best to set up a new court on the European model, but they soon found that Mexico was a far cry from Vienna or Brussels. Orders were disregarded, appointments forgotten, punctuality unknown. Efficient government was out of the question, finances rapidly descended into chaos – and were not helped by the Emperor's compulsive building. Scarcely had he finished the redecoration of Chapultepec in his own lavish taste than he began constructing a broad, tree-lined avenue stretching all the way from the palace to the city. Now known as the Paseo de la Reforma, it is still one of the most superb thoroughfares of the world, and the glory of the capital; but at the time it was an extravagance that Maximilian could not begin to afford. He had the French army to support, to say nothing of the right-wing Mexicans whose backing he needed – though as the weeks went by he came more and more to abominate their views. He himself was a liberal, considering his upbringing and the standards of the time; but they blocked all his liberal ideas, almost before he had time to express them. They even allowed him to feel their disapproval when he began a series of long provincial journeys, during which he would dress in Mexican style and chat with the peasants in the villages through which he passed.

Gradually, as the months went by, these tours grew longer and more frequent, and it became increasingly clear that Maximilian was growing discouraged, and that the problems of government were beginning to bore him. An able and diligent administrator while things went his way, he lacked the determination and the staying power to beat down stubborn opposition. It was so much easier to set off on another expedition to some distant province, showing himself to his subjects and, he probably imagined, gaining much local information that might prove useful in the future. But

Charlotte, remaining behind as Regent at Chapultepec, was not deceived. He wrote to her regularly, but interested as she may have been in his long and enthusiastic descriptions of the beauty of the country and its people, she noticed how rarely he mentioned the political and economic issues they had to face. Meanwhile, ministers and staff alike found her far more capable than her husband, who continued to spend money like water and hardly seemed to realise that his country was in the throes of civil war. Soon, too, he discovered another terrestrial paradise – Cuernavaca, only some fifty miles from the capital but 2000 feet lower, and possessed of one of the most perfect climates in the world.

At Cuernavaca Maximilian was in his element – reading, collecting insects and planning grandiose schemes for the country, all oblivious of the fact that both he and it were already heavily in debt. Charlotte, too, tried to be happy; she always did. But she knew perfectly well about the pretty young gardener's wife who was paying secret visits to her husband and was shortly to bear the son that she herself could never give him. This continued childlessness was beginning to prey on her mind. Something that in Europe would have been considered simply a misfortune was seen in Mexico as a shame and a humiliation, a subject for obscene songs and lampoons – something that Maximilian's enemies would never allow him, or her, to forget.

Thus their lives gradually grew apart, with the Emperor spending more and more time on tour or at Cuernavaca while the Empress governed from Chapultepec or on occasion travelled separately, protected by a detachment of French *zouaves*. But how much longer would the French remain? For the moment they were still holding Juarez at bay, keeping him and his men constantly on the move; but they could not be everywhere at once, and as soon as they left a conquered town the *Juaristas* – their numbers swelled after the end of the American Civil War by bands of Confederate refugees – would move in again, often with dreadful reprisals. In short, the situation had reached a stalemate. The French, at their present strength, might contain Juarez; they could never defeat him.

Napoleon III, now bitterly regretting that he had ever involved himself in the Mexican enterprise, sought only a means of withdrawing his army without loss of face.

Fortunately for him, Maximilian had rashly agreed before his departure to accept the responsibility for its maintenance; equally fortunately, within a year of his arrival, he found himself obliged to confess that this would no longer be possible. It was just the excuse for which Napoleon had been looking. His letter, which reached Mexico late in 1865, came as a shattering blow but hardly as a surprise:

Your Majesty's own statement that you are unable to contribute to its maintenance leaves me with no other choice than to withdraw my army. The evacuation, which will begin as soon as possible, will be carried out gradually and in such a way as not to upset public opinion or endanger the interests we both have at heart. . . . It may cause Your Majesty some temporary embarrassment . . .

Maximilian's reaction to these last words can be imagined. Napoleon was abandoning him, quite possibly to his death. His reply was cold and defiant:

I propose that you withdraw your troops immediately from the Mexican continent; I, guided by my honour, shall for my part try to defend my empire with the help of my new countrymen.

For Charlotte, however, defiance was not enough. Napoleon was entirely responsible for their having come to Mexico in the first place; he could not be permitted to shuffle off his moral obligations so easily. She herself would go to Paris, confront him and force him to keep his promises. In the summer of 1866 she left for Europe.

For some three months after her departure Maximilian remained firm in his resolve. Then, in October, there arrived a telegram which caused him more concern than Napoleon ever could. Charlotte was gravely ill. The nature of her illness was not described; yet the fact alone was enough to decide the Emperor on a course of action which he had until that moment resolutely rejected – abdication. Within forty-eight hours he had started for Vera Cruz; but when he reached Orizaba, about two-thirds of the way to the coast, he gave orders to stop. Was this what Charlotte,

Entry of Juarez into Mexico City, 1867

in sickness or in health, would have wished? Surely not. And what about his duty to Mexico, and his Habsburg honour? There and then, at Orizaba, he put the issue to a specially-convened Council of State; and it was they who decided that he should remain, as he put it, like a sentry at his post. Almost with relief, it seemed, he returned to Mexico City. Chapultepec he found already stripped of its furnishings, so he moved back into the old Palace. From one of its windows, hidden behind a curtain, he watched when, on 2 February 1867, the French army marched out of the capital; as it disappeared from view he turned to an aide and murmured, 'At last – we are free.'

And he was right. For the first time he could look down on a Mexico devoid of foreign bayonets. Though militarily he might be weaker, morally he was in a stronger position than ever before. His effective strength was reduced to a mere 9000 men – but they were all of them Mexicans. With this *national* army

behind him, he could for the first time confront Juarez on his own terms. One thing, however, was clear: he could not remain in the capital, with all its spies, conspiracies and intrigues. He must retire to some conservative stronghold and fight from there. On 13 February 1867 he left for Queretaro.

Queretaro was one of the oldest – and, incidentally, one of the most beautiful – cities of colonial Mexico, and one which from the outset had been staunchly loyal to the imperialist cause. Strategically, it was rather less suitable; the *Juaristas* found it all too easy to position themselves in the surrounding hills, and within a week of the Emperor's arrival the city was effectively under siege. Maximilian, however, had recovered all his former spirit. He had established his headquarters in the old Spanish convent of La Cruz – almost a fortress in itself, it was by far the most easily defensible building in the city – and despite frequent, if spasmodic, republican attacks was marching about through the town showing a disregard for danger that at times seriously alarmed his staff.

Alas, courage was no longer enough. Though the besiegers repeatedly proved unable to force their way into the convent, by the middle of May the situation in Queretaro had become untenable. The aqueduct on which it largely depended for its water supplies had been cut; food was practically non-existent. Somehow, Maximilian and his army must force their way out into the open country. A plan was carefully laid for one of the senior generals, Tomás Mejía, himself a pure-blooded Indian, to arrange a noisy diversion by all the 3000 Indians in the city while they did so. It might have worked; but just twenty-four hours before it was due to be put into effect, one of the Emperor's most trusted officers betrayed him. His name was Colonel Miguel Lopez. In the early hours of the morning of 15 May, the bolts of a small door in the garden wall of the convent were quietly drawn aside; the wall itself was breached; and the Republicans poured in. Maximilian was immediately awake. He dressed quickly and, accompanied by one of his aides, slipped out of the building with barely a moment to spare.

Beyond the town to the West was a gentle rise in the ground known as the Cerro de las Campanas – the Hill of the Bells. There it seemed just possible that the Emperor might be able to regroup his army and save something from the *débâcle*; but when he reached it an hour later it was plain to him that the position was hopeless. Nearly all his men were dead, captured or in hiding; he, with the few who had managed to join him, was now surrounded and under heavy fire. An officer was despatched to the Republican camp with a white flag. Its commander hurried out, and Maximilian delivered up his sword. The Empire was finished.

The convent of La Cruz, which until a short time before had been Maximilian's headquarters, now became his prison while word was awaited from Juarez as to what was to be done with him. At last it came. With his two senior surviving generals, Tomás Mejía and Miguel Miramón, he was to be tried by court martial. The decision can have caused him no surprise; but when he also learnt that the trial would be

held publicly in the local theatre, he refused pointblank to attend. Since he was by now quite seriously ill with dysentery, his doctor's certificate was accepted, and he was not present when the tribunal met on 12 June. It was just as well, for the result was a foregone conclusion: all three were sentenced to death by firing squad.

When the telegraph flashed the news to the chanceries of Europe, public opinion was outraged. Appeals for the Emperor's life flowed in from all sides – even from Garibaldi in Italy and from Washington, where the United States Government, guided by the Monroe Doctrine of European non-intervention in American affairs, had always opposed Maximilian. Juarez, however, remained immovable as ever. The appeals may even have hardened his heart still further, for he was now above all determined to show the world that his country was no longer to be swayed by any outside pressures: Mexico, from now on, was taking orders from no one.

Thus it came about that at half-past six in the morning of 19 June the Emperor Maximilian and his two most faithful Mexican supporters were driven from the Capuchin monastery in which they had spent the last period of their confinement to the place of execution – that same Hill of the Bells on which he had made his surrender a month before. The firing squad was already waiting. The Emperor, cool and utterly composed, shook hands with each man in turn, handing each a gold piece and reminding him to take careful aim. Just before the signal was given to fire, he called out in Spanish: 'I forgive everyone. I pray that everyone will also forgive me, and that my blood, which is now to be shed, will bring peace to my new country. Long live Independence! Viva Mexico!' They were his last words.

Maximilian died bravely and magnificently; but he died a failure. He was doomed from the start, for Mexico had no room for moderates. The ultrareactionaries who had summoned him to power had hoped for a despotic absolutism as in the old Spanish days; Maximilian's liberal dream of enlightened constitutional rule shocked and horrified them. Similarly his monarchist ideals were anathema to the re-

(Above) *The firing squad;* (inset) *the waist-coat worn by Maximilian at his execution.* (Left) *Maximilian's last moments in the Capuchin monastery, as portrayed in propagandist terms by Laurens.*

publicans. Moreover his enemy Juarez possessed two immense strengths which he himself lacked. One was the power of concentration, the sheer stamina that enables a man to endure any amount of hardship or discouragement without even momentarily losing sight of his ultimate objective. The other was simpler still: Juarez was a Mexican. The days of the Conquistadors were past. Europeans could no longer, whatever their motives, hope to carve out Empires for themselves in the New World. It was in Paris and at Miramar, not on the Hill of the Bells, that Maximilian's fate had been sealed.

And Charlotte's too — less violent, perhaps, than her husband's but far, far worse. Her own personal calvary had scarcely begun. She had arrived in Paris in August 1866 looking, as her lady-in-waiting described her, 'like a walking ghost'; the empress Eugénie, coming to call on her at the Grand Hotel, was horrified to find that the fresh young girl she remembered had turned, in only two years, into a sallow, haunted-looking old woman.

But also a determined one. Napoleon, himself a sick man and unable, in his guilt and embarrassment, to face her righteous indignation, had sent word that he was confined to bed and could not therefore receive her; but Charlotte brushed Eugénie's lame excuses aside. She would return the call on the following day — 'and if the Emperor refuses to see me,' she added with a grim smile, 'I shall break in on him.'

The threat was not lost on Eugénie, nor, it seems, on the Emperor when he heard it; for when Charlotte arrived at Saint-Cloud at noon on 11 August, both were waiting to receive her. Napoleon, suave and slippery as ever, tried to take the easy way out: the responsibility was no longer his — the decision lay with his government. But Charlotte would have none of it. Returning uninvited the next day she abandoned the logical, well-documented approach of the previous day and broke into a frenzy of vituperation. Her anxiety for her husband, together with her frustration and rage against the man who had betrayed their trust, had unhinged her mind. Sobbing and screaming hysterically, she was half-carried from the Palace. That night she wrote to Maximilian: 'I have achieved

150

THE MEXICAN MARTYR !

'The Mexican Martyr'; cartoon in The Tomahawk, 3 August 1867

nothing. . . . No power can aid us, for he has Hell on his side. He is the Devil in person. . . . He had an expression so hideous, it made my hair stand on end; it was the expression of his soul.'

One last shred of hope remained — Pope Pius IX in Rome. By the time she arrived there, Charlotte was incapable of rational pleading. Her audience was private and unrecorded; we only know that she emerged silent and distraught, and immediately ordered the removal of the papal guard of honour from her hotel. Her mental state was now deteriorating fast, as her thoughts became fixed on a single fear: poison. At the hotel she refused all food but oranges, eggs and nuts — which she could see from the unbroken peels and shells had not been tampered with — or chickens, killed and cooked by her one trusted maid in her presence. Early in the morning of 30 September she

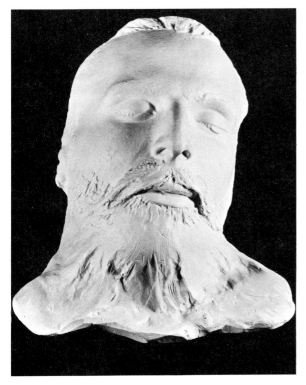

drove with her lady-in-waiting to the Trevi fountain, then knelt at the edge and drank the water from her cupped hands, crying triumphantly, 'Here at least it will not be poisoned.'

An hour later, in the Vatican, Pope Pius was sitting at breakfast; suddenly the Empress burst in and hurled herself at his feet, imploring protection against the assassins who were closing in on her, then plunging her fingers into his cup of chocolate and sucking them. Nothing could induce her to leave. That night she spent in the Vatican Palace – perhaps the first woman in its history to do so. Only on the following evening, when she suddenly fainted after another brainstorm, was she carried, unconscious, back to the hotel. For her frantic attendants it must have seemed an age before her brother, the Count of Flanders, arrived to escort her back to Miramar. There, a doctor was waiting. His name was Riedel, and he was the Director of the Vienna Lunatic Asylum.

Whether Charlotte ever knew of her husband's fate is an open question. She was still at Miramar when the

(Left) *Maximilian's death-mask;* (below) *his funeral barge leaving Mexico*

news reached Europe, but strict orders had been given that throughout the palace there should be no word spoken of the tragedy nor any sign of mourning. A month later she was taken back to Belgium. She was twenty-seven years old.

And for another sixty years she lived on. Tranquil now, but withdrawn into a world of her own, she never regained her reason and could endlessly confuse the lovely moated castle of Bouchout where she spent her last years with others she had known, at Miramar and Chapultepec. But never did her clouded mind forget her imperial past; and every afternoon, as she took her daily drive through the castle park, the gardeners and groundsmen would stand to attention, doff their hats, and cry 'Viva la Emperatriz!' as the carriage clattered by.

The funeral procession at Trieste

The Historian and *Chronicle*

John Hale

What can the academic historian bring to the making of films for reasonably wide audiences? What can he gain from making them that is relevant to his academic work? For the process is one of giving and taking. I learned something of how it works from making three programmes for *Chronicle*, all directed by Ken Shepheard. They were, respectively, about Renaissance Venice, Florence and Rome. All represented exhilarating but nerve-wracked holidays from archives and lecture rooms. None was as successful as it should have been. Yet all were better than they might have been had they not been created under the *Chronicle* influence: popularised seriousness, going to the dead past with the imperative 'bring it back alive'. These formulae, however, pulsed with inner contradictions. In addition there was the day-by-day struggle for *lebensraum* between words and images, between what is true because it is complex and what is useful because it can be grasped and remembered.

The first surprise was the difficulty of finding enough visual material to bring the age and its people to life. First, buildings. It is true that Italy retains a greater percentage of buildings constructed before 1550 than does any other country; hence the uniquely grave task Italy faces in preserving its heritage. But there are not so many as I had come to expect. Deluged by visual impressions the eye has to select. Tests made in exploring the psychology of vision have shown how this works. If a coin is held at an equal distance from a rich man and a poor one, it will seem bigger to the latter. If an estate agent, a botanist and a Don Juan undertake the same journey in the same time their accounts of it will differ: the estate agent will stress the condition and saleability of houses, the botanist the contents of gardens, the Don Juan will have looked most closely at the girls' legs.

Similarly I had, on my travels in Italy, screened out much that was later than or irrelevant to my chief interest and was shocked to find, when trying to choose a street scene or panorama for the screen, that I had been ignoring anomalies and eyesores all my life. Leaving aside the signs and drainpipes and parked cars and overhead wires that had plagued my attempts to photograph individual monuments, there were suddenly, as I looked with this new end in view, sleazy nineteenth-century tenements, even whole garages and cinemas that I had never noticed before, though I must have seen them. Nor had I noticed how much later (and often how distressing) were the façades of buildings I had walked through so many times in order to enjoy their Renaissance interiors. Now exteriors became of equal, of superior importance because interiors were usually too expensive and too time-consuming to light for film. Nor, mopping up in culture-tourist vein the palaces and churches, had I noticed how few ordinary houses of the period remained, and how very few were free from the accumulations or remodellings of later centuries. It took not my own eye, but the television camera, to reveal my blindness.

Of course there was a gain in this. An assumption was challenged, a love promoted from ritual to reappraisal, a sense of chronological process deepened. These were both academic and personal gains, sharply seasoned with a healthy sense of loss. But they complicated the construction of the visual plot, for our aim throughout was to show the viewer only what might have been visible *then*.

Secondly, people. However shopworn the phrase has become, it is still tempting to think that the Renaissance was somehow bound up with 'the discovery of the world and of man', and it is not just tempting to

153

think that Renaissance artists had learned how to record with a convincing naturalism the scenes and people of their day: it is true. The mastery of rendering observed reality in two dimensions was one of the successes so triumphantly noted by Vasari in his *Lives of the Painters*. And sculptors, too, had learned to recreate the sense of real presence that had been achieved by the marble portraitists of ancient Rome. Why, surely – I thought at first – the age had documented itself; no problem, let the rostrum camera roll.

But it is not like that. Art's gift to documentary television is *genre*, the painting of everyday life, everyday scenes. And *genre* did not appeal to Renaissance artists, especially to the finest of them, whose work, being most cherished, has been most likely to survive. Indeed, why should an artist, working in an atmosphere of competition and experiment, do anything as limiting as simply copy appearances, save as a preliminary study for something finer that could show his mind and imagination at work? The identifiable landscape, the minutely recorded interior, the flower and food piece, the topographical view: these all represented aspects of *genre* that were only taken seriously and brought to a high degree of finish later on – much to the advantage of documentaries on the seventeenth and later centuries, but of no use to me. Even in the minor arts – engraving, woodcut, intarsia, majolica – the designer was beguiled by paler reflections of the same impulses that pushed sculptors and painters aside from the mere slice-of-life: impulses to normalise, idealise, classicise, to use art to go beyond, not to drop into step with nature.

I began to realise why coffee-table evocations of the Renaissance used, over and over again, the same bits and pieces, a background to a religious painting here, there a book illustration or a detail from a painted wedding-chest. To be interested in one's world is not necessarily to be concerned to record it, warts and all. I come to envy those who could use film clips, old photographs or, perhaps best of all, the graphic journalism of magazines like the nineteenth-century *Illustrated London News*.

No illustration can communicate in its fulness the sense of being there, of something actually happening.

However exact, unposed, convincingly accidental the image may be, we know it is an image of some event at which we were not present and so it cannot satisfy the instinct to believe only in what we touch or see for ourselves. And the more we are educated by television into realising that film and still photography are activities that themselves have a history, have heroes and prostitutors, are subjects to be studied in their own right, the less conviction they carry as evidence of the actual. So the Victorian illustration of a news event has more empathic immediacy than an image captured by a lens: the formalised firing squad for Maximilian in Mexico than the newsreel camera showing the stagger and slumping of Kennedy in his funeral limousine. Some space for the imagination to say 'there – it must have been like that' is necessary before we fully believe. And television, burdened by its wooing of those who seek to be diverted at all costs from the reality of unpaid instalments and unjoyful beds and incomprehensible politics, becomes ever less capable of purveying a sense of the real.

This reflection is natural for the historian who works for television. For his professional business is with evidence, with facts and what they mean. All facts have to be manipulated if the context in which they are inserted – the history book – is to be readable. And in television, whose facts are images, the same transformations obtain, even more alarmingly, if the product is to have a wide appeal. So the historian can learn, from placing his images in a film, how he may have cheated by placing a fact in a book in a position that exaggerates its lustre, by forcing it to make a specific point.

For the temptations to cheat with images are more glaring. In the first place the images are fewer, and each has to 'last' longer, for the film has to please as well as inform and cannot be stopped or reversed, whereas the writer can rely on the reader to adjust his turning of the pages to the speed with which he absorbs the narration and the facts that give it flesh and credibility. And in the second place the images that are left in the film are not necessarily those around which the film-making was planned. A key image can be muffed and then scrapped. Another, less essential or even downright irrelevant, can prove so irresistible that it has to be written in, and the argument trimmed to absorb it. Yet again, there simply may be no image to illustrate a point and it will have to be dropped.

There are thus three temptations: to make an image 'mean' more than it should; to invent a significance for an image that is only there because of its glamour; and to make an argument look sound while it actually has a hole in it. These temptations also occur in the writing of a book. There is the irresistible quotation, for instance, which can be given a significance it should not really bear. There is the flash of organising insight which may squeeze the facts into patterns that merely throttle them into confessing what the historian thinks they ought to mean. There is the temptation to fill a gap by implication rather than with evidence. During the process of seeking and marshalling the many thousands of facts that go into a book these temptations can be yielded to almost imperceptibly; they are diminished in significance by the mass of the material, and by their dispersal amid the multiplicity of decisions that have to be made. But working for television brings one's hidden procedures into a simplifying and pitiless light. If it to some extent encourages fraud, it also exposes it.

So the historian has three lessons to learn: the extent to which his optical vision is blinkered by his dominant interest; the discrepancy between the sense of reality conveyed by written and visual evidence; and the relationship between the scattered fragments and the design into which they are reassembled.

Is there more to learn? Intelligibility, accessibility: these qualities, essential for a documentary programme, are also encouraged by the challenge of the back rows of a lecture theatre or the questioning implicit in a tutorial or seminar – though the real or fancied sophistication of undergraduates prevents them from asking the grandly straightforward questions one has to anticipate on the lips of an average, interested television viewer.

Simplify, clarify: these television imperatives are a call to mental order stronger than classroom relationships can demand. But they also summon one to judgment at the bar where wait the dead whose experience one is purporting to convey; experience that was, to individuals, or to whole generations, neither simple nor clear. Treated as tax- or cannon- or diseasefodder while they lived, must they now undergo the last indignity of being served up as entertainment? Can television time, jerking impersonally along on the studio clock, do justice to time as subjectively felt by *people*? 'Time travels in divers places with divers persons. I'll tell you who Time ambles withal, who Time trots withal, who Time gallops withal, and who he stands still withal.' Thus Shakespeare: and our own knowledge. But 'simplify, clarify', these words, so admirable in themselves, can, as the escapement of television time, become the 'tick-tock' of impending treachery. Television is better at recreating events than experience, better at telling a story than revealing what that story meant to its protagonists. It is a peremptory medium and its summons to cut the cackle means that there are wide areas of feeling to which it – or at any rate documentaries about the past – cannot give a voice. Not for me, alas, are the interviews with survivors or participants, the stuttered utterance, the heavily breathing pause, the glance of appeal, that enables the contemporary documentary to trump the simulacra of the real deployed by the drama department.

The gradual realisation that television is better at telling stories than revealing states of mind was valuable. My inclination as a historian is to assemble evidence that can be sorted out to yield answers to the question: what was it like to be alive then? Yet without a sense of narrative, of chronological flow somewhere in the background, the answers seem detached from the experience they purport to describe. To analyse his material and to bridge gaps by reference to enduring human traits, the social historian needs from time to time to limber up in the intellectual gymnasium run by the social sciences, to practise especially on the equipment provided by the social psychologist and the social anthropologist. But he also needs exercise in narrative, and working for television makes this form of work-out compulsory. It can thus provide a form of retraining that is not necessarily prompted by lecture or classroom.

A smaller lesson, but one that will take more time to describe, is the way in which experience of television can bring home a danger every historian knows he must avoid: the over-weighting of isolated pieces of evidence. When planning the programme on the history of Venice, I wanted to illustrate a very early description of how the lagoon dwellers had lived. Early in the sixth century AD, Cassiodorus had referred to their houses as being 'like the nests of sea-birds, built half in water, half on land'. It seemed a frail hope, but if such a construction could be found it would make an effective visual point about the age before the Venice of brick and stone and marble began to appear.

Ken Shepheard could not come to direct the reconnaissance, so I went to Venice to do it alone. On the launch that ran from the airport to the city I talked to the young ticket collector. He turned out to be a keen duck-shooter in his spare time, who knew the lagoon well and had a boat of his own. He was due for some days of leave, and I asked him to provide my transport.

I left the planning of the lagoon sequence till the end, and when the final day arrived it was densely foggy. Hoping nevertheless that it would clear and that meanwhile my charts and Agostino's experience would enable us to find our way, we set off, just after dawn, muffled against the January cold and damp, in his tiny motorboat. It lay low in the water and for the first two hours water, for a few yards around, was all we could see; a faint thickening in the vapour meant a channel marker to skirt, a more booming echo of the motor, the bulk of an unseen islet. Guided by shadows and sounds we pushed cautiously northwards through the fog, tracing a course which seemed to make sense on the chart. By ten o'clock the fog, though paler, was as thick as ever and there was no island where there should have been one – the island of bones, to which remains from the cemetery island of S. Michele are transferred when all the plots there are filled up. We nosed this way and that, raced the engine and then cut it to hear any echo the better, but there was no variation, nothing but water and the tent of fog that moved and stopped as we did.

There was nothing particularly disturbing about being lost, though the lagoon had come to seem menacingly large and lonely. The fog would lift. We had wine and grapes and cheese. It was the passage of time that made me nervous; before the sun set we had not only to reconnoitre the island of S. Andrea with its fortress in the centre of the lagoon, but to coast all the way to Chioggia looking for a location for the film's conclusion – the city's continuing fight for survival against the seas pounding on the lagoon's fringe, the *Lidi*.

We would have to give up Cassiodorus' bird's nest and turn back for S. Andrea, hoping that at least by noon the visibility would improve. But without the bone island as a fixed point of departure, even to reach S. Andrea, over two hours away in sunlight, seemed all too uncertain. Agostino, catching my restlessness, set off in a wide reckless arc as though longing for the satisfaction of ramming something solid.

He nearly did: a sudden paling in the fog ahead of us was followed by a snatching away of tier after tier of gauze to reveal a creek with clear water and slimy banks. Hardly had the engine screeched into reverse than the fog started billowing towards us again, but not before I had seen, ahead and on the bank of the creek, a large shack entirely built, roof and walls, of reeds. Whether fisherman's or hunter's shelter, it was near enough to Cassiodorus' bird's nest to serve. Another stirring in the vapour enabled Agostino to identify the islet itself – dingy, spongy and deserted enough to serve as a perfect site for a piece of sound recording. It was called, somewhat ludicrously, Montagna d'Oro, Mountain of Gold and I knew that I could guide the team there when the time came to film. 'House of Reeds', I marked on the chart with a sense of triumph. *Venice – the Most Serene Republic* was going to get off to a marvellously evocative start.

We had brilliant weather the following April, cool but so crystalline that even from the low gunwale of our heavy *topo* we could see the whole width of a lagoon that now seemed very small, highly populated – and hideously noisy: every snarl from every speed-boat, every put-put from every prawning boat carried to our sound equipment with new-minted clarity. The

Mountain of Gold was now not evocatively dingy but sordid. Its muddy flanks were gaudy with unbiodegradable plastic refuse. As time after time I trudged brightly towards the camera along the track we had painstakingly cleared of disposed-of junk I was all too aware that my voice was now in competition with a pile driver thuddingly proclaiming its contribution to mainland prosperity. I fluffed my way through take after take, hated by the cameraman, openly loathed by the recordist. And in Ken's courteous but clamped expression I could read the lesson he was repeating to himself – never let them do the recce by themselves. But there was one grain of comfort; wait till they see the House of Reeds!

We managed at last to get some commentary recorded, leaden but audible, and loaded up and set off for the site where reproach would turn to congratulation. It was late now, dangerously late perhaps for the light, but the noisy boats were fewer and the pile-driver silent. Finger on chart, eye on the grassy lumps (how had we missed them all?) that broke the water and involved one vain landing and search after another while the light faded, I was able at last to point and, with a catch in my voice, announce 'There it is!'

And there was a catch. The house was there. It was covered with reeds. But these were tacked over a bijou residence for bathing parties. There were curtained windows, an uncompromising stuccoed chimney stack; and the staring front door bore a poker-work plaque lettered with the Italian equivalent of *Mon Repos*.

With reproachful self-control the camera crew lay in the mud and manoeuvred a few blades of grass to hide this monstrosity's architectural pretensions. Ken wordlessly indicated a couple of short takes. No one looked at or spoke to me. I ate alone in a trattoria that in years of knowing Venice had always been a source of solace. That night it provided none.

As it happened, the shot was evocative enough to cover the quotation from Cassiodorus. My reputation, in ruins on the lagoon, was partially saved in the cutting room. But while the disgrace faded, the moral remained all too clearly defined: never assume that you have found what you looked for until you have checked its context. How often, in the exploration of the foggy lagoon of an archive's holdings, a phrase gleams, while time runs out, as the perfect reflection of a hunch or a need. Never use it as the sufficient image of some wished-for conclusion. Always go back. Always confirm.

If working for television can be helpful in this and in the other ways that I have indicated, what has television to gain from the professional historian? As soon as the question is posed I know that I can offer only a personal, and therefore partial answer. What, then, have *I* to offer in return for money, challenge, travel, a sometimes rewarding, often merely debilitating tension, the pleasure of watching the dedication and expertise of others?

I find this difficult to answer, mainly because I think that television is overwhelmingly best-suited to dealing with recent and contemporary history. Then the faces can be seen to speak, the bodies to move; the settings are familiar, if only from newsreel or newspaper; above all the viewers' memories can cover the necessarily bare bones of hasty narrative with a nostalgic semblance, if not an actual sense, of verisimilitude. But the remoter past is, simply, past. To its recreation on screen the average viewer brings little from his experience apart from slogans 'No Popery' and caricatures 'Sir Walter Raleigh was the Man with the Cloak'. At best they will be unreverberative; at worst positively misleading.

Television, it seems to me, is better at advertising history than at purveying it. It can provide trailers – glamorous, poetic, enthralling – for the Real Thing, but the Real Thing must be a book. Only a book can do justice to history's complexity. To clarify the remote past is to falsify it.

Even during the Renaissance this was a live issue, the nub of a controversy between the age's greatest historians and political thinkers, Niccolo Machiavelli and Francesco Guicciardini. To the former, the past was primarily important as a source of examples of what action to take in the present: faced by a political problem, the wise statesman thumbs through the history of ancient Rome, locates a comparable problem and imitates the measures that led to its solution. To

Guicciardini this was doubly simplistic. To follow Machiavelli's doctrine of imitation, the past had first to be schematised to the point of unreality. In the second place, situations and their causes and personalities are so fraught with contingencies and complexities that they can never recur in a form that makes imitation possible. Problems may recur, but their context never. The past teaches only by recording human experience and nourishing wisdom, not by offering answers. And when Guicciardini, having written two unfinished histories of Florence located in a past remote from his own experience, finally settled to his masterpiece, it was an account of the history of Italy in his own times. Here he could at last do justice to the reality of the past, and offer a sympathetic guidance through the overwhelming freight of detail that alone could remind his readers what it had been like to have lived through the forty catastrophic years 1494 to 1534. He turned, in fact, to what television can do so well: tell a story which is effective because its complexity rings true to its audience's own experience of life, and which can rely for its success on a measure of collaboration with that experience.

In a sense, recent history is weighty gossip, the public version of private experience. The remoter past, tapping no such willingness on the audience's part to participate, is doomed, when measured out in thirty- or fifty-minute doses, to appear merely anecdotal or picturesque: diverting, possibly intellectually good for you, but only fraily capable of extending – as good history should – the individual's self-awareness. That takes time: time to recreate an environment and a set of feelings that the viewer will come to accept as a valid alternative to his own, a world that can be not merely observed but entered. And this is where historical time is worsted by television time.

So my aim has to be limited: to instruct, cajole, entertain, get the 'feel' of the subject as right as possible, and infuse the programme with enough sense of urgency to give at least some of it a chance of lingering in the memory. It is a thoroughly worthwhile aim. But is it one that requires the services of an academic historian?

A good deal of what he has to offer could, after all, be passed on, stage by stage as the final script took shape, to a professional scriptwriter. The clearer the story to be told the more this is likely to work well. But to succeed, the relationship would have to be much closer than the usual one between writer and adviser, because each stage – even during the shortening or pepping-up of a passage while filming or dubbing – can involve the intrusion of an image or a phrase which would mar the sense of overall rightness that it is the historian's job to ensure. And collaborations of this sort can be uneasy in personal terms, and expensive.

Of course, *Chronicle* has had notable successes with writers with strong historical interest and knowledge who are not academic. But restricting myself to my own experience, I would say that the academic is especially useful when the story line is not particularly obvious, and when the programme needs to evoke and explain and analyse as well as describe. Here the sense of rightness, and a knowledge of source material that it is difficult for a programme researcher to acquire in the time, can give life and the stamp of truth. He is also – perhaps more controversially – useful as a 'talking head'. Not so much on account of personal presentability as because he can communicate a sense of commitment to the study of history that can only be conveyed by someone who devotes all or much of his career to it. That he can be seen as well as heard to be moved by his subject is part of the 'advertisement for history' function I have referred to, and which Paul Johnstone's standards and the energetic devotion of his colleagues have sustained with such conspicuous success.

Silbury Hill

R. J. C. Atkinson

The excavation of Silbury Hill in 1968–70 was one of the largest operations mounted by *Chronicle* under Paul Johnstone's direction. I offer this account of it as an affectionate and admiring tribute to his memory, and to his great achievement in presenting archaeology on television.

Silbury is one of the largest prehistoric earthworks in Europe, and stands like a huge grass-grown plum-pudding beside the Bath Road, a few miles west of Marlborough in north Wiltshire. Its base covers more than five acres, or not much less than Trafalgar Square in London, and its top would come about three-quarters of the way up Nelson's Column there. Its enormous size has attracted the curiosity of archaeologists for more than two centuries; but it has deterred most of them from digging into it. The earliest exploration, in 1776, took the form of a vertical shaft dug from the centre of the flat top, but apparently without result. The most ambitious was a narrow tunnel, dug in 1849 from the base of the mound on the south side to the centre and around it. The records of this showed that near the centre the remains of the contemporary vegetation were preserved in a quite unprecedented way.

The idea of a new excavation, sponsored by the BBC, was first put forward by John Irving, then a television and radio producer in Bristol. We discussed this in 1960; but I then felt that the cost would be so great, and the results so speculative, that if the money were available it could be used better on an alternative project offering a better hope of archaeological reward. With my friend Professor Stuart Piggott, I put up a scheme for the complete re-excavation of a number of Neolithic and Bronze Age barrows near Stonehenge, which had been only cursorily examined

150 years before. In the end, however, it became clear that there was insufficient money for either project, and both were dropped.

Five years later the Silbury project was revived by *Chronicle*, but this time as Silbury or nothing. No alternative scheme would be considered. After some heart-searching, but in the belief that a new excavation would provide evidence that could be found nowhere else, I agreed to direct the excavation, subject to agreement on the funds to be provided for two or for three seasons of work. Early in 1966 we had obtained the permission of the owner, Lord Avebury, and of the official guardians, the Ministry of Works. Thereafter the detailed planning went ahead, though slowly at first, because until October 1967 almost all my spare time was absorbed by my duties as Dean of the Faculty of Arts of my College.

The main objectives on which we settled were, first of all, to re-open the tunnel of 1849 and follow it to the centre and beyond; secondly, to examine the surrounding ditch, both on the north side, where it was known to be waterlogged in the lower levels throughout the year, and on the south side, where it was narrower, and probably shallower and drier; and thirdly to excavate part of the flat top of the mound and of the marked terrace below it, and some at least of the other shorter and narrower terraces which could be seen elsewhere. We also planned to re-open the large trench cut into the base of the mound in 1922 by Sir William Flinders Petrie, the famous Egyptologist, opposite the causeway at the east end of the south ditch.

For this programme of work an experienced local archaeologist, Major Lance Vatcher of the Avebury Museum, agreed to act as deputy director. The tun-

159

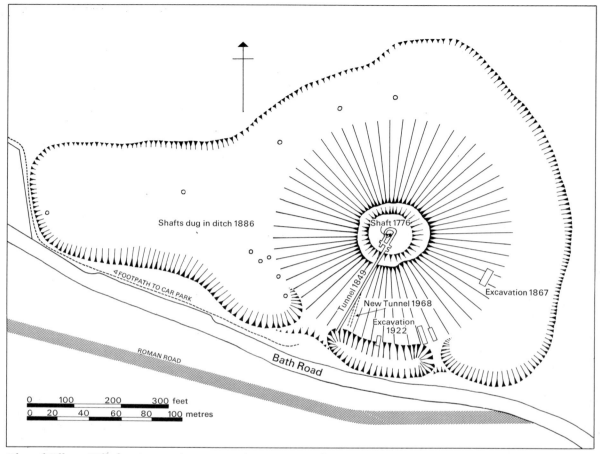

Plan of Silbury Hill showing previous excavations

Within the plan:
Shafts dug in ditch 1886
Shaft 1776
FOOTPATH TO CAR PARK
Tunnel 1849
New Tunnel 1968
Excavation 1867
Excavation 1922
ROMAN ROAD
Bath Road

0 100 200 300 feet
0 20 40 60 80 100 metres

nelling was to be done by mining students from University College, Cardiff, directed by Dr John Taylor, then a lecturer in our Mining Department, with one of his research students, Mr Collis James, as his deputy. The archaeological team was to be recruited from Cardiff and other Universities. The post of information officer, essential for a project which was going to attract huge numbers of visitors, was filled by another local resident, Commander Jan Davies RN, who had until recently been the Director for Wales of the National Trust's Project Neptune. These were all most fortunate choices, and I can hardly express adequately my thanks to all my colleagues, including many whom I have no space to name here, for their part in this very unusual and demanding project. We were equally fortunate in our liaison with BBC West in Bristol, initially through Mr James Dewar and later through Mr Ray Kite. *Chronicle* itself, personified by Paul Johnstone and David Collison, gave us unfailing support, both in high-level discussions within the BBC, sometimes of a somewhat Byzantine nature, and in our numerous local difficulties.

The planning involved unusual requirements, not encountered in a more conventional excavation. For the tunnel we needed quantities of steel mining-arches and special mining-timber, a compressor to power the forced-ventilation fan and the air-tools used at the working face, and an electric supply for lighting, as well as a workshop with various pieces of equipment and a GPO telephone and a water-supply. Because work underground would be done in shifts, as in more conventional mining, we had to provide caravans, hot showers and a kitchen and mess-hut for the tunnelling teams. To explore the structure of the mound and the waterlogged ditch we had to commission specialists equipped with drilling-rigs and geophysical instruments. To deal with the well-preserved vegetation, snails and insects which we expected to find we had to engage resident and visiting experts, and provide a laboratory for them on the site.

In addition, the position of Silbury alongside a very busy trunk road (the parallel section of the M4 motorway had not then been built) made it necessary to exclude visitors by fencing a long stretch of the road, and to provide a new carpark near Avebury, with a long access-path which also had to be fenced securely, to prevent short cuts over private land. All this took a great deal of time and effort.

Whilst these plans were being made, two preliminary investigations were put in hand. The first was the radiocarbon dating of a deer-antler pick-axe found in earlier excavations. The second was the making of a contoured plan of the mound and ditch, and the insertion of numerous reference-pegs, by the Geography Department of the University of Bristol.

Fenced-in area of the excavation, seen during the first televised broadcast in April 1968

This was later supplemented by a very detailed contoured plan, plotted by the Department of Surveying and Photogrammetry at University College, London, from air-photographs specially taken by Meridian Airmaps Ltd.

The news of the forthcoming excavation was released at a BBC press conference in London in the middle of September 1967, with a television link from the site. My colleagues and I sat in the rain on a bale of straw, with the mound looming dimly behind us, and answered as best we could our unseen questioners in London. It was an uncomfortable start. Four days later the first *Chronicle* programme was transmitted, in which I described what we hoped to do (subsequently published, in rather different form, in *Antiquity*, XLI, December 1967, 259–62), and appealed for information from viewers who in their youth had crawled along the old tunnel of 1849, the mouth of which fell in during the first World War and was not sealed up again until 1923. This appeal produced about forty replies, some of which were recorded for use in future programmes.

At the end of March 1968, the huts and site-services began to be installed at Silbury, and a platform erected in front of the tunnel-entrance, with a scaffold bridge across the adjacent ditch. The excavation itself started on the evening of 7 April, preceded by an opening ceremony at which I cut the first turf with an inscribed spade and declared Silbury open, up to a point. The second *Chronicle* programme, previously recorded, was transmitted that night. The aim of this first two-week excavation was to drive a new tunnel into the mound, starting above and to the east of the entrance of the old one, so as to intersect the latter about twenty-two yards inside the mound. The outer part of the old tunnel was known to have collapsed, and its re-opening would have been difficult and hazardous.

We started in uncomfortable circumstances. The caravans provided for us were too few and too small; and a spell of intense frost, unseasonable for early April, froze our water supply and prevented the tunnelling teams from having hot showers at the end of their shifts. It took some days to return to proper

The late Bill Curtis, the senior miner

working-conditions. Meanwhile, within the first few hours, we encountered the first of many revetment-walls of chalk blocks, dividing the mound internally, which turned up as the tunnel progressed. A few days later, we cut through the carefully-laid filling of what proved to be a huge ditch buried beneath the mound, some fourteen yards wide. This was completely unexpected, and showed at once that beneath the present mound a smaller and earlier 'Silbury' lay concealed.

For this initial work we had the invaluable guidance of Mr Bill Curtis, a retired South Wales miner of great experience, who built almost single-handed a concrete portal for the tunnel mouth, with the date cast in the centre of the lintel, behind which at a brief foundation ceremony I buried a sealed bottle containing the names of the team. Sadly, this was his last contribution to a lifetime in the mining industry, for he did not live to see our work resumed in the summer. His portal survives beneath the turf as a memorial to his skill and as a puzzle for the excavators of the future. According to plan, we reached the old tunnel after ten days' work, and within a few inches of where we expected to find it; but it was blocked by a roof-fall, so that we could go no further. Thereafter we stopped work, and handed over the site to the BBC's riggers for the first live outside broadcast from Silbury by *Chronicle*.

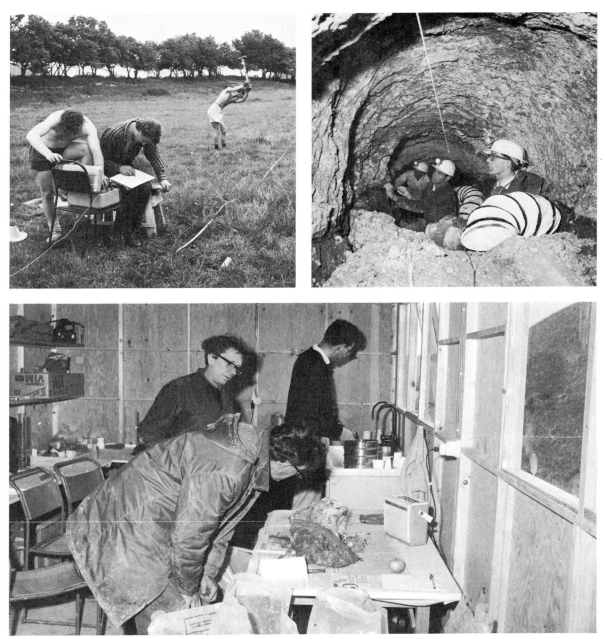

(Top left) *Measuring the depth of the ditch by echo-sounding;* (top right) *John Taylor, Lance Vatcher and Richard Atkinson inspecting the old tunnel;* (bottom) *examining samples in the laboratory on the site.*

This was a disconcerting operation, though we got used to it on later occasions. Miles of cable were laid for cameras, lights and microphones. The tunnel was floored with thick plywood sheets, so that camera-dollies could travel down it smoothly, without bumping; and the cameras were fitted with mirrors, to give a view of the sides. Powerful lights of up to 2000 watts each were installed, to which, after some initial singeing, we learned to give a wide berth; and enormous vehicles, filled with electronic equipment, were manoeuvred into perilous positions on the edge of the plunging ditch. In the end the riggers overcame all the difficulties, and the programme went on the air according to plan. For the viewers it may have been something of an anticlimax. For us it was the successful culmination of our initial work, and a start for the next stage.

During the university summer term the project was shut down for ten weeks. We began again on 29 June, with a number of separate investigations of different parts of the site starting simultaneously. This was the busiest part of the whole programme of work. The excavation of the tunnel, now following the blocked tunnel of 1849, went ahead at first with wheelbarrows for removing the spoil, as before. We had decided meanwhile to replace these with a diesel-powered mining tractor fitted with an hydraulic shovel; but, before this could be used, the platform and bridge outside the entrance had to be strengthened to take its weight. Simultaneously we started a trench on the lower slope of the mound, east of the tunnel, to find the level of the undisturbed natural chalk; and a party of students from the Geology Department at University College, Cardiff, led by Dr C. R. K. Blundell, began a seismic (echo-sounding) survey of the huge silted ditch round the base of the mound, to determine its depth and profile.

They brought with them too a drilling-rig which was hauled, not without difficulty, to the flat top of the mound, to which a water supply had also to be laid to flush the bore-hole. A second and larger drilling-rig, generously put at our disposal by Stanley Pugh and Co. Ltd of Bridgend in Glamorgan in return for expenses only, was likewise installed on the top of the mound, together with a compressor to flush the bore-hole with compressed air. This successfully provided an almost continuous series of cores of the mound material to within five yards of its base.

On 5 July the morning shift broke through into the still-open part of the tunnel of 1849, some thirty yards within the mound. Extra ventilation ducting was immediately installed to blow out any foul air, and thereafter Lance Vatcher, John Taylor and I were able to explore the whole of the old tunnel from the break-through inwards. This gave us a fascinating first view of the structure of the base of the mound, to which all our efforts so far had been directed; but I must confess that during the whole of this exploration I was almost rigid with fear, and at one point had to sit down and compose myself before following my companions through a narrow hole, little bigger than a large badger's earth, where the unsupported roof had collapsed and almost blocked one of the side tunnels dug in 1849.

For about thirty-five yards from the break-through the old tunnel survived to about half its original height of two yards. Most of the roof had collapsed, filling the lower part; but in places it survived, with the marks of pick-axes still visible. At several points we could see in the sides the bases of steeply-rising walls of chalk blocks, like the ones we had already found in our own tunnel; and in one place there was a large dump, resting on the old ground surface, of clay the colour of milk chocolate containing weathered fragments of chalk, which we immediately named 'Toblerone'.

We already knew that this material formed a thin weathered layer on the surface of the natural chalk, so that we were at once able to identify this dump (tentatively, though this later proved correct) as the first material skimmed off from the top of the main ditch round the mound. It thus marked the outer edge, at ground level, of the first chalk mound excavated from the buried ditch which we had previously found at Easter. Seeing this deposit for the first time gave me one of those rare and satisfying moments at which a single observation provides an instantaneous flash of illumination, and a whole series of muddled ideas suddenly falls into a coherent pattern.

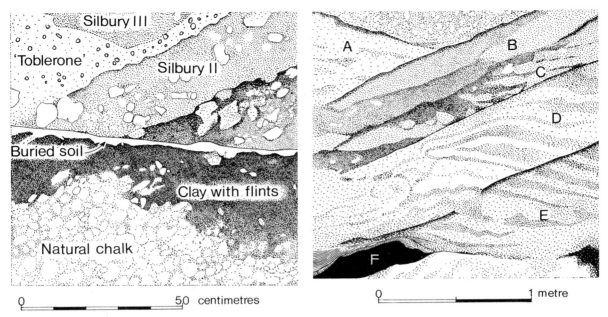

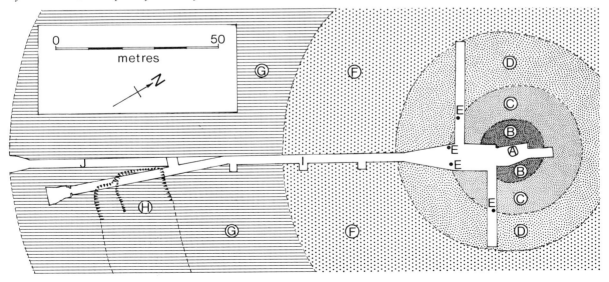

(Top left) *Section at the junction of Silbury II and III at the base of the mound.* (Top right) *Section of the outer part of the mound of Silbury I. A, chalk mound of Silbury II. B-E, complex outer layers of Silbury I. F, mouth of a lateral tunnel of 1949.* (Below) *Diagrammatic plan of the internal structure. A, base of the shaft of 1776. B, central low mound of clay-with-flints. C, covering mound of turf and topsoil. D, the four outer complex layers of Silbury I. E, stake impressions. F, chalk mound of Silbury II. G, chalk mound of Silbury III. H, buried ditch of Silbury II. I, tunnel of 1968-69. J, outer part of tunnel of 1849.*

Beyond this stretch a massive fall of the tunnel roof had left a space only eighteen inches high, through which we had to wriggle like snakes. Thereafter the height increased, until at the centre we found ourselves in a domed space, some four yards across and high enough for us to stand upright, formed by the collapse of the junction of the main tunnel with shorter tunnels to either side.

The sides of this open chamber presented one of the most astonishing sights that I have ever seen, and one of a kind encountered in dreams rather than in waking life. We already knew from the work of 1849 that at the centre of Silbury there was an inner core, or primary mound, composed of turf and dark topsoil. Now it was at once clear that this innermost mound had been covered by a series of conical shells or cappings, each about five feet wide horizontally and each built up from the bottom in narrow horizontal bands of widely different and contrasting materials, all evidently excavated from the flood-deposits in the neighbouring valley. The effect was of finding oneself inside an enormously complicated and highly-coloured layer cake of gigantic size.

Some of the bands were of black marshy soil; others of white chalk gravel, abraded and rounded in a flash-flood; others again were of ochre-coloured flint gravel; and many were of mixtures of these. Furthermore, in places the white chalk had been stained to a brilliant orange tint, by percolating water laden with dissolved iron compounds. The boundaries between each of the four complex cappings were quite sharp, showing that one was completed before the next outside it was begun from the bottom.

Nothing remotely resembling this extraordinary construction has ever been found in any other prehistoric earthwork, and it was immediately clear to us that the unique size of Silbury was matched by unique methods of building it, of which the chalk-block walls had already given us a hint. After this fantastic experience (and I use the word in its real sense, because it had more in common with fantasy than with normal life) I came gratefully out into the daylight, to face Paul Johnstone and his wife behind a film camera on the platform and give a rather incoherent account of what I had seen.

The next day some of us explored the remainder of the old tunnel, between the break-through and the outside of the mound. Here there had been huge roof-falls and only a short stretch of the original tunnel survived, with a pair of recesses cut in the chalk walls for candles. Elsewhere the open space rose and fell like a switch-back, ending at the outside with a green-painted wooden door covered with sheet iron, installed by the Office of Works nearly fifty years before, and covered on the outside by soil and turf. At the top of a large roof-fall further inwards a part of the east wall, about the size of a grand piano, had cracked away and seemed ready to fall at any moment. As I said at the time, this was not a place to linger; and for that reason we were not able to record the exposed structure of the mound by conventional measured drawings, though much was done on film by our photographer, Mr Malcolm Murray of the Department of Archaeology in the University of Edinburgh, both here and in other hazardous parts of the old tunnel.

During the next week the drilling-rigs were brought down from the top of the mound, and the smaller one bored into the filling of the south ditch, in preparation for a section to be cut by hand the following year. At the same time the seismic survey of the main ditch was supplemented by borings with a Mackintosh Percussion Tool and with a bucket-auger, carried out mainly by my sons Timothy and Giles. This enabled specimens from the silt at various depths to be examined on the spot in the site laboratory; and our resident environmental archaeologist, Miss Barbara Hart-Jones, at that time one of my own students, was able to show that the contained snails were almost all water-snails, not land-snails. It was clear from this that the ditch had been water-filled for a long time (probably from the middle or later part of the Bronze Age onwards, or from somewhere between 1500 and 1000 BC), and that most of the silt had been washed in by a stream, in the form of chalk mud, and had not been weathered off the sides of the mound. Subsequent borings identified the point where this stream had broken through the northern edge of the ditch, depositing a fan of eroded flint gravel in the lower levels of the silt.

As a result of two or three weeks of intensive investigation, therefore, we knew by the middle of July the main outlines of the initial and subsequent history of Silbury, and most of the rest of our work was devoted to filling in the gaps and refining the details. For the rest of the season we drove the tunnel inwards towards the centre, increasing its width and height once we had passed the edge of the primary mound, which again was marked by a large heap of 'Toblerone' clay, from the upper levels of the buried quarry-ditch. By 22 July we had reached the edge of the turf mound recorded in 1849. When we removed some of this for examination in the laboratory, we were astonished to find that the grass was still green (though much darker than living grass) and so well preserved that every species of the grasses, mosses and weeds could be identified. The same was true of the ants and other insects. It was difficult not to believe, when one looked at them under a low-power microscope, that at any moment they might scuttle off into the nearest crevice. I had always hoped that the preservation of organic remains near the centre would be unusually good; but this exceeded all my expectations. The following day we found the first of a series of impressions of pointed wooden stakes, driven into the old ground surface at the edge of the mound of turf. These must have supported a low hurdle fence,

The end of the BBC tunnel in 1968, with mining materials stored for the next season.

Impression of a stake supporting the fence which probably enclosed the ceremonial area before the building of Silbury I. Scale of centimetres.

perhaps erected at the very beginning to mark out an area for some special ceremony.

The final live outside broadcast of the season, preceded by three days of rigging and rehearsals, went out on 27 July. By that time the tunnel had advanced to within a few feet of the estimated centre of the mound. During the remaining fortnight we surveyed the flat top of the mound with geophysical instruments, in preparation for an excavation there the following year. This was partly frustrated by the chicken-wire embedded in the surface, put down in 1966 to hold together new turf then laid to repair erosion. At the end of this first season we felt that we had done what we set out to do, and that many of the results exceeded our expectations. I summarised these later in an article in *The Listener*. Early in 1969 the detailed planning began for the next season.

At this point it became clear that the BBC was not going to be able to fund the programme of work that I had put forward at the outset, and Paul Johnstone had the melancholy task of telling me this and of asking me to cut my estimates for 1969 by no less than forty per cent. This meant abandoning two major investigations which could (and probably would) have greatly increased our understanding of Silbury. The first was the re-excavation of Petrie's deep cutting into the base of the mound opposite the south-east causeway. This was the only place where we could hope to obtain, rapidly and economically, a large and continuous exposure of the structure of the mound. The second was the excavation of part of the main ditch on the north side, within a water-tight coffer dam formed by the injection of special plastics. It was all the more galling to have to give these up, because for both projects I had had generous offers from commercial firms of equipment and materials either free or at very low cost.

Furthermore, there would not be enough money to reinforce the tunnel at the end of the excavation, as we had originally intended, so that it could remain open underground (though blocked securely at the entrance) for examination and possible extension by the archaeologists of the future.

Nothing is to be gained now by analysing in detail the reasons for this drastic reduction in the scope of our programme when it was but half completed. With hindsight my own fault is clear. I ought to have built in to my estimates much larger sums for contingencies which the unprecedented character of the work made it impossible to foresee. On the BBC's side there were two major causes – a general retrenchment of expenditure at the time, and a significant degree of over-spending in the first year. Some of this was unavoidable, because of unexpected demands for extra fencing of the path for visitors from the Avebury car-park, and for the strengthening of the platform and bridge to take the mine-tractor; but a good deal of it arose from the placing of contracts for site-works which were not always adequately supervised, so that mistakes were made which had later to be rectified expensively.

When work began again at the end of June 1969 our reduced objectives were to extend the tunnel to and beyond the centre, and laterally to east and west, to find the limits of the primary mound; to cut a broad section across the south ditch; to excavate about one-eighth of the flat top of the mound, to look for con-

Excavations at the top of Silbury Hill in June 1969, seen from a helicopter.

temporary or later structures; and to investigate selectively the main terrace below the top, and some of the minor ones further down the slope. The resumption of the tunnelling was delayed, because during the intervening ten-and-a-half months various collapses had occurred, the electrical system had been affected by percolating water, and some of the arches near the centre had become dangerously overloaded by further falls in the old tunnel above them.

All this had first to be made good. Thereafter the side tunnels to east and west were driven a little beyond the edge of the primary mound, confirming the complex character of the outer cappings and revealing further stake-impressions at the edge of the turf stack. The main tunnel was extended northwards, encountering on the way the lower filling of the Duke of Northumberland's shaft, which continued downwards for at least five feet below the old ground surface and was about five feet in diameter. This filling contained, incidentally, a small colony of living earthworms, whose ancestors must have been thrown into the shaft when it was refilled in 1777. Beyond this, during the recording of material for the final television broadcast, the tunnellers found the sealed stoneware jar, or time-capsule, deposited by their predecessors in 1849. This contained an inscribed lead plaque, contemporary coins, various manuscript accounts of the work and a poem specially composed for the occasion.

The excavation of a broad section of the south ditch went initially more slowly than we had hoped, because at the top there was a thick deposit of Roman rubbish, containing over a hundred coins of the fourth century AD, all of which had to be carefully recorded. Moreover because of the hot weather, and the reflection of the heat by the chalk sides, the working conditions were severe. Temperatures of 90°F or more were often recorded, and salt tablets had to be provided for the diggers. There was a corresponding increase in the sales of the Red Lion at Avebury!

We found that the south ditch, itself divided from the main ditch by causeways of solid chalk, was also divided in the middle by a causeway at a lower level. The silting showed that very little of it had been eroded from the slope of the mound, and that most of it had been weathered by frost from the southern side, which extended beneath the Bath Road (A4). Furthermore, the builders had evidently taken unique precautions, as they had done in the interior of the mound, to ensure stability and prevent collapse. The inner side of the ditch had been cut to much the same slope as that of the mound above it; but the builders

Part of the terrace near the top of Silbury Hill, showing a chalk-block retaining wall.

clearly realised that if it were left exposed subsequent frost-erosion would under-cut the base of the mound and precipitate a landslide. They therefore protected the inner side of the ditch with horizontal layers of clay and chalk in a series of large steps, each about a yard high and a yard deep, revetted on the outside with timber. Nothing like this has ever been found in any other prehistoric earthwork; but it worked. There were no landslides.

On the top of the mound we opened a rectangular area, stretching from the centre at one corner to the northern edge, which revealed at a shallow depth the tops of chalk-block walls, and part of a deep soil-filled trench dug in the early part of the eighteenth century for the planting of trees. From this we made a narrower cutting from the top across the main terrace on the north side and a smaller short terrace below it. The main terrace proved to be an original neolithic feature, revetted on the inside by a chalk-block wall and extending inwards, under the topmost level of the mound, as a surface trampled smooth by workers carrying baskets of chalk rubble and blocks of chalk and sarsen. Both terraces had much later been cut back to a vertical face, revetted by timber secured with iron nails. We were fortunate in being able to date this event by the finding on the lower terrace of a silver farthing (a quarter cut from a silver penny) minted about AD 1010 in the reign of Ethelred II ('The Unready'). Clearly an attempt had been made to fortify Silbury as a strong-point against the Danes who were raiding deeply into southern England at this time from across the North Sea.

By the end of this season, early in August, we had been able to confirm most of our earlier ideas about the initial building of Silbury, and to extend our knowledge of its later history; but for television viewers, perhaps, our final programme was something of a disappointment. We had found no crock of gold at the centre, which all too many of them falsely expected; and what we had found, satisfied with it though we were ourselves, was of a kind to appeal more to archaeologists than to the general public.

Meanwhile, as I had suspected at the beginning of the year, we had had neither the time nor the money to

complete the excavation on the top of the mound. Paul Johnstone made valiant and ultimately successful efforts to secure for us the small sum necessary for finishing this part of the work (£450). At the same time, in November 1969, the tunnel was refilled solidly by blowing back the dumped material by compressed air. This was a sad end to an otherwise successful enterprise, and a poor reward for all those who had laboured in the tunnel, often under much more dangerous conditions than those of conventional mining.

For three weeks in July and August 1970 about a dozen of us camped in an adjacent derelict bungalow to complete the excavation on the top of the mound. This showed that at the summit, as at the bottom, the chalk rubble had been deposited in a series of separate dumps, each revetted circumferentially and radially by retaining-walls of chalk blocks; we found four such circular walls, and traces of a fifth, each separated from the next by a little more than two yards, with the intervening material raked out horizontally as each basketful was dumped. Clearly the builders' obsession with stability continued right to the top of the mound.

From these three seasons of excavation we can now reconstruct in outline the sequence of events during the building and the later history of Silbury. Some time in August, in a year around 2500 BC, a centre point was chosen and marked out, and a low fence was built around it, ten yards away. The area had recently been heavily grazed and had been trampled bare in places, either by cattle or by periodic meetings of a dense crowd of people.

Something then happened within the circular fence, though we shall never know what it was. It could have been a burial at the centre; but this is exactly the area destroyed by the shaft sunk in 1776. Thereafter the centre was covered by a low mound of gravelly clay, and turf was cut from the surface outside the fence and stacked within it, with loose surface soil piled on top, probably to a height of about five yards. This in turn was covered by four concentric layers of mixed soils and gravels dug out from the valley floor nearby and carried up in baskets, each

Silbury Hill from the north-west. The extension of the 'moat' to the right may have provided material for Silbury IV.

layer being built up in horizontal bands from the bottom upwards. This completed the primary mound (Silbury I), with a diameter of forty yards and a height of seven or eight.

Then the excavation began of a large quarry-ditch at a distance of forty yards from the base of the primary mound. This was thirteen yards wide, with vertical sides up to seven yards deep. Two gaps were left in it, to the south-east and south-west, to give access to the interior. The excavated chalk was piled over and around the primary mound to form Silbury II. When this had reached a diameter of eighty yards, and before the ditch had been dug to its full depth, the builders changed their minds. A new and much larger ditch was started further out, and the ditch already excavated was carefully filled up. The chalk from this new ditch, again with two gaps for access, was piled over Silbury II to form the present mound (Silbury III).

This was probably built in successive flat-topped layers, rather like a wedding-cake, each layer being five to six yards high and each finished before the next was put on top of it, with the outer edge revetted by steeply-rising walls of chalk blocks. This shape, like a stepped cone, would allow the outer margins of each layer to consolidate before they had to bear an extra load. This would have been good engineering, in keeping with the builders' concern for stability.

Finally the main ditch was extended to the west as a quarry of about two-and-a-half acres, about five yards deep, to provide the extra material for filling up the steps (Silbury IV). This had to be done from the bottom upwards; but for some reason the topmost step was never filled and is still visible today. Even after nearly five thousand years of weathering, Silbury is still very close in shape to a true cone. Clearly, as it was built up, the original centre point was projected upwards, so that each new layer could be laid out accurately around it. Thousands of years later, in the first century AD, the builders of the Roman road from London to Bath used Silbury as an aiming-point, but carried their road round the ditch to the south. Later still, probably after AD 300, a small Roman settlement grew up close by, and the south ditch was used as a rubbish

dump. Finally, about AD 1010, the Saxons of the area made an attempt to fortify parts of Silbury with timber defences, but we do not know whether they were ever tested in action. Certainly they were not destroyed by fire. Thus ends the long archaeological history of this extraordinary monument.

The presentation of the Silbury dig on television, over a period all told of four years, was an exercise of exceptional difficulty, because of the number of recordings at intervals on film and videotape, and the fairly frequent live outside broadcasts whilst digging was in progress. Moreover, especially for the latter, the conditions on the site were of exceptional difficulty because of poor access and restricted space for parking vehicles, as well as the very confined nature of the tunnel underground. Though those of us who were 'performers' were often hindered in our archaeological work, sometimes for days at a time, we all retain a real admiration for the professional skill and perseverence by which the difficulties of presentation were overcome.

From the start, however, the project ran the risk of raising expectations too high, because of the unique character of the site, its enormous size, our ignorance to begin with of its date, structure and purpose, and above all because of the sheer weight of publicity that it received. Inevitably, when spectacular finds failed to appear, the public felt a sense of anti-climax. Subsequently I have often heard people speak of it as a flop, or even a fiasco (especially if they were ignorant of my own part in it); and similar sentiments have appeared in the press.

For me and my colleagues, however, it was very far from that. We were able to achieve almost all that we set out to do, and when we were frustrated it was by lack of money, not lack of evidence. We gained a very detailed picture of the prehistoric flora and fauna, which no other site could have provided; and we found evidence for a degree of empirical understanding of civil engineering and of soil-mechanics which no one had previously suspected to exist at so early a date, some 500 years or more before the building of Avebury or the raising of the great stones of Stonehenge. Above all, Silbury showed us a whole prehistoric community in action, for to build it must have taken at least 500 people at least ten years, and probably more. Most prehistoric sites of this early date are family affairs, which do not allow us to see much beyond the family level of organisation. It is only the great works like Silbury and Stonehenge that give us some insight, directly, into the *communities* of our remote ancestors. Despite the disappointment of the public at large (and some disappointments of our own), the Silbury dig was a success, and a success that we owe to *Chronicle* and to Paul Johnstone in particular. Would that he could read these words!

The Contributors

R. J. C. ATKINSON has been Professor of Archaeology at University College, Cardiff since 1958, and has been broadcasting on radio and television, for *Chronicle* and other archaeological programmes, since 1952. He has directed excavations on many prehistoric sites in Britain, and has made a special study of Stonehenge.

DAVID COLLISON worked on *Chronicle* from 1966 to 1973. In addition to 'Lost World of the Maya' his films included 'Cracking the Stone-Age Code' (megalithic astronomy), 'The Tree that put the Clock Back' (the new radio-carbon dating) and two film biographies of Sir Mortimer Wheeler. Subsequently joined David Attenborough for 'Tribal Eye' and Magnus Magnusson for 'BC: The Archaeology of the Bible Lands'.

GLYN DANIEL is Disney Professor of Archaeology and Head of the Department of Archaeology in the University of Cambridge and a Fellow of St John's College. He was Chairman of *Animal, Vegetable, Mineral?* for nine years and then Advisor to *Chronicle* until Paul Johnstone's death. He has been a Director of Anglia Television since the inception of that company. He is at present President of the Royal Anthropological Institute. He edits the journal *Antiquity* and the two series *Ancient Peoples and Places*, and *The World of Archaeology*.

BASIL GREENHILL has been the Director of the National Maritime Museum since 1967 and under his Directorship the Museum has been completely reorganised and redeveloped. He is a member of the Council of the Maritime Trust, the Ancient Monuments Board for England, the *Great Britain* Trust and President of the International Congress of Maritime Museums. He is Chairman of the Governors of Dulwich College Picture Gallery.

JOHN R. HALE, Professor of Italian at University College since 1969, is Chairman of the Trustees of the National Gallery. He has published a number of books including *Machiavelli and the Italian Renaissance*, *Renaissance Europe* (edited) and most recently *Florence and the Medici*. He is also a regular broadcaster on radio and television. He wrote and narrated for *Chronicle* three full-length documentaries on

the histories of Florence and Rome as well as the programme on Venice which is the subject of his contribution to this book.

R. G. HARRISON, Derby Professor of Anatomy at Liverpool University since 1950, was Visiting Professor of Egyptology at the University of Cairo in 1972, and in 1970 was first Celebrity Lecturer at the British Academy of Forensic Scientists. As well as the 1969 *Chronicle* film of the 'Tutankhamun Post-Mortem' he presented an ITV film in 1973 on 'Tutankhamun Kinship'. His publications include *A Textbook of Human Embryology*, *Sex and Infertility* and chapters in *Cunningham's Textbook of Anatomy*.

KENNETH HUDSON spent seven years at the University of Bristol, five at the University of Bath and twelve with the BBC. He is now following a more active life as an author and museums consultant. His thirty-five books include eight on industrial archaeology, with three more to appear in 1978–79.

PAUL JORDAN read Archaeology and Anthropology at Cambridge, specialising in the Stone Age, and has worked on the *Chronicle* programme since 1969, where he has in particular written and produced films about ancient Egypt. He is the author of *Egypt – The Black Land*.

HENRY LINCOLN is a full-time writer. Since the transmission of 'The Lost Treasure of Jerusalem?' in 1972, he has concentrated on research into the story of Rennes-le-Château. His second *Chronicle* film on the subject, 'The Priest, the Painter and the Devil' was broadcast in 1974 and sketched in the later discoveries. The full truth of what lies behind the mystery is yet to be known.

MAGNUS MAGNUSSON, born in Iceland, came with his family to Edinburgh at the age of nine months. After working in newspaper journalism he became a freelance writer and broadcaster – as the latter he was the first presenter of *Chronicle*. He has translated Icelandic Sagas for Penguin Classics, and is editor of *The Bodley Head Archaeologies*, to which he has contributed two books of his own: *Introducing Archaeology* and *Viking Expansion Westwards*. He is also

174

Further Reading

author of *BC – The Archaeology of the Bible Lands*, the book of the television series of that name. In 1975 he was elected Rector of Edinburgh University.

TONY MORRISON is a zoologist, writer and film maker. During the past seventeen years he has explored remote parts of South America and has been an occasional contributor to *Chronicle*. He is a member of the Flamingo Survival group of the I.C.B.P. Smithsonian Institution, and was in the Falkland Islands with his wife Marion, filming wildlife, when plans were completed for the salvage of the *Great Britain*.

JOHN JULIUS NORWICH was educated in Canada, France and England, and served for twelve years in the Foreign Service before becoming a full-time writer. His many BBC documentaries include 'The Fall of Constantinople', 'The Conquest of Mexico' and a six-part series on the antiquities of Turkey. He has written books on the medieval Norman kingdom of Sicily, and in addition to travel books has published the first volume of a history of the Venetian Republic: *Venice, the Rise to Empire*. Lord Norwich is Chairman of the *Venice in Peril* fund, and a member of the Liberal Party in the House of Lords.

COLIN RENFREW is Professor of Archaeology in the University of Southampton. He has excavated on several prehistoric sites in Greece, and in the Orkney Islands. One of his special interests is the megalithic architecture of Western Europe. It was in order to learn more of the circumstances in which great stone monuments are erected by non-urban communities that he visited the Pacific in company with David Collison (Director, *Chronicle*), Magnus Magnusson and a *Chronicle* camera crew.

RAY SUTCLIFFE read history at Cambridge, subsequently working as Historian for the LCC Historic Buildings Department before joining the BBC in 1964. As a founder member of the *Chronicle* unit from 1966, he has specialised in programmes on Industrial and Maritime Archaeology. He is Chairman of the Council for Nautical Archaeology and a Vice President of the Society for Nautical Research.

The Return of the SS Great Britain
The Great Iron Ship Euan Corlett (Moonraker Press 1975)
Isambard Kingdom Brunel Rolt (Longmans, first published 1957)
The Great Britain K. T. Rowland (David and Charles 1971)
The Saga of the Great Britain J. O'Callaghan (Hart-Davis 1971)
The Return of the Great Britain Richard Goold Adams (Weidenfeld and Nicolson 1976)

The Archaeology of the Boat
A History of Seafaring based on underwater archaeology George F. Bass (Thames and Hudson 1972)
The Graveney Boat: National Maritime Museum Archaeological Series No. 3 V. H. Fenwick, editor (Oxford: British Archaeological Reports 1978)
Archaeology of the Boat; a new introductory study Basil Greenhill (Adam & Charles Black 1976)
Ships and Shipyards, Sailors and Fishermen Olof Hasslof and others, editors (Copenhagen: Rosenkilde & Bagger 1972)
The Archaeology of Ships Paul Johnstone (Bodley Head 1974)

The Tutankhamun Post-Mortem
The Tomb of Tutankhamen Howard Carter (Cassell Vol 1: 1923; Vol 2: 1927)
Tutankhamen Christiane des Roches–Noble Court (Michael Joseph 1963)
Akhenaten Cyril Aldred (Thames & Hudson 1968)

The Ashes of Atlantis
Atlantis, The Truth Behind the Legend A. G. Galanopoulos (Nelson 1969)
The End of Atlantis J. V. Luce (Paladin 1970)
Voyage of Atlantis J. W. Mavor (Collins 1973)
The Pegasus Story of Atlantis Helen O'Clery (Dobson 1971)

Glozel
Antiquity:
1927 'L'Affaire Glozel' by O. G. S. Crawford
1930 'Glozel Forgeries' by Vayson De Pradenne

1974 'Thermoluminescence and Glozel' by Hugh McKerrell and others
Archaeological Fakes Adolf Reith (Barrie & Jenkins 1970)
France before the Romans G. Daniel, S. Piggot, C. McBurney (Thames and Hudson 1974)

The Lost Treasure of Jerusalem . . .?
L'Or de Rennes Gérard de Sède (Julliard 1967, republished as *Le trésor maudit de Rennes-le-Château*, J'ai lu 1969)
Henry Lincoln is currently working on a book-length treatment of the subject.

The Lost World of the Maya
The Rise and Fall of Maya Civilisation J. E. S. Thompson (Oklahoma University Press 1977)
Maya Archaeologist J. E. S. Thompson (Robert Hale 1975)
Maya Hieroglyphs Without Tears J. E. S. Thompson (British Museum Publications 1972)
The British and the Maya Elizabeth Carmichael (British Museum Publications 1973)
Islands out of Time
Before Civilisation Colin Renfrew (Penguin Books 1976)
Stonehenge R. J. C. Atkinson (Penguin 1960)
The Island Civilisations of Polynesia R. C. Suggs (Mentor Books 1960)
Ancient Polynesian Society Irving Goldman (University of Chicago Press 1970)
Archaeology of Tonga W. C. McKern (Bulletin of the Bernice P. Bishop Museum, Honolulu, no. 60)
Easter Island Alfred Metraux (André Deutsch 1974)

The Industrial Archaeology Dilemma
The Archaeology of the Industrial Revolution Brian Bracegirdle and others (Heinemann 1973)
Industrial Archaeology in Britain R. A. Buchana (Penguin 1972)
The BP Book of Industrial Archaeology Neil Cossons (David & Charles 1975)

Exploring our Industrial Past Kenneth Hudson (Hodder & Stoughton 1975)
World Industrial Archaeology Kenneth Hudson (Cambridge University Press 1978)
Food, Clothes and Shelter: Twentieth-Century Industrial Archaeology Kenneth Hudson (John Baker 1978)
Industrial Archaeology: An Historical Survey Arthur Raistrick (Methuen 1972)

Maximilian
Imperial Adventurer Joan Haslip (Weidenfeld & Nicholson 1971)
The Mexican Empire H. Montgomery Hyde (Macmillan 1946)
The Cactus Throne Richard O'Connor (Allen & Unwin 1971)
Maximilian and Carlota Gene Smith (Harrap 1975)

The Historian and Chronicle
The Imperial Age of Venice D. S. Chambers (Thames and Hudson 1970)
Venice – The Rise to Empire John Julius Norwich (Allen & Unwin 1977)
Culture and Society in Venice Oliver Logan (Batsford 1970)
Venice Peter Lauritzen (Weidenfeld & Nicolson 1978)

Silbury Hill
Stonehenge and Avebury R. J. C. Atkinson (HMSO 1959)
Antiquity:
1967 'Silbury Hill'
1968 'Silbury Hill 1968'
1970 'Silbury Hill 1969–70' all by R. J. C. Atkinson
Silbury Hill R. J. C. Atkinson (BBC Publications 1968; supplement 1969)
The Archaeology of Wessex L. V. Grinsell (Methuen 1958)
British Prehistory: A New Outline ed. Colin Renfrew (Duckworth 1974)
Pre-Roman Britain Thomas Stanley (Studio Vista 1965)
The Avebury Monuments L. and F. Vatcher (HMSO 1976)